Ultimate Tailwind CSS Handbook

Build sleek and modern websites with immersive UIs using Tailwind CSS

Kartik Bhat

orangeava.com

First published: August 2023

Published by: Orange Education Pvt Ltd, AVA™

Address: 9, Daryaganj, Delhi, 110002

ISBN: 978-93-88590-76-1

www.orangeava.com

Om sahanaavavathu | sahanaubhunakthu |
Sahaveeryamkaravavahai | Tejaswi naavadheethamastu maa vidvishavahai ||

Dedicated to

All my teachers, beloved family, and my friends

About the Author

Kartik Bhat, basically a scribbler in Kannada language. Born in the year 1994. He has pursued a bachelor's degree in computer science and engineering from Visvesvaraya Technological University Belagavi (Karnataka- India) in the year 2016. Has 5+ years of experience in web applications development and hands-on knowledge in various front-end and back-end technologies. As a part of startup teams, he has worked on multiple ways of full stack web development, and experienced different front-end libraries, back-end/API technologies. Since 2021, he has been working on projects comprising user interface development using Tailwind CSS. Currently lives in Dharwad (Karnataka - India) and works as Senior Software Developer.

About the Reviewer

Soroush Sohrabi is a Senior Front-End Web Developer with 10 years of experience. He is a growth seeker and thrives on challenges. Soroush has the privilege of working directly with more than 6 Asian and 3 European companies, where he brings his expertise to create exceptional web experiences. His mastery lies in designing readable and scalable code that adheres to clean code principles. With a strong background in UI and UX designing, Soroush combines aesthetics and functionality to deliver user-centric solutions. He is passionate about staying up-to-date with the latest industry trends and technologies, constantly seeking opportunities to expand his skill set. Soroush's dedication to excellence and his ability to tackle complex projects makes him a valuable asset to any team.

LinkedIn profile:

https://www.linkedin.com/in/soroshism

Acknowledgement

I wish to thank the people who supported me in the journey of writing this book. My family fully encouraged me to write this book by motivating me to keep dedicated time to write this book, without compromising the content quality.

I am grateful to mention those mentors, guides, and the companies where I worked in my professional career that has given me knowledge in the field of web development, of course that is the foundation for this book too. My friends and colleagues really have a special role in my learning phase.

Also, I am thankful to the gratitude to the editorial team at Orange AVA for their continued guidance throughout the process for quite a long time to complete this book. I gratefully acknowledge Mr. Soroush Sohrabi for his kind and valuable technical review of this book.

Preface

Development of complete website, without writing single line of CSS directly. Looks curious right? Yes, Tailwind CSS makes it possible. Being a CSS framework, it provides a complete feature set to develop a website from scratch. It just needs you should have basic knowledge of HTML, CSS. Even if you don't know these as well then, this book is for you. Begin with it.

This book provides an approach to the development of website and user interface components using Tailwind CSS. Begins with the introduction to HTML and CSS, which are foundation of website development. Then we explain concepts in Tailwind CSS and utilities available in it.

Further we develop a simple website that comprises six webpages using Tailwind CSS, here we will not write single line of CSS directly, Tailwind CSS manages itself. Then we push the developed code to GitHub and chain it with GitHub Pages deployment. This deploys the code so the user can access it using its URL. At last, we are providing some user components developed using Tailwind CSS.

Chapter 1 will explain basic concepts of HTML, CSS so that new readers can get basic foundation for further reading and experienced readers can get quick glance prior to core context. Then we will explain installing methods of Tailwind CSS to get started with it.

Chapter 2 will cover detailed explanation on principle concepts of the Tailwind CSS. These will describe how Tailwind CSS proves to be a good fit for user interface development easier and faster.

Chapter 3 will cover customization, base style available in Tailwind CSS as a utility class, here we cover layout building mechanism, spacing, and sizing mechanisms too.

Chapter 4 details styling mechanism like typography, border, transition and transforms so on related utility classes available in Tailwind CSS. These are related to element specific styling.

Chapter 5 will introduce website development flow, by explaining each user interface component we build a complete web page. In this chapter we will build homepage, gallery page and a menu page, where each webpage contains different user interface components.

Chapter 6 will provide continued information of advanced usage of Tailwind CSS in the development of user interface components. In this chapter as well, we are developing three web pages, blogs page, contact us page and faq page that completes full website. Then we are deploying a website under github pages.

Chapter 7 provides standard practices you need to keep in mind while developing website or more precisely user interface components. Then we are providing some examples of user components developed using Tailwind CSS.

Downloading the code bundles and colored images

Please follow the link to download the
Code Bundles of the book:

https://github.com/OrangeAVA/Ultimate-Tailwind-CSS-Handbook

The code bundles and images of the book are also hosted on
https://rebrand.ly/pubn0jv

In case there's an update to the code, it will be updated on the existing GitHub repository.

Errata

We take immense pride in our work at Orange Education Pvt Ltd and follow best practices to ensure the accuracy of our content to provide an indulging reading experience to our subscribers. Our readers are our mirrors, and we use their inputs to reflect and improve upon human errors, if any, that may have occurred during the publishing processes involved. To let us maintain the quality and help us reach out to any readers who might be having difficulties due to any unforeseen errors, please write to us at :

errata@orangeava.com

Your support, suggestions, and feedback are highly appreciated.

DID YOU KNOW

Did you know that Orange Education Pvt Ltd offers eBook versions of every book published, with PDF and ePub files available? You can upgrade to the eBook version at **www.orangeava.com** and as a print book customer, you are entitled to a discount on the eBook copy. Get in touch with us at: **info@orangeava.com** for more details.

At **www.orangeava.com**, you can also read a collection of free technical articles, sign up for a range of free newsletters, and receive exclusive discounts and offers on AVA™ Books and eBooks.

PIRACY

If you come across any illegal copies of our works in any form on the internet, we would be grateful if you would provide us with the location address or website name. Please contact us at **info@orangeava.com** with a link to the material.

ARE YOU INTERESTED IN AUTHORING WITH US?

If there is a topic that you have expertise in, and you are interested in either writing or contributing to a book, please write to us at **business@orangeava.com**. We are on a journey to help developers and tech professionals to gain insights on the present technological advancements and innovations happening across the globe and build a community that believes Knowledge is best acquired by sharing and learning with others. Please reach out to us to learn what our audience demands and how you can be part of this educational reform. We also welcome ideas from tech experts and help them build learning and development content for their domains.

REVIEWS

Please leave a review. Once you have read and used this book, why not leave a review on the site that you purchased it from? Potential readers can then see and use your unbiased opinion to make purchase decisions. We at Orange Education would love to know what you think about our products, and our authors can learn from your feedback. Thank you!

For more information about Orange Education, please visit **www.orangeava.com**.

Table of Contents

CHAPTER 1

Getting Started with HTML, CSS, and Tailwind CSS

Introduction

In this chapter, we are going to learn about the definition of a website, and the basic principles behind the development of web pages. This chapter gives brief knowledge on the structure of a webpage and the technologies used for it by explaining the core concepts of HTML and CSS. Then, we will learn about Tailwind CSS, and its installation variants, and discuss applying it to our project.

Structure

In this chapter, we will cover the following topics:

- Defining website
- HTML
- What is CSS?
- Let's begin with Tailwind CSS
- Installation and setup
- Standalone CLI: Use Tailwind CSS without Node.js

Defining website

A **website** is a document that has a certain link that can be accessed or visited on a browser. More precisely, a website is a document, which can be opened using the internet, where we can find information about a person, company, place, and so on.

This can be the basic definition of a website that everybody can interpret. Technically, a website is a set of documents built using various programming languages, each of which has its unique role.

When you refer a specific entity as a website, it is a collection of web pages interconnected by hyperlinks, where all of them are present under a single hood called **domain**.

> **Domain is a name that you need to visit a website, which begins with www and ends with `.com`, `.uk`, `.in`, and so on. Technically, domain in called as URL - Uniform Resource Locator that act as a mask for an IP-address, where website is located.**

A website is a set of web pages. A **web page** is a document that represents a part of the data that comes under the website.

Consider the following example:

There is a website that gives information about certain places, and there are some parts present on that website like address, about, contact, and so on. These parts are said to be web pages. These represent specific information about that place's website.

Website and its representation

We are now aware that the website is an entity, and it runs on a browser. Hence, the *browser* is a medium between website data and visitors. Representation of data is a key point for every successful website. So, *what does this representation mean?* It's a way users can conveniently access and experience the website on various devices.

The usage of a website on various devices matters a lot behind the success of a website. As a layperson, you may have noticed that the same website has a different interface when accessed from a desktop computer and a mobile device, *isn't it?*

It is ultimately true that it can be inconvenient when a website gets loaded on a mobile device with an interface of a desktop. Mobile devices have a vertical orientation of usage, whereas desktop or laptop devices have a horizontal orientation. It is necessary to make the website look clean and effective on all types of devices, in both orientations.

Most of us have mobile devices and internet access in today's digital trend. According to a recent survey on website visits, visits from mobile devices (*more than* 50% - increasing every year) are more than visits from desktop devices. This highlights the importance of ensuring a website's appearance on various devices. Thinking and implementing this approach is called the **Mobile First** approach. Here, the development concentrates on creating user-friendly experience on mobile devices and to further larger devices.

Tailwind CSS has made this approach easier. We will learn more about it in upcoming chapter.

Types of websites

We can distinguish websites into two major types:

- Static website
- Dynamic website

A **static website** consists of webpages with statically added data. These data are added straight to the web pages that will be displayed on a browser and are often added during the development phase of the website (when there are no frequent changes made). For example, a simple website showing information on places, animals, and so on.

Dynamic websites are those where data comes dynamically from other sources and are systematically displayed on webpages. As and when data changes from external sources, it will be rendered on these web pages, with different data being loaded dynamically in the same place on a webpage.

For example, websites such as job posting sites, news sites, and so on.

In this book, we are going to explain the development of a static website from scratch until its deployment. We have chosen a static one because we are focusing more on the design of the website rather than the display of dynamic data from external data points.

Webpage: a technical aspect

A page or a document, which consists of several lines of code, is termed as a web page. When the browser engine reads and understands the code written on the page, its visual representation will be loaded on a browser window. So, *what kind of code does the browser understand?*

Web pages are written in HTML language. HTML cannot be called a programming language as we are not creating any complex logic here. It is called **markup language**.

> **Markup language is a standard text-encoding system. It comprises easily understandable keywords, names, tags, and so on, which are used to structure the webpage.**

HTML

HTML is considered as a standard markup language for those documents, which are meant to be displayed on web browsers.

Figure 1.1: *Full form of HTML*

HTML was initially released in 1993. With the progressive improvements over the years, it is currently running with the 5th version (5.3 as of October 2022) known as **HTML5.** Files that hold HTML code have the extension `.html`.

HTML provides a sufficient number of built-in tags/elements to easily structure the webpage as per expectations which can be easily rendered on most current-day web browsers.

When you see a website loaded on a browser window, then it is nothing but an HTML document that gets rendered on the browser engine. HTML code or document or file is a set of arrangement of tags in a specific order to obtain a structure to display data.

HTML tags are *reserved keywords* enclosed with open–close angular brackets, meant to render a specific structure. Most of the tags are declared with *open* and *close* tags called **block** tags (open–close tags are interchangeably called *start–end* tags). Some of them can be used with single tags, which are called **inline** tags.

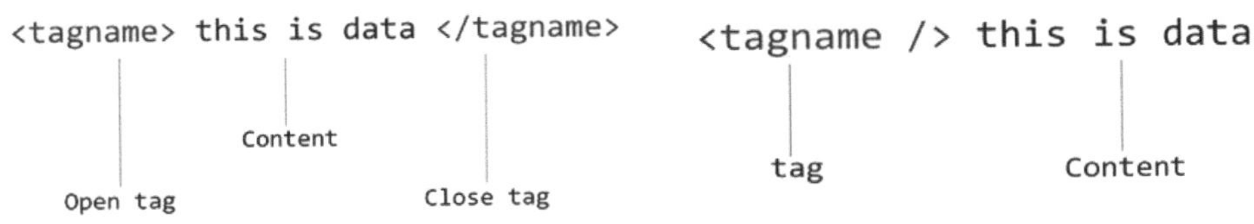

(a) (b)

Figure 1.2: *(a) HTML block tag; (b) HTML inline tag*

Here, we are providing the most used HTML tags or elements throughout this book. You will also get knowledge on different sets of HTML tags from some external sources:

Some commonly used HTML tags/elements			
Tag	**Description**	**Tag**	**Description**
<head>	Head part of HTML	<title>	Defines Title of Document of Browser
<body>	Defines the whole body of the HTML Document	<main>	Defines the main section of the Document
<div>	Division block	<p>	Paragraph
<h1>	Heading - 1	<h2>	Heading - 2
 	Line break	<hr />	Horizontal line
<table>	Defines table	<img />	Defines image
<td>	Table data	<tr>	Table row
<b>	Bold element	<span>	Span element
<a>	Hyperlink	<link>	To refer external CSS files
<script>	To refer to JavaScript code	<header>	Defines header part of Document
<footer>	Defines footer part of the Document	<figure>	Used to define image
<ol>	To begin ordered list	<li>	To define list item

Table 1.1: *Common HTML tags*

By looking into these tag names, you can understand how easy it is to write an HTML document, *isn't it*? HTML comes with an easy-to-use set of built-in keywords.

Let's look into the simple structure of an HTML document; as we are using HTML5, it is specifically an HTML5 document:

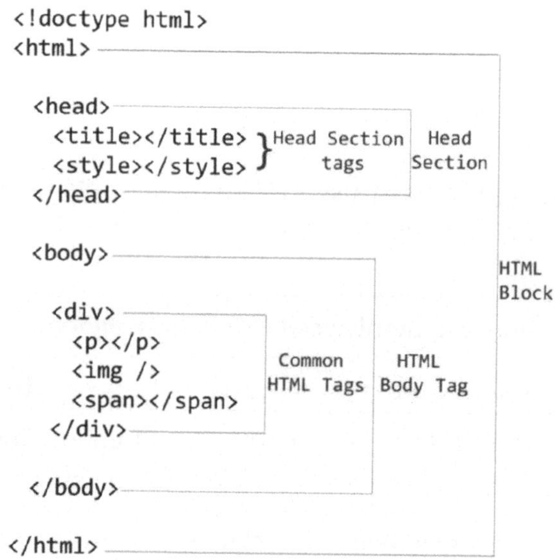

Figure 1.3: *Sample HTML document*

Let's learn some tags:

- **<!doctype html>**: This is an indication tag. When we include it in a document, the browser understands that the document is using HTML5 for structuring the page.
- **<html></html>**: This is a mandatory tag that must be present in an HTML document. All other HTML tags should be present within this paired tag.
- **<head></head>**: This paired tag is used to refer to external files (**`.css`**, **`.js`**) and the title of the document.
- **<body></body>**: The body tag is the main part of the document and it holds all the tags that are meant for page structuring.
- **<div></div>, <p></p>, <img />**: These are the tags that are added in a sequence to create a specific structure of the page, and they are the core part of an HTML document.

It is a general practice to define <style></style> tag within the <head></head> tag but it will not create a problem if you define it outside of it. The style tag brings the expected style to the document.

When you visit a website from a browser, you are allowed to view the code that is responsible for the visualization. Yes, it is available in the browser itself.

If you are using Windows, by right-clicking on a webpage, you get a pop-up menu, and then by clicking **Inspect**, you get the following:

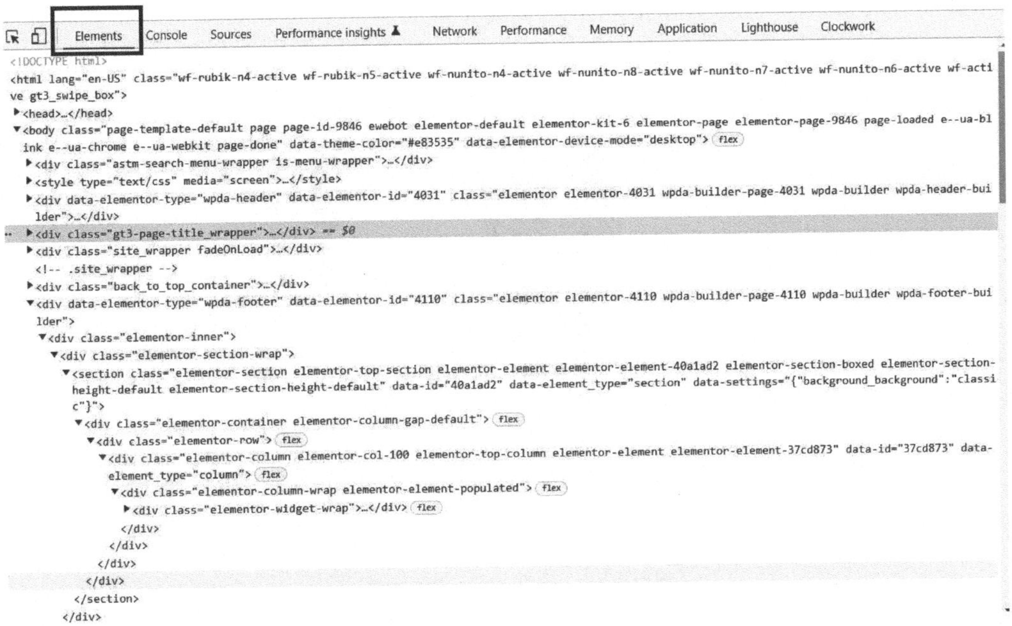

```
Elements  Console  Sources  Performance insights  Network  Performance  Memory  Application  Lighthouse  Clockwork
<!DOCTYPE html>
<html lang="en-US" class="wf-rubik-n4-active wf-rubik-n5-active wf-nunito-n4-active wf-nunito-n8-active wf-nunito-n7-active wf-nunito-n6-active wf-acti
ve gt3_swipe_box">
 ▸<head>…</head>
 ▾<body class="page-template-default page page-id-9846 ewebot elementor-default elementor-kit-6 elementor-page elementor-page-9846 page-loaded e--ua-bl
  ink e--ua-chrome e--ua-webkit page-done" data-theme-color="#e83535" data-elementor-device-mode="desktop"> flex
   ▸<div class="astm-search-menu-wrapper is-menu-wrapper">…</div>
   ▸<style type="text/css" media="screen">…</style>
   ▸<div data-elementor-type="wpda-header" data-elementor-id="4031" class="elementor elementor-4031 wpda-builder-page-4031 wpda-builder wpda-header-bui
    lder">…</div>
   ▸<div class="gt3-page-title_wrapper">…</div> == $0
   ▸<div class="site_wrapper fadeOnLoad">…</div>
    <!-- .site_wrapper -->
   ▸<div class="back_to_top_container">…</div>
   ▾<div data-elementor-type="wpda-footer" data-elementor-id="4110" class="elementor elementor-4110 wpda-builder-page-4110 wpda-builder wpda-footer-bui
    lder">
     ▾<div class="elementor-inner">
       ▾<div class="elementor-section-wrap">
         ▾<section class="elementor-section elementor-top-section elementor-element elementor-element-40a1ad2 elementor-section-boxed elementor-section-
          height-default elementor-section-height-default" data-id="40a1ad2" data-element_type="section" data-settings="{"background_background":"classi
          c"}">
           ▾<div class="elementor-container elementor-column-gap-default"> flex
             ▾<div class="elementor-row"> flex
               ▾<div class="elementor-column elementor-col-100 elementor-top-column elementor-element elementor-element-37cd873" data-id="37cd873" data-
                element_type="column"> flex
                 ▾<div class="elementor-column-wrap elementor-element-populated"> flex
                   ▸<div class="elementor-widget-wrap">…</div> flex
                  </div>
                </div>
              </div>
            </div>
          </section>
        </div>
```

***Figure 1.4**: HTML code from the browser*

In this snapshot, a set of tags is arranged in a specific order to create the structure of a page. You can also observe that these tags have various attributes like **`class`**, **`id`**, and so on, which provide style and interactivity to the page.

Styles and interactivity

HTML is meant for structuring the page but has limitations in terms of design parameters and user interactivity. To overcome it, we need to combine other technologies with HTML such as:

CSS: All visualization enhancement aspects, such as *color patterns*, *margins*, *borders*, *shadow*, can be achieved with this technology. As you read before, the term **Mobile First Approach** requires this CSS for its implementation. In the next section, we will provide brief information on the core concepts of CSS which are very much essential for understanding the working of Tailwind CSS.

JS: JavaScript: It is a scripting tool required to handle interactivity with the visitors of the website. Interactivity includes actions such as *clicking*, *hovering on an element*, *submitting a form*, *fetching dynamic data from external sources*, and so on.

The following diagram helps you understand the importance and capabilities of **HTML–CSS–JS** for the creation of webpages:

Figure 1.5: *What is HTML-CSS-JS*

Throughout this book, we will learn how to apply **Tailwind CSS** to create a website from scratch. We are going to develop a static website, where the focus is purely on creating a web page rather than dynamic data fetching and handling through JS - which is beyond the scope of this book. However, to make some simple interactions with the page, we will explain the required JS concepts while developing web pages.

Although it is not mandatory to know JS, knowing some basics will help you to grow your knowledge to make a web page more interactive.

A web page is said to be *complete* or *perfect* if it has a proper structure with suitable visual enhancements and interactivity.

Here is a reference HTML page you can use to test chunks of code mentioned throughout the book:

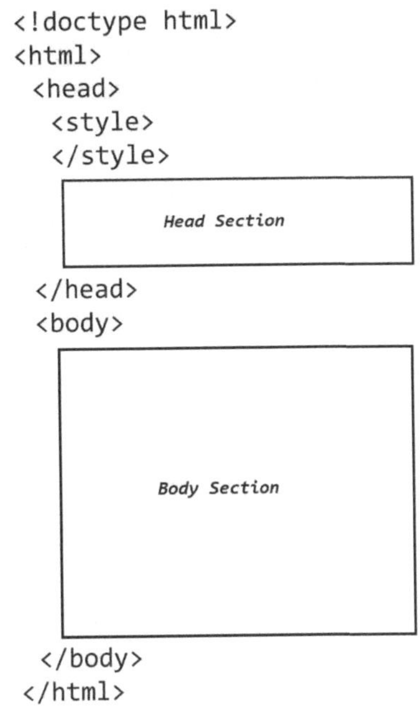

Figure 1.6: HTML *reference document*

As we are approaching website development, we strongly recommend that you follow the preceding syntax while writing a code to gain more confidence. This practice makes you well-versed with code than by just reading it in a book.

Cascading Style Sheet (CSS)

This chapter provides a brief explanation on fundamentals of CSS along with HTML, which is the foundation to understand and apply Tailwind CSS.

CSS is a visual enhancement technology that is applied to HTML documents to produce aesthetically neat webpages. CSS was developed by the **World Web Consortium (w3c)** in 1996. Currently, it is running *third* of it, called **CSS3**.

In this section, we cover typical aspects of CSS, such as types of CSS, how it works with HTML, and the *Box Model*.

What is **Cascading Style Sheet (CSS)**? It can be elaborated as follows:

- **Cascading**: An arrangement or a sequence
- **Style**: Appearance
- **Sheet**: Set of rules

So, CSS can be defined as a document or a piece of code that defines a set of rules in a sequence to create some stylish appearance. CSS is a context that has no importance as an independent entity. These written set of rules need to be referred to somewhere to create a visual impact of it.

Visual Impact – Yes, this is how CSS has its identification. In general, if a website appears to be visually appealing, it means that CSS has been used to achieve that appearance. On that website, CSS is used to create various colors, shadow effects, margins, padding, text decorations, and so on.

Applying CSS in web development involves adding a set of design rules to the webpage, that is, to the HTML document. CSS rule will be adopted by HTML tag whenever it gets rendered on a web browser.

The preceding paragraph clearly states that CSS needs a channel to be visualized, and the HTML document plays as a channel for it. *How does HTML adopt these rules provided by CSS or what CSS needs to get it visualized on the screen?* **Selectors.**

Selectors

Selector is an entry point for a particular CSS rule. *It's the way we can define a rule!* Without selectors, we cannot say a piece of CSS as a rule that affects the visual representation of data on an HTML webpage:

```
selector {
  property : value ;
  property : value ;
  property : value ;
  property : value ;
  .
  .
  .
}
```

Figure 1.7: *CSS rule format*

color: green ;
background-color: blue ;
width: 10px ;
height: 20px ;
	div {
	    color: green ;
	    background-color: blue ;
	    width: 10px ;
	    height: 20px ;
	}

It has no meaning (improper rule)	*It has proper meaning (proper rule)*

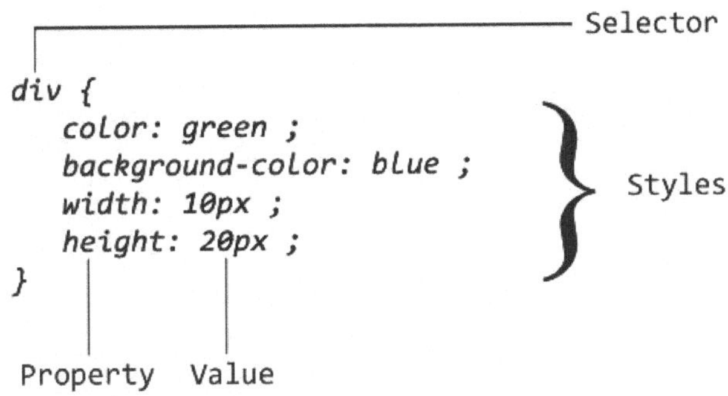

Figure 1.8: *Example of CSS rule*

Now you can define the meaning of the CSS rule.

Set of styles (*property – value pair*) defined within a selector scope, which targets tags present on HTML document.

The preceding code sample demonstrates how CSS rules can be written. A CSS *rule* is considered a rule whenever it has a proper *selector* mentioned in it. Without that, the styles written in CSS will have no effect on any part of the HTML document.

Types of selectors

As we have understood, a CSS rule should contain a selector to make visual representations of styles defined. So, *what these selectors can be? Can you guess?*

If you know where the CSS rule will be projected for its execution, then you can answer it immediately. Yes, it is HTML, more concisely, a selector can be an HTML tag, the ID property of an HTML tag, the class property of an HTML class, and so on.

Let's take a look at some important selectors of CSS. Do note that you need to read and understand them better from other external sources for your convenience:

Tag or element selector: Here, the HTML tag also known as an **element**, is used as a selector to apply style rules. When the HTML page is rendered on the browser, these rules will be applied to all instances of that element used as a selector:

```
p {
  color: red ;
}
```

Here **<p></p>** tag is used as a selector to apply font color as **red** on the HTML page, if there are ten **<p>** tags on the HTML document then this CSS rule will be applied to all.

ID selector: The **id** attribute of HTML tag is used as a selector for projection of CSS rules. As, we use the **id** attribute as a unique identifier of tag on the HTML document, the rules with **id** selectors will affect only that tag (an HTML document can have multiple tags with the same **id**):

```
HTML -
<p id="paragraph"> It is first paragraph </p>


CSS -
#paragraph {
        color: green ;
}
```

For **id** selectors, CSS requires the **# (hash)** symbol along with the ID of the HTML tag. Here, those elements having **id="paragraph"** receive **green** as their text color from CSS rule.

Class selector: The class attribute defined with an HTML tag is used for CSS rules projection. This is one of the most important selectors that you need to keep in mind, as Tailwind CSS refers to the same approach for its execution:

```
HTML -
<p class="description"> description of the paragraph </p>
CSS -
.description {
```

```
        color: blue ;
}
```

For class selectors, CSS requires **.** (**dot**) symbol along with the class attribute of the HTML tag. Here, those elements having **class="description"** will receive a **blue** color as their text color from the CSS rule.

Pseudo selectors: These are special types of selectors, where based on a certain condition of the HTML tag, receive projected styles from the CSS rule. Conditions include *on hover*, *on visited*, *on focus events* or *on enabled – disabled states* or *only first-child*, *last-child* of the element. This has an important scope as well on Tailwind CSS, Do understand it better from external sources for your convenience:

```
HTML -
<p id="paragraph"> It is first paragraph </p>
CSS -
#paragraph:hover {
        color: green ;
}
```

For pseudo selectors, CSS requires the **colon** (**:**) symbol in between the **selector** keyword and the condition for an HTML tag. Here, the elements having **id="paragraph"** will receive **green** as their text color from the CSS rule when we *hover* the mouse over it. We expect you to read and understand more about these selectors' sections for your ease of understanding.

Styles – (property-value pairs)

Style rules are at the heart of CSS rules!

These will define the visual enhancements that you need to project on the HTML's part. The selector leads the rule and *property-value pairs* which define the actual style to be represented.

In each rule, there is a *property-value pair*, where the **Property** field holds one of the many keywords defined in CSS for design-related things and the **Value** field holds an arbitrary value supported by the respective **Property** field:

Property	Value
height, width, padding, margin	digit with (**px**,**rem**,**em**)
background-image	url
text-indent	center, left, right
color, background-color	any color (**hex**, **rgb**, color name)
display	Block flex, none

Table 1.2: Property – value pairs of CSS rule

CSS Box Model

CSS considers every element as a *box* with certain properties. These properties are combined and called as **CSS Box Model**. The following figure shows its components:

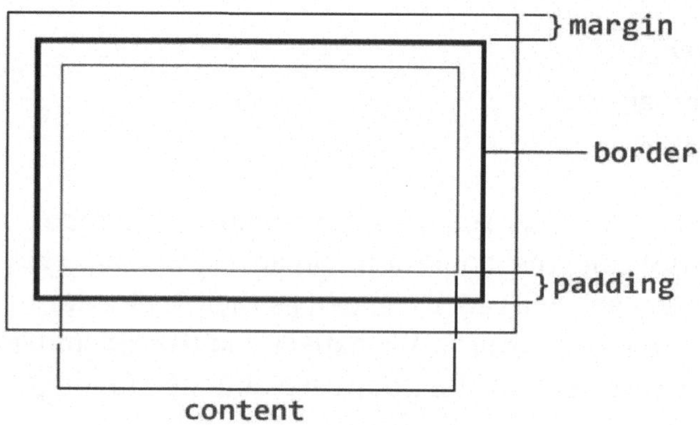

Figure 1.9: *CSS Box Model*

The box model contains *four* components:

- **Margin**: It is the space between the border of an element and other elements around it.
- **Border**: It is the boundary line of an element.
- **Padding**: It is the space between the boundary line and the actual content.
- **Content**: It is the area that holds the data to be rendered (image, paragraph, and so on).

As CSS focuses on the Box Model, it is important to understand the Box Model in detail. Manipulation is directly performed on the Box Model to make an element look good aesthetically.

Except for content, all others can take a value as a number for all directions or each direction separately.

The following tables depict various ways to define the box model participants to give different effects:

```div { padding : 1px }```	```div{ padding-top: 1px ; padding-right: 1px ; padding-bottom: 1px ; padding-left: 1px ; }```

Table 1.3: *This adds padding of 1px for all directions.*
(left column represents the shorthand form of the right column)

```div { margin : 10px 20px ; }```	```div { margin-top : 10px ; margin-bottom: 10px ; margin-left: 20px; margin-right : 20px; }```

Table 1.4: *This adds a margin of 10px for vertical direction and 20px for horizontal direction*

Types of CSS

Types of CSS are not differentiated based on version or syntax. They are based on how we use CSS on a webpage. Let's take a brief look at each.

In website development terminology, a webpage is a place where our CSS is referenced. It is the place where we can visualize those sets of style rules.

Inline CSS

This method is for adding CSS to a webpage where those style rules are declared within the **`style`** attribute of an HTML tag.

This type of CSS has effects only on that tag or the children tags within that tag. This way of adding CSS makes the handling of styles more difficult when the number of tags on a webpage grows.

For example:

```
<div style="background-color: yellow; color: blue">
            This has yellow background and blue text
</div>
```

In this example, you can see that this kind of CSS doesn't require any selectors, as it directly targets an HTML tag, so we can consider it a *tag* or *element* selector:

- **Advantage**: Easy-to-apply styles to a specific HTML element without disturbing the other elements.
- **Disadvantage**: Code loses readability as each tag gets its style.

Internal CSS

It's an approach of adding CSS to the webpage where rules are written as a separate section of the page, within the **<style></style>** tags of the HTML document. These rules can affect targeted HTML elements throughout the document. These kinds of CSS rules are helpful to create generalized rule sets that can affect multiple similar sets of selector parameters within the context of the HTML document.

Since all style rules are on the same page, the web page will render along with the HTML code and CSS code. It's a best practice to keep these styles (**style** tag) before the **body** element. This is because when there are many style rules declared, by declaring them after the **body** element, on a partial load of pages, the HTML elements may render without an expected style until the page loads completely. If we declare them before the body, then only after executing all style rules, the HTML elements will be rendered.

For example:

CSS:

```
<style>
   div {
          margin: 2px ;
   }
```

```
        #paragraph {
              color: green ;
        }
        .box {
              padding: 3px;
        }
    </style>
HTML:
    <body>
        <div> This is block 1 </div>
        <div> This is block 2 </div>
        <div> This is block 3 </div>
        <div> This is block 4 </div>
        <p id="paragraph"> This is paragraph </p>
        <div class="box"> It is the box </div>
    </body>
```

In this block of code, the style related to the **`div`** selector (**`tag`** selector) gets projected to all four instances of **`div`** on the page and **`#`** paragraph (**`id`** selector) related style will be projected only to instances of the **`p`** element. **`class`** selector **`.box`** affects the **`div`** element with class **`box`**.

- **Advantage**: Code readability increases and rules can be generalized within the document.
- **Disadvantage**: While creating a website, these rules cannot be accessed outside the current document.

External CSS

This is the most used CSS type when developing a website. Here, all CSS rules are kept in a separate file with an extension **`.css`**, which is then referred to within the HTML document.

Like internal CSS, using different types of selectors, we can write various CSS rules for HTML elements. By using the **`<link />`** tag of HTML, the external CSS file will be added to the current document:

style.css

```
div {
        margin: 2px ;
}
#paragraph {
        color: green ;
}
.box {
        padding: 3px;
}
```

page.html

```
<html>
        <head>
                <link href="style.css" />
        </head>
        <body>
                <div> This is block 1 </div>
                <div> This is block 2 </div>
                <div> This is block 3 </div>
                <div> This is block 4 </div>
                <p id="paragraph"> This is paragraph </p>
                <div class="box"> It is the box </div>
        </body>
</html>
```

Compared to adding CSS using an internal CSS approach, we can observe the same result, except CSS rules are present in some external files with the extension **`.css`**.

This approach makes rules generalization easier, as we can refer to this external CSS file in any number of HTML documents, where we want similar style rules to be applied. Rules are written only once but referred to at multiple places wherever we want the same style to be visualized. This is a *developer-friendly approach* to keep the code cleaner.

Media queries

Again, we are mentioning the word *Mobile First Approach.*

The previous section explains the importance of presenting websites on different kinds of devices, *right?*

We need to adopt the mobile-first approach to ensure we are developing a website that renders perfectly on various devices.

As this deals with the aesthetics of the website, we need to handle it in CSS. This can be done using media queries.

Media query is the CSS rules will be changed based on the condition we are mentioning. These conditions can include **screen resolutions** and the **min-max height** of the device.

> **Devices are often differentiated by their dimensions, more specifically their screen resolutions. Desktops, laptops, mobiles, tablets, and so on, each has their unique screen resolution.**

We often write our code on a desktop or laptop and consider it as correct based on the output we see on that resolution. But it may not be the case when we look at the same website on devices with various dimensions/screen resolutions.

Therefore, it is important to make design adjustments to the webpage to make it accessible effectively on all devices. Mentioning screen resolution as a condition for CSS rules is nothing but writing a media query for the web page. Media query will be along with keyword **`@media`**:

```
@media only screen and (max-width: 600px) {
        body {
                background-color: blue;
        }
}
```

Here you can see a typical example of how a media query is written. The CSS rule called **`background-color`** as **`blue`** will be projected on the body element of an HTML document only when the browser window/device resolution is **`600px`** *wide* or *less*:

```
@media only (min-width:360px) and (max-width: 800px) {
        div {
```

```
            width: 10px;
            height: 30px
        }
}
@media only (min-width:801px) and (max-width: 1200px) {
        div {
            width: 20px;
            height: 50px
        }
}
```

In this example, the same CSS rule on the **div** element is set to different values based on different screen resolutions. Devices with a screen resolution between **400px** and **800px** have one set of values while those with a resolution between **801px** and **1200px** have a different set of values.

Key points to remember

When you mention all three different types of CSS on the same HTML document for the same element, **inline CSS** has the *highest priority* to apply style rules to that element. In the absence of inline CSS, internal CSS takes priority. Style rules defined in external files are overridden by style rules defined within the document scope for the same selector.

In the absence of any style rules for some element, it will inherit style rules from its *parent element*. So, while applying CSS to elements with *children*, the same rules will imply to those children as well (except for Box Model parameters):

```
CSS Rules
        .data-box {
              color: green;
        }
HTML Elements
        <div class="data-box">
              Heading Text
              <p>paragraph</p>
              <div>simple text</div>
```

```
        <p style="color:red;">red colored text</p>
    </div>
```

Here the text color of all the text present under **<div>** with class **data-box** will be **green**, as they inherit from the parent, except the last **<p>** element, as it has its own style rule defined for the **color** property.

CSS rules are *case-insensitive*. While writing rules, we must provide proper text for **selector**, **property**, and **value** fields, else CSS cannot identify the rule for visualization:

div {
    font-size: 10px;
    color: red;
}
	DIV {
	  Colour : red
	  FontSize: 20cm;
	}

Properly defined rules	Improper defined rules

Table 1.5: *CSS styling method*

The keywords you are using on an HTML document should be the same while writing CSS rules for it. CSS searches for the selector on the HTML document and adds style to it when it is rendered on the web browser.

If you write CSS rules with the same selector and the same property but different value fields, the one that is written later will be considered for targeting an element of the HTML document. CSS reads code from *top to bottom*, adds styles for the respective selectors, and keeps only the recently read style rule for the element:

```
CSS Rules
    #paragraph {
        color: green;
        font-size: 10px;
    }

    #paragraph {
        color: red;
    }
```

```
HTML Element
        <p id="paragraph">
                This is paragraph text
        </p>
```

When this code got rendered on the web browser, it visualized the **`<p>`** element with **`color`** as **`red`** and **`font-size:10px`**. You can observe CSS has overridden only similar properties on similar selectors (**`color`** property on the preceding code sample) and those are defined only once and are added as a style on HTML document.

How to override the default behavior of considering only the last definition of a rule among multiple definitions written before in the code? CSS has a solution for it - **`!important`**.

`!important` is the keyword to be added to the style rules among multiple definitions, which one needs to be projected on an HTML element. When CSS encounters the symbol **`!`** **(exclamation)** **`important`**, it considers this definition as a *high priority* for projection and ignores any other similar definitions written either before or after it:

```
CSS Rules
        #paragraph {
                color: green !important;
                font-size: 10px;
        }
        #paragraph {
                color: red;
        }
```

In this code sample as per default behavior, an element with **`id`** as **`paragraph`** should get a style where **`color`** is **`red`** but as we applied **`!important`** keyword on similar definition written before. So, CSS projects this style to that HTML element.

Introducing Tailwind CSS

Now we are at the actual focus of this book. The knowledge you earned in the previous section is the basic knowledge to digest upcoming concepts. Remembering these concepts is very essential throughout reading this book:

Figure 1.10: *Tailwind CSS Logo*

Tailwind CSS is an *open-source* CSS *framework*, authored by *Adam Wathan* and *Steve Schoger*, under the name *Tailwind Labs* as development activity. It was first featured in the year *May* 2019.

After various enhancements with different aspects of user interface development, currently, *version* 3.3.2 is running in the market, attracting a big number of web developers' interest. They believed in and achieved an intuitive way of applying styles to HTML documents with a faster development experience.

Tailwind CSS has more than *61k stars* (as of Oct 2022) on *GitHub*, which shows that it is gaining and winning interest these days for its support of the rapid building of **user interfaces (UI)**. It is called the **Utility-First CSS framework**.

Utility First CSS? It is nothing but low-level utility classes to build expected visualization on HTML documents. By using these low-level utility classes, you are not restricted to stick with any predefined components; instead, you are free to build any kind of custom designs of your wish.

Utility classes are self-explanatory classes; there is no need of remembering complex names to apply it on HTML document. Tailwind CSS comes with a set of such class names that are named according to their intended purpose. These can also be called *single-purpose* CSS *classes*, and each one of them has a corresponding CSS rule.

Need of Tailwind CSS

Tailwind CSS is popular because of the faster development experience for its users. Then, *how it makes the development process faster?*

Developing a fit and fine webpage as you know requires knowledge of HTML and CSS on a primary note. You will create a structure using HTML and then make it visually impacted, with multiple device-friendly activities using CSS. *Right?* As a primary definition on the development of a webpage, it is correct up to the point.

As you read that Tailwind CSS provides utility classes to development, using these classes alone you can create a complete user interface of your wish without writing any CSS rule directly for your HTML document.

Yes, writing a huge set of CSS rules is not required to achieve various aspects on HTML documents, such as *color patterns*, *responsive design*, and so on. In fact, you can completely avoid writing any inline, internal, or external CSS rule when you are with Tailwind CSS. Amazing, *isn't it?*

This book is meant for educating you on this approach itself. We will develop a complete website without worrying about directly writing a CSS rule by ourselves. You are going to enjoy website development alongside reading this book.

A webpage that has a cleaner look and can convey all the information of the webpage on various devices without disturbing the user experience is said to be a responsive website.

Applying Tailwind CSS on HTML

HTML has a set of elements to define the structure of a webpage, most of these elements or tags can hold various attributes for different purposes. An internal or external CSS can be mapped into these using **`class`** attributes.

It is that simple to mention class names to the elements that are already provided by Tailwind CSS:

This sentence has good design, has background color and center-aligned

```
<div class = "bg-gray-300 text-center font-bold italic underline">
        This sentence has good design, has background color and
center-aligned
</div>
```

```
div {
  background-color: #d1d5db;
  text-align: center ;
  font-weight: bold ;
  font-style: italic ;
 text-decoration: underline ;
}
```

***Table 1.6**: Glimpse on Tailwind CSS flavoring*

From *Table* 1.5, you can easily understand how Tailwind CSS makes our work easier and saves the time we spend on writing CSS rules. Chaining different class lists on the class attribute of the HTML element yields those style rules that were applied when it got rendered on a web browser. It's a work that is already done behind the scenes to experience a faster development process.

Apart from lots of prebuilt classes for rapid development, Tailwind CSS supports a high level of customization that is required for complex design patterns. This is one of the reasons that makes Tailwind CSS compete with popular component-based frameworks.

Advantages of Tailwind CSS

Tailwind CSS produces class names that are named almost to the intended purpose. There is no need to remember these class names, which makes the learning curve easy.

User interface - it is a technical term for what a website user sees on a web browser. Designing this user interface is done using CSS, which visualizes the styles. In our case, applying Tailwind CSS makes it faster.

When using Tailwind CSS, it is not mandatory to write our own CSS rules set, which avoids direct interaction with CSS files as we get most of the things done from pre-built classes themselves.

To implement a responsive design of a webpage, we need to keep many aspects into account and address them carefully (**header**, **footer**, **menu**, **popup**, and so on). In such scenarios, the CSS rules set grows to multiple sets of lines. Tailwind CSS provides a cleaner approach for this, with breakpoint-oriented class names excel to target different device resolutions.

Being a low-level CSS framework as its learning curve is not so steep, it is easy to get adopted by groups of people working in a broader context. Tailwind CSS helps to define systematic coherence in design.

Tailwind CSS's production version of CSS file contains only those sets of CSS rules that have been referred to through class names in the HTML document, not all the hundreds of pre-built class names supported in the framework. It boosts the loading time of CSS into the browser.

As you are free to develop any design of your wish, there are scenarios where you need to use the same pattern in multiple places on the same page or other web pages of the same website. Tailwind CSS allows you to prepare a component and reuse it anywhere on your website, it enhances the **Don't Repeat Yourself (DRY)** strategy, which keeps code cleaner.

In the coming chapters of this book, we are using the latest version of Tailwind CSS to make you learn recent and advanced features and its brief example and for website development.

As of *April* 2023, the latest version of Tailwind is **Tailwind CSS v3 (3.2.3)**.

Installing and setting up Tailwind CSS

Tailwind CSS is written in JavaScript and distributed as an NPM package, which means you need to have a node environment running for Tailwind CSS to work.

Your system needs to have **NodeJS** installed before you begin with the installation of Tailwind CSS in your system:

- **NodeJS: It is a JavaScript runtime environment that executes JavaScript code outside a web browser.**
- **NPM: Node Package Manager, for NodeJS.**

Follow these steps:

1. Let's create a folder to begin with our installation. We will name it `TailwindCSSProject`.

   We suggest using VS code for code writing, although it is up to you to use your convenient IDE for code writing. (VS code is user-friendly and the useful features are already inbuilt).

   NodeJS is an environment and NPM is a package manager. As NPM works with a command line, you must execute a specific command to download packages for your work. In this case, we are downloading or installing our Tailwind CSS using NPM commands. It is called Tailwind CSS **Command Line Interface (CLI)**.

2. Open the project folder with VSCODE and open the terminal. If you already installed NodeJS, you can run the following command:

   ```
   node -v
   ```

3. You can see the version of the same as a response. Installation of NodeJS also installs `npm` by default. If you run the following command, you can see its version as well:

   ```
   npm -v
   ```

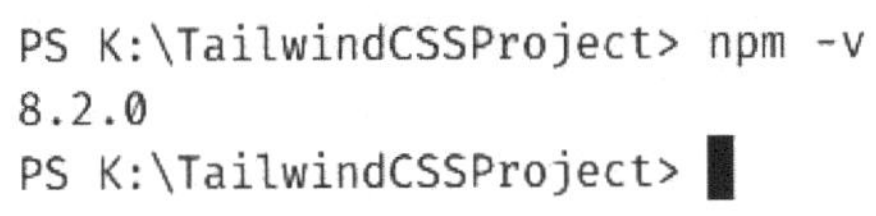

(a)

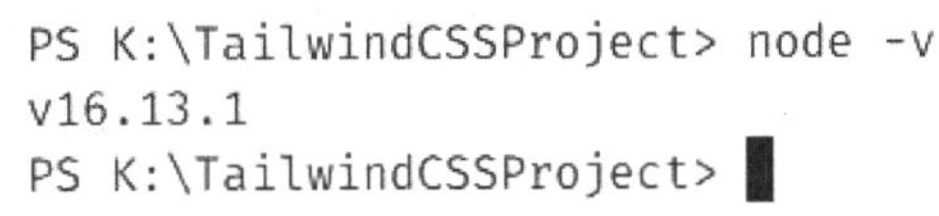

(b)

***Figure 1.11**: (a) NodeJS version, (b) NPM version*

It flags you are good to go with the installation of Tailwind CSS on your system/project. Observe that there are no files present in your folder (**`TailwindCSSProject`** folder).

4. Now run the command:

   `npm install -D tailwindcss`

   It installs all required files from the server and then you can observe the **`node_modules`** folder and **`package.json`** file created in your folder. These are related to the NodeJS environment:

   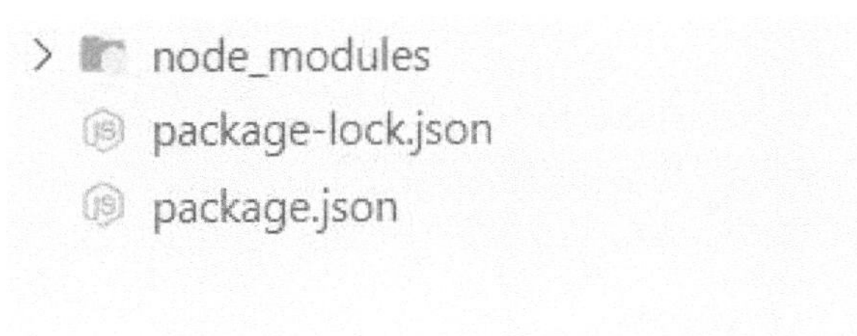

   ***Figure 1.12**: Node environment files*

   If you open these **`node_modules`** folders, then along with other folders you can find the **`tailwindcss`** folder. It confirms you have successfully installed **`tailwindcss`** on your system.

   Now it's time to create a configuration file for Tailwind CSS, configuration is done using the file itself. As Tailwind CSS is written in JS, this file should also be in JS itself.

5. Now run the following command:

   `npx tailwindcss init`

This creates a **`tailwind.config.js`** file in your project folder:

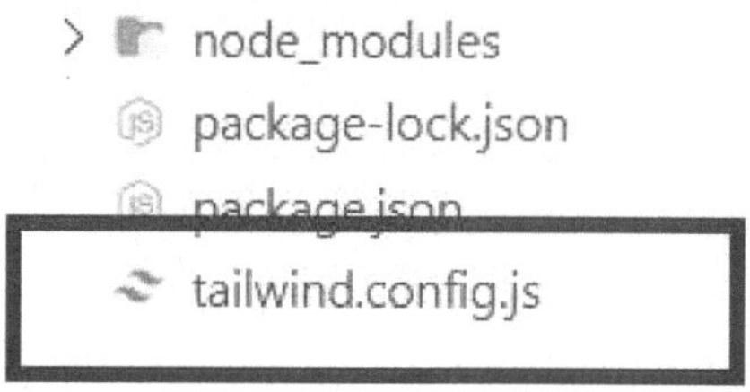

***Figure 1.13**: Tailwind CSS config file*

6. Now, open, and edit the content section of this config file to listen to HTML files of our project. This investigates the place where Tailwind needs to search for its utility classes. It is important to mention the path of your HTML files (folder hierarchy) / project user interface files where you are applying Tailwind CSS:

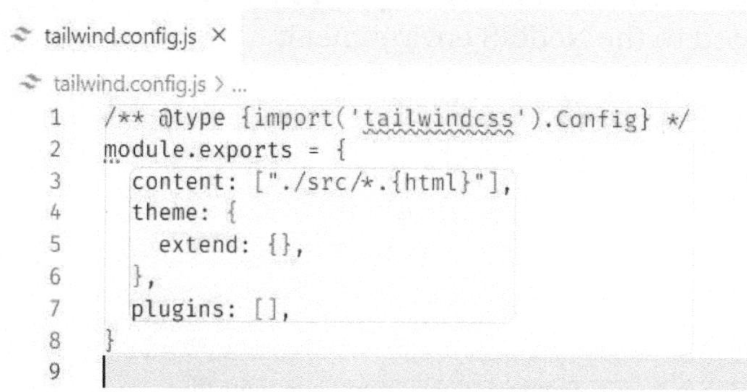

***Figure 1.14**: tailwind.config.js file*

Here we are placing **`.html`** files within the **`src`** folder in the **`project`** folder. Within that folder, tailwind can read a file with any name that has the extension **`.html`** (* indicates any file name).

Apart from the **`content`** section, other two sections are present in that config file, namely, **`theme`** and **`plugins`**. Here, **`theme`** section is used to configure custom classes with Tailwind CSS, here we can define custom class names and require CSS style to be linked with it. Further, these class names can be used within HTML documents like other Tailwind CSS classes. **`plugins`** section can hold a reference to those external features developed to support common development elements like forms, aspect ratio, and so on, which will be explained in detail in further chapters:

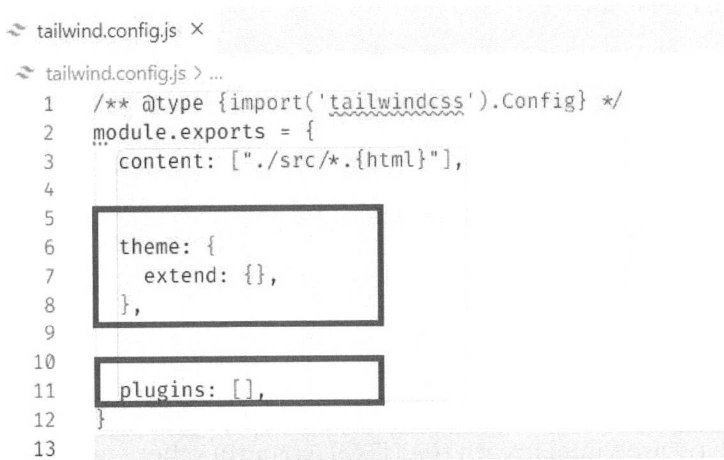

Figure 1.15: *Other section of the config file*

7. Create a **.css** file within the **src** folder to refer to all those features provided by Tailwind CSS, then we will refer to this **.css** file in our HTML files. Then add the following line to that empty file:

   ```
   @tailwindcss utilities;
   ```

   > **What this @ symbol in CSS: @ symbol is called as At- *rule*, this instructs CSS how to behave, for example, `@charset "utf-8";`**
   >
   > **Here we are using rule `@tailwindcss` as a rule for CSS.**

   Here, we are referring to all those utility classes provided by it in our CSS file. When it gets rendered on the browser, it holds all those utility classes in it. This line also adds utility classes of those plugins added to support Tailwind CSS.

   It completes setting up Tailwind CSS on your project. Now you are free to use those all-utilities classes from Tailwind CSS in your HTML documents.

8. Create a sample HTML document to test if Tailwind CSS is working or not:

   ```
   index.html
   <!doctype html>
   <html>
   <head>
   ```

```
  <meta charset="UTF-8">
  <meta name="viewport" content="width=device-width, initial-
scale=1.0">
</head>
<body>
  <h1 class="text-4xl font-semibold italic">
    This is sample text
  </h1>
</body>
</html>
```

Hope you are familiar with the HTML structure, here we are adding three utility classes on the **h1** element present with the **body** element.

Whenever we load this page on a browser, it should render text with *4×l size*, semi-bold thickness with italic style. *Right*? Understand that class names are named for the intended purpose. *Isn't it*?

Now, this code as-is cannot render styles on the browser. *Why can you guess*?

We are missing a CSS file that holds/listens to all these utility classes' CSS rules, and that says what to visualize for what.

Before that, *is it good to load all Tailwind CSS utility classes even though we are using it*? No, *right*? Tailwind has a solution for it. It provides a command to create a compiled CSS file that holds only those CSS rules related to those classes we have used in our HTML files. In the preceding case, only those CSS rules of classes *text-4xl*, font-semi-bold and italic should be added as a style.

9. Run the following command to achieve that:

   ```
   npx tailwindcss -i ./src/style.css -o ./style/output.css --watch
   ```

   --watch option indicates command is running to observe changes we are making on HTML files to identify utility classes and adding related CSS rules to the **output.css** file which we need to refer to in our HTML document. After running this command, it automatically generates the output.css file.

   Add/refer **output.css** file to **index.html** file within **head** section using the **link** tag:

```
<link href="output.css" rel="stylesheet">
```

As a curious factor, you can open this **`output.css`** file to verify which all CSS rules are added for utility classes we have utilized in **`index.html`**.

> **Until the preceding command keeps on running/watching all your changes on the HTML file, it will create a set of CSS rules dynamically on the `output.css` file.**

It's time to run this **`index.html`** file on the browser:

***Figure 1.16**: index.html on browser*

We now have an appropriate style rendered on the browser.

Apply Tailwind CSS using CDN

Whenever we are using NodeJS runtime environment we stick with **`npm`** to manage Tailwind CSS installation. Even though it is a suggested approach it is not the only way to use Tailwind CSS.

TailwindCSS's **content delivery network** (**CDN**) is equally capable of bringing results to the table. CDN is a mechanism where we are referring to some content that is available in the network using an URL. The setup process is a bit different compared to the above suggested, but it is not so difficult to adopt.

Add the following **`script`** tag at the head section of **`index.html`**, CDN is served using the **`script`** tag:

```
<script src="https://cdn.tailwindcss.com"></script>
```

> **Remove that link tag used to refer to compiled CSS from `output.css` while using the CDN approach of Tailwind CSS. Replace that `link` tag with a CDN `script` tag.**

Yes, now it is done. Refresh the **`index.html`** file on your browser and you will get a similar effect.

Then, how to configure more with CDN?

Add the **theme** sections of the **tailwind.config.js** file as a JavaScript code in **index.html** within **<script></script>** tag just after CDN. You can customize it as you wish:

```
<script>
    tailwind.config = {
      theme: {
        extend: {
          colors: {
            clifford: '#da373d',
          }
        }
      }
    }
  </script>
```

Plugins can be added as a GET parameter on the CDN URL that will bring utility classes of respective plugins under the same CDN reference.

For example:

```
<script src="https://cdn.tailwindcss.com?plugins=forms,typography"><script>
```

Forms and typography are the *first-party plugins* of Tailwind CSS. Any other *third-party plugins* cannot be used in this way.

Standalone CLI - Tailwind CSS without Node.js

As you know Tailwind CSS is built using JavaScript, except for the CDN approach, which always requires NodeJS to run behind to compile Tailwind CSS classes for our project.

It is acceptable if you are completely utilizing this environment for your project for various aspects, but there are scenarios where NodeJS is not a common thing for development. In such cases, the usual installation enforces people to be there with NodeJS environment to use Tailwind CSS, which is an entirely different ecosystem they need to adopt.

In *December* 2021, Tailwind CSS announced a tooling mechanism that provides full feasibility of using Tailwind CLI in a *self-contained executable* format, where there is no interference of NodeJS or NPM. It is called a **standalone CLI build**.

From GitHub, you can download the supported executable for Windows, Mac, and Linux accordingly. Then instead of running CLI commands as `npm` commands, you can run them using Tailwind form and everything remains the same.

To init Tailwind CSS in your project you can run the following command:

```
./tailwindcss init
```

These commands create a config file of Tailwind CSS in your project. Similarly, to compile the class names you can run the following command:

```
./tailwindcss -i input.css -o output.css -watch
```

There is no change in other parts of the command except the need for the `npm` prefix.

When it comes to the config file, it is acceptable to use the same syntax for the `plugin` section as we use in the NodeJS environment.

We can use a project called `pkg` by *Vercel* that makes a Node.js project into an executable that can be run without installing Node.js on the system by bundling all the parts your project needs right into the executable itself. That's how it is possible to utilize the full power of JavaScript in our project.

If your project is already running on the NodeJS ecosystem, then there is no point in using Standalone CLI. If you only need a JavaScript environment to use Tailwind CSS, it would be a better option without creating complexity in your project, for example, Rails, Phoenix, and so on.

Tailwind CSS in production

Tailwind CSS is more widespread than any other similar framework because of its production size. When we minify our output CSS file, it becomes *less than* 10 KB even for bigger projects. Following is a command to minify the output CSS file:

```
npx tailwindcss -o output.css --minify
```

Conclusion

To apply Tailwind CSS effectively in website development for its user interface creation, the information covered here can be considered as a basic foundation. Understanding and exploring the concepts discussed above makes you feel more confident with Tailwind CSS, a better approach for a faster development experience.

In the next chapter, we will cover the core concepts of Tailwind CSS. Let's be ready to explore.

CHAPTER 2
Design Principles for Tailwind CSS

Introduction

Being a CSS framework or a tool to create user interfaces, we are learning core concepts that Tailwind CSS conveys for the development process. There are many factors involved to develop a design of a website, and since Tailwind CSS exists to make it easier to approach them, we are categorizing each one for easy comprehension. We keep the explanation simple because we try to utilize most of the resources while developing the website.

Structure

In this chapter, the following topics will be discussed:

- Utility classes
- Events
- Responsive design
- Dark mode
- Re-usage of style
- Creating custom styles
- Function and directives

Utility-first classes

In the previous chapter, we already had a glimpse of how utility class is applied to HTML by avoiding writing CSS rules directly just by adding various classes for HTML elements. Now let's see a detailed view of it.

We prefer you add HTML and CSS rules to the model HTML document provided in the previous chapter so that you can run on browsers easily to visualize the styles of your wish.

Here, we are seeing a traditional way of creating user interfaces or by specifically a component (use either internal CSS or external CSS for testing this code).

HTML

```
<div class="mainBlock">
        <div class="innerBlock">
                <div class="contentBlock">
                        <div class="colorBlock"></div>
                                <div class="textBlock">
                                        <h2>Information</h2>
                                        Lorem Ipsum is simply dummy text
                                        of the printing and typesetting industry.
                                </div>
                        </div>
                </div>
        </div>
</div>
```

CSS rules

```
.mainBlock {
       background-color: #6b7280 ;
       padding: 0.5rem ;
       width: 18rem;
}
.innerBlock {
       border: 1px solid #030304 ;
```

```
        border-radius: 5px ;
}
.contentBlock {
        display: flex ;
}
.colorBlock {
        margin: 0.5rem ;
        background-color: #16a34a ;
        border-radius: 50%;
        width: 5rem ;
        height: 3rem ;
}
.textBlock {
        padding: 0.5rem ;
        color: #ffffff ;
        font-size : 12px ;
}
```

These HTML and CSS combinedly produce the following effect on the browser window:

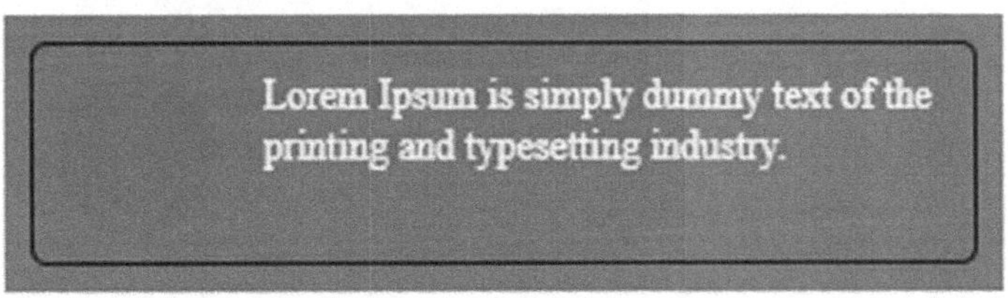

Figure 2.1: *Output of traditional approach of CSS*

Here, you can observe there is an outer block with gray color then inside that there is another block with a black border, then within that, there is a green box and white text one beside another. *Right*? a simple component.

Now let's create it using utility-first classes provided by Tailwind CSS. Pretty sure you admire it.

It's an alert that we are not using any CSS rules directly to design the component. It's just an HTML block of code.

HTML

```
<div class="bg-gray-500 p-2 w-72 m-2">
    <div class="border border-gray-900 rounded-md">
      <div class="flex">
        <div class="bg-green-600 h-12 w-24 rounded-full m-2">

        </div>
        <div class="text-white text-xs p-2">
          Lorem Ipsum is simply dummy text
          of the printing and typesetting industry.
        </div>
      </div>
    </div>
</div>
```

After running this HTML on the browser, we will get the following result. We can hardly identify the difference, *isn't it*? (Except the font family all other styles remain the same):

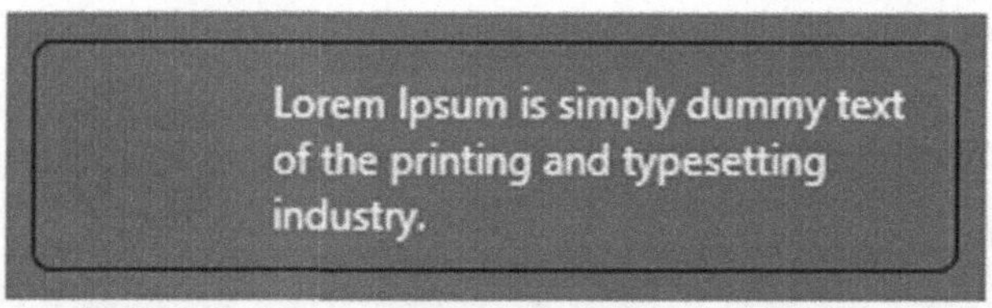

Figure 2.2: *Output of Tailwind CSS approach*

If you look at HTML document, for the first time if you are looking into Tailwind CSS utility classes applied, you may say it is creating a mess to the readability of the HTML code. Until you know the importance of each class.

The preceding HTML document shows everything is done by providing utility classes as a class attribute value of the element.

When you feel comfortable with the usage of utility classes you will agree that you are not wasting time defining CSS rules and giving an unrelated name to the class to refer to it. You can feel that your CSS stops growing bigger than the actual HTML elements of the file. Moreover, you feel safe while changing **style** property as you are just changing the class name rather than changing CSS rule itself.

While using these utility classes provided by Tailwind CSS, you may get a question in your mind about using inline CSS itself in the name of utility class names. If you just started utilizing utility classes, it is common that you doubt it:

- If you use inline styles, then it is a localized rule set on that element. Further, you cannot reuse that rule on other elements, but utility classes are a part of a design system. You can reuse the same class name to build an *impactable design*, where CSS rules are defined only once.
- Inline styles are only meant for styling purposes. You cannot handle responsive design code there, but there are utility classes for handling responsive design that really save your development time to target each aspect ratio separately to write CSS rules.
- Inline CSS is incapable of handling state events like *hover*, *focus*, and so on. There is support for these as well in Tailwind CSS utility classes.

Hope you got clarity on the distinction between inline CSS and utility classes. Now you feel charged to continue with the usage of utility classes with more comfort and fun.

Events and states

Whenever you are building a webpage some events play an important role from a user experience perspective. **Events**, more precisely we can say interactivity of the user with the web page. Interactivity on an HTML page means hovering on elements, clicking on buttons, text selection, and so on. Similarly, **State** is a status or condition of an HTML element like *disabled*, *first child*, *even children*, *first-letter*, *first-line*, and so on.

Let's look at a simple example:

```
<button class=" w-36 py-3 rounded bg-green-300 hover:bg-blue-400
active:bg-red-500 ">
      Simple blockD
</button>
```

You can see the following output on the browser. On load, the page button renders with **green** color. When you hover on it will be changed to **blue** and when you click on it will be changed to **red** color. Got *it*? How utility classes provide support for interactivity:

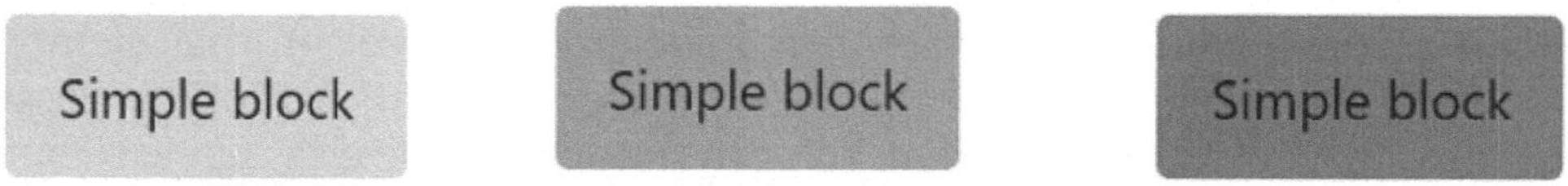

Figure 2.3: *Events utility classes (normal state, hover event, and click state)*

From the example, you can understand that these *state* and *event*-related classes have a format event name and as usual class name separated by colon.

If you want to add multiple styles on interactivity, you need to prepend an event name with a colon with each of those classes.

For example, on hover if you need to change the text color and background color then you need to add class like hover:bg-green-500 hover:text-white.

The following table shows simple examples of various event- and state-related utility classes:

First child and last child: Style will be added to only first and last accordingly:
`<div>`
`  <div  class="first:font-bold`
`              last:italic">one</div>`
`  <div class="first:font-bold`
`              last:italic">two</div>`
`  <div class="first:font-bold`
`              last:italic">three</div>`
`  <div class="first:font-bold`
`              last:italic">four</div>`
`</div>`
	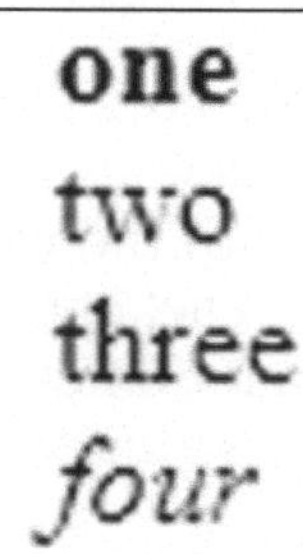
	
	Figure 2.4: *First and last child elements styling*
	(Here you can observe: the first child of the parent got bold style and the last child got italic style among all children.)

odd – even child: Style will be applied to odd or even child accordingly:

```
<div class="w-36 text-white">
 <div class="my-1 odd:bg-green-500
           even:bg-blue-500">one </div>
 <div class="my-1 odd:bg-green-500
           even:bg-blue-500">two</div>
 <div class="my-1 odd:bg-green-500
           even:bg-blue-500">three</div>
 <div class="my-1 odd:bg-green-500
           even:bg-blue-500">four</div>
</div>
```

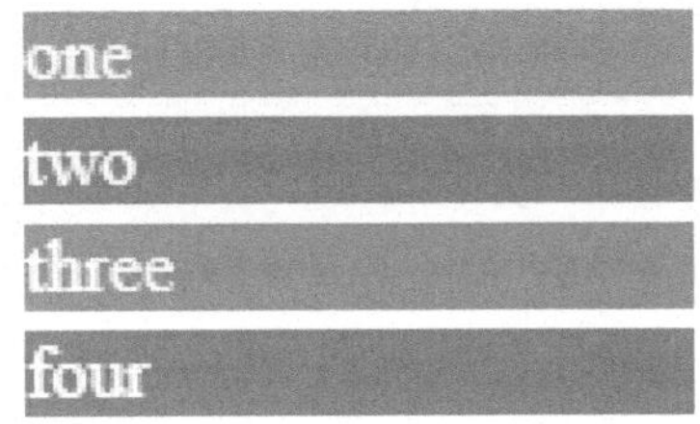

Figure 2.5: *Styling odd – even child elements*

(Similar to first – last child example, based on position within the parent element, odd or even children can be styled accordingly.)

Form element states: For example, **`required`**, **`invalid`**, **`disabled`**:

```
<input type="number" required
    class="required:bg-red-200 my-1" />
<br />
<input type="number" disabled
   class="disabled:bg-green-200 my-1" />
```

Figure 2.6: *Form elements styling*

Based on the state we mention, input element style will be reflected on it.

group: Based on interactivity with parent element style will be added to its children:

```
<div class="group w-24 p-5">
   <div class="bg-gray-100
             group-hover:bg-green-500">
       Text1
   </div>
   <div class="bg-gray-100
              group-hover:bg-red-500">
       Text2
   </div>
</div>
```

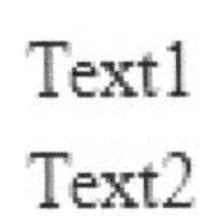

Figure 2.7: *group elements styling*

(When you hover on parent element of these two elements, background color of these will be changed accordingly, group class is mandatory for the parent element.)

peer: Style will be added to the peer or sibling element:

```
<input type="email" class="peer"/>
<p class="mt-2 invisible text-sm
          peer-invalid:visible
          peer-invalid:text-red-600 ">
        invalid
</p>
```

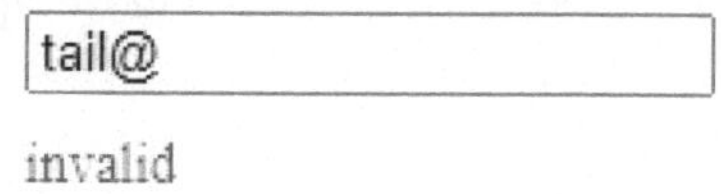

Figure 2.8: *Peer elements styling*

(Based on valid data on input element peer element **p** will be shown and hidden, peer class on deciding element is mandatory.)

before – after : These are used to style contents after or before the current element:

```
<span class="after:content-['am']
             after:text-green-500">
        I
</span>
<br />
<span class="before:content-['I']
             before:text-red-500">
        am
</span>
```

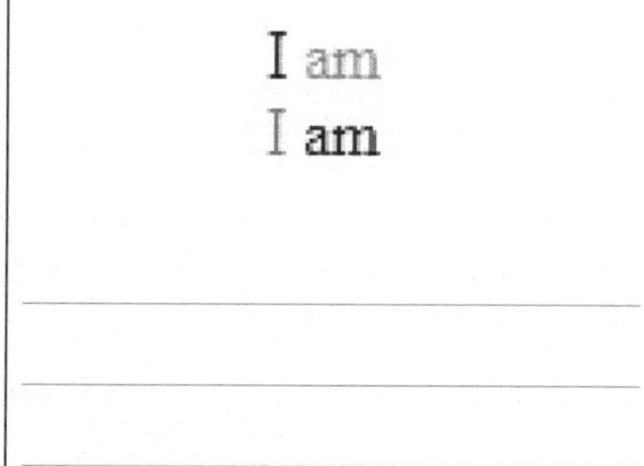

Figure 2.9: *Styling before- after elements*

(Here, in the first case, **am** with **green** color will be added after text **I** of the element, similarly in second case **I** with **red** color will be added before text **am** of the element.)

Placeholder: Before entering any characters within the input field placeholder text can be shown to convey what to enter, this can be styled using utility classes:

```
<input class=" placeholder:italic
               placeholder:text-red-500"
     placeholder="Enter name" />
```

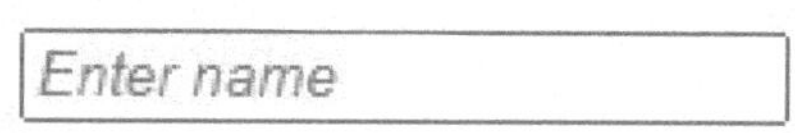

Figure 2.10: *Styling placeholder text*

(You can observe placeholder text color has styled with color **red**).

Marker: List style items will be styled using marker:

```
<ul class="marker:text-blue-500">
   <li>one</li>
   <li>two</li>
   <li>three</li>
   <li>four</li>
 </ul>
```

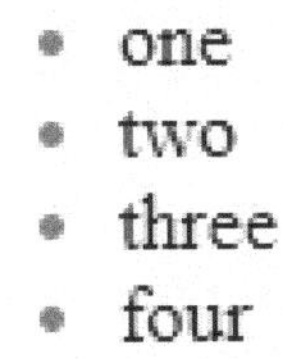

Figure 2.11: *Styling list item text*

(Listing item style has color **blue**, mentioned on parent element.)

Selection: Styling selected text using mouse cursor or keyboard – text-selection:

```
<div class="selection:bg-green-600
            selection:text-white w-36">
  <p> I am learning TailwindCSS, it is
     fun way to learn, basics are easy,
     Let's build website
  </p>
</div>
```

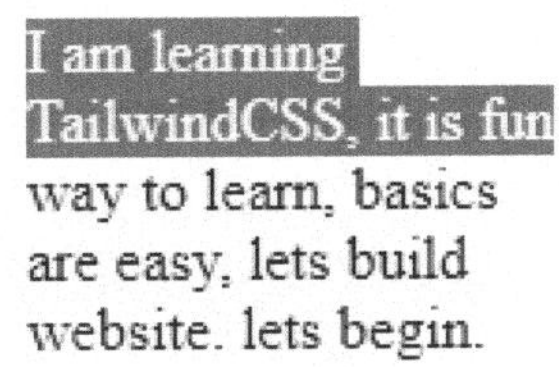

Figure 2.12: *Styling selection text*

First Line – First Letter: Style can be added to the first line or first letter of the element:

```
<p class="first-line:bg-green-500">
    I am learning TailwindCSS, it is
    fun way to learn, basics are easy
</p>


<p class="first-letter:text-3xl">
   I am learning TailwindCSS
</p>
```

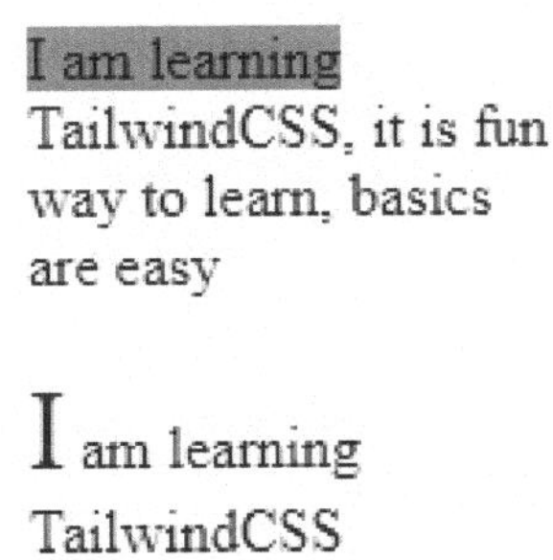

Figure 2.13: *Styling selection text*

(First line of the upper text gets **green** as background color and the first letter of the lower text has a *bigger* font size.)

Viewport: Styles can be added based on the viewport of the device.
`(portrait and landscape)`
`<div class="portrait:hidden">`
`  I am Desktop`
`</div>`
`<div class="landscape:hidden">`
`  I am Mobile`
`</div>`
	I am Mobile
	(a)
	I am Desktop
	(b)
	Figure 2.14: *Styling based on viewport*
	(*Figure (a)* got hidden whenever page got rendered on mobile *viewports – portrait.*
	Figure (b) got hidden whenever the page got rendered on desktop *viewports – landscape.*)

Print: Specific style can be added to content when they get printed:
`<p class="text-green-500`
`        print:text-red-500">`
`      I am learning TailwindCSS`
`</p>`
	I am learning TailwindCSS
	Figure 2.15: *Styling based on viewport*
	(Here you see that text is in **green** color when the page gets loaded on browser, but on print it will be printed in **red** color – (try *ctrl* + *p*).)

Table 2.1: *Examples of different events and state styling*

Apart from these ways, style can be applied using aria attributes and data attributes that we can use on HTML elements.

Not all sets of utility classes can be used with every state and event, only some of them which are used frequently and meaningfully are supported. Still, we could write custom classes to achieve it if we needed to.

> **You can chain multiple states and events with a single class, for example:**
>
> **placeholder:hover:text-green-500**
>
> **When hovering on placeholder text it will be changed to green, each state/ event is separated by : (colon).**

Responsive design

Being an emerging CSS framework, Tailwind CSS provides a smoother way of achieving responsiveness on a website. As we need to follow, *Mobile First approach* to build website, to make it feel good on different kinds of devices right from mobile to larger displays, Tailwind CSS's utility classes provide target breakpoint keywords to prepend with usual classes so that style variants will be added accordingly to create adaptive user interfaces.

Let's look into Tailwind CSS default breakpoints list; here you can understand **breakpoints**, **maximum width of the screen** on which they can work, and **CSS media query** of that breakpoint:

Breakpoint name	Breakpoint width	Equivalent Media query

sm
(for **smaller** width devices)
	640px	`@media (min-width: 640px) {`
		`// CSS Rules`
		`}`

md
(for **medium** width devices)
	768px	`@media (min-width: 768px) {`
		`// CSS Rules`
		`}`

lg
(for **large** width devices)
	1024px	`@media (min-width: 1024px) {`
		`// CSS Rules`
		`}`

xl
(for **extra-large** width devices)
	1280px	`@media (min-width: 1280px) {`
		`// CSS Rules`
		`}`

2xl
(for **double extra-large** width devices)
	1536px	`@media (min-width: 1536px) {`
		`// CSS Rules`
		`}`

***Table 2.2**: Tailwind CSS responsive design breakpoints*

Along with these breakpoint classes, we are free to use any of the utility classes to make any variation in style for different device viewports. Changing the color of **div** on mobile, width on larger devices can be basic usages.

The following example shows changing color of the background in different devices:

```
<div class="h-36 w-36
```

```
        bg-pink-500
        sm:bg-red-500
        md:bg-green-500
        lg:bg-gray-500
        xl:bg-blue-500
        2xl:bg-gray-200">
</div>
```


***Figure 2.16**: Change of div color in responsive design*

When you run the above code it adapts different colors in different devices, the figure shows color of **div** with 2×*l* breakpoint.

If you haven't mentioned any breakpoint, it means a common utility class, which influences all kinds of breakpoints. If you mention utility class with only **sm** breakpoint that style will be applicable to all devices equal to or above **sm** breakpoint. Similarly, if you mention utility class with **md** breakpoint, then style will be applicable to all devices having width as **md** and above breakpoints.

> **If you want to style only smaller devices and all larger devices should obey the same style, then no need to mention utility classes for all breakpoints.**
>
> **`sm:bg-green-500 md:bg-red-500`**
>
> **green background is applied for only smaller (`sm`) devices and all other devices equal to or above `md` (`lg, xl, 2xl`) get red as their background color.**

Targeting a breakpoint range

As you read previously, if you mention breakpoint with a classname, it will be applied to all the preceding breakpoints. But there is a possibility we can provide a range of breakpoints for a particular class. So that utility class we will apply to that range of devices:

- **sm:bg-green-500**: Applies green as background from **sm** breakpoint.

- **sm:max-lg:bg-red-500**: Applies red as background color between **sm** and **lg** breakpoints.
- **Targeting a single breakpoint**: There are situations where we need to apply class for a particular resolution. There, by targeting the next resolution with a utility class we can achieve it.
- **sm:max-md:flex**: Flex will be applied to resolution with **sm** width devices.
- **md:max-lg:font-semibold**: Font semi bold, will be applied to resolution with **md** with devices.

Dark mode

These days dark mode is one of the popular features among the latest operating systems. Now it is more common than designing a website in a dark mode to go along with a default design of the operating system.

Tailwind CSS comes with this feature to make dark mode design development easier. As like other things responsive design, event and state the dark mode can be applied similar to them. Mentioning the **dark** keyword before our utility class and a colon in-between.

Let's have a simple example:

```
      <div class="dark">
            <div class="h-10 w-10 bg-green-400 dark:bg-red-500"></div>
</div>
```

This will render a **green** box on browser windows with a **default** or **light** mode, try switching your browser mode to **dark**, then you can see a red-colored box.

If you wish you can make this light/dark mode shifting manually on your webpage instead of relying on the operating system's behavior. To make that you can make the following changes to your Tailwind configuration file.

On **tailwind.config.js**:

```
module.exports = {
  darkMode: 'class',
}
```

Then to make dark variants to work with our usual variant it is mandatory to mention **dark** class to the parent element. Now, manual toggling can be achieved by adding/removing this class with parent element using JavaScript.

HTML

```
<div class="flex justify-center w-40" id="parentDiv">
      <div class="flex flex-col">
            <div class="flex justify-center" >
                  <div class="h-10 w-10 bg-green-400 dark:bg-
red-500"></div>
            </div>
            <button class="bg-blue-400 mt-5" onclick="changeMode()">
change mode
</button>
      </div>
 </div>
```

JavaScript

This code should be added between **<script></script>** before closing the body element:

```
function changeMode() {
      var element = document.getElementById('parentDiv')
      if(element.classList.contains('dark')) {
            element.classList.remove('dark')
      } else {
            element.classList.add('dark')
      }
  }
```

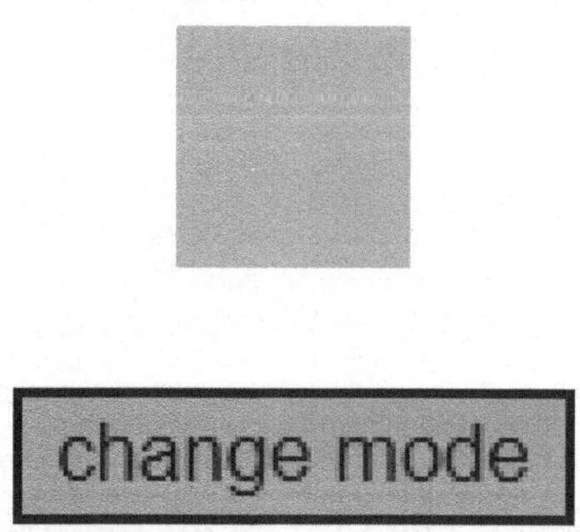

***Figure 2.17**: Changing light/dark mode*

In the preceding HTML chunk, you observe that there is no dark class added to any of the elements, but we have a *dark* variant style defined for an element to change its background color (**green** for light mode – **red** for dark mode). In JavaScript, we are handling adding and removing of **dark** utility class to the element which has ID **parentDiv** to toggle between *dark* and *light* mode. Each time when you click on a button present in the HTML (change mode), it calls the JavaScript function. It adds/removes class dark to/from the element. The color of the **div** changes accordingly.

Reusing styles

Assume that we are showing 10 *square boxes* with the same design, *what will be the primary approach for this*? Adding the same classes to each element.

But at the beginning of learning the Tailwind CSS approach itself somewhere, you already suspected that these Tailwind CSS utility classes were creating a mess with the readability of the HTML document.

You may agree on the usage of the same set of utility classes on a set of elements to obtain the same style:

```
<div class="flex justify-center gap-2">
      <div class="h-20 w-20 bg-green-500 border-2 border-green-900
                  rounded-2xl hover:bg-blue-600 active:bg-gray-300">
      </div>


      <div class="h-20 w-20 bg-green-500 border-2 border-green-900
                  rounded-2xl hover:bg-blue-600 active:bg-gray-300">
      </div>
      <div class="h-20 w-20 bg-green-500 border-2 border-green-900
                  rounded-2xl hover:bg-blue-600 active:bg-gray-300">
      </div>
      <div class="h-20 w-20 bg-green-500 border-2 border-green-900
                  rounded-2xl hover:bg-blue-600 active:bg-gray-300">
      </div>
      <div class="h-20 w-20 bg-green-500 border-2 border-green-900
                  rounded-2xl hover:bg-blue-600 active:bg-gray-300">
      </div>
      <div class="h-20 w-20 bg-green-500 border-2 border-green-900
                  rounded-2xl hover:bg-blue-600 active:bg-gray-300">
      </div>
```

```
    <div class="h-20 w-20 bg-green-500 border-2 border-green-900
                rounded-2xl hover:bg-blue-600 active:bg-gray-300">
    </div>
    <div class="h-20 w-20 bg-green-500 border-2 border-green-900
                rounded-2xl hover:bg-blue-600 active:bg-gray-300">
    </div>
    <div class="h-20 w-20 bg-green-500 border-2 border-green-900
                rounded-2xl hover:bg-blue-600 active:bg-gray-300">
    </div>
</div>
```

***Figure 2.18**: Multiple elements with the same style*

Hence, to make a similar style, we are writing/repeating the same pattern to make code readability more difficult.

In *real-time projects*, while displaying similar items we usually follow looping mechanisms where we define style elements within the loop so that it will repeat that many times programmatically:

For example:

```
for loop begins (loop for 10 times)
    <div class="h-20 w-20 bg-green-500 border-2 border-green-900
               rounded-2xl hover:bg-blue-600 active:bg-gray-300">
</div>
for loop ends
```

Here, an element with a specific set of utility classes got rendered for 10 *times*, with the same style effects as for loop executes for 10 *times*.

Code editor support – multi cursor editing

If you are using such elements with the same set of classes on it within the same HTML document then there are powerful code editors, which provide support for editing multiple lines at the same time by providing multiple cursor support, where users can create multiple blinking cursor points to add or edit characters. Example: **VSCode**, **JetBrains**, and so on.

Using frameworks

While developing projects with **React**, **Vue**, **blade**, and so on technologies, where you can be able to create components for frequently using HTML block. In such cases, applying utility classes to elements present in those components keeps the code cleaner. Along with the page structure and logic, keeping respective styles abstracted using components is a popular approach in modern technologies.

CSS abstraction

Whenever we are using elements with the same set of styles in different files then those styles can be abstracted using CSS. Those elements get the same class name, and that class name will be used to add styles from CSS.

HTML file 1	HTML file 2	External CSS

<div class="box">
    This is file 1
</div>
	<div class="box">
	    This is file 2
	</div>
		.box {
		  background-color: green ;
		  color: white
		}

***Table 2.3**: CSS abstraction*

When you render those two separate HTML files, the element gets rendered with the same style – the basic functionality of the external CSS approach.

Extracting classes with @apply

It is a feature provided by Tailwind CSS to create a generic style block that can be used anywhere in your project. It's a way out of the box feature, where we are defining CSS rule not by *key-value pairs*, but instead with those set utility classes provided by Tailwind CSS. Yes, it is that simple.

Open your **input.css** file from the **src** folder of your project. There you can see only line **@tailwind utilities;** as we used only utility classes till now. Add the following statement next to it to make component addition possible:

```
@tailwind utilities;
```

Here, we can see a simple example of how components look like. We are extending the component structure of the Tailwind CSS, then as a part of extending, we are defining a CSS rule with utility classes that are required to form an expected generic style:

```
@layer components {
  .btn-primary {
    @apply   py-2 px-4 bg-blue-500 text-white font-semibold rounded-lg
            shadow-md hover:bg-blue-700 focus:outline-none focus:ring-2
             focus:ring-blue-400 focus:ring-opacity-75;
  }
}
```

We can use this **.btn-primary** class anywhere in our project, it loads/applies all these respective lists of utility classes to the element of the HTML document.

Let's try this approach to create a similar result as we saw in *Figure 2.14*.

Add this in **input.css** file:

```
@layer components {
  .box {
 @apply h-20 w-20 bg-green-500 border-2 border-green-900 rounded-2xl
              hover:bg-blue-600 active:bg-gray-300;
  }
}
```

HTML block

```
<div class="flex justify-center gap-2">
      <div class="box"></div>
      <div class="box"></div>
      <div class="box"></div>
      <div class="box"></div>
      <div class="box"></div>
      <div class="box"></div>
      <div class="box"></div>
      <div class="box"></div>
      <div class="box"></div>
```

```
    <div class="box"></div>
</div>
```

Simple. *Right? Do you agree that now HTML has more readability?* Adding only class **box** to all elements renders all those related utility classes referred behind class **box**. You can try this to match a similar result.

Advantages of this approach

The advantages of this approach are as follows:

- Remembering utility classes are enough to create a component.
- Altering style is not scarier. You need to change it in only one place.
- You can still add more utility classes to HTML elements, along with generic class.

> **Do not create reusable components as you wish in your project, it is highly not recommended. Just to create cleaner HTML, you should not follow this approach. Create a component only if it is required and will be used frequently in your project. As you create more components for simple designs, it violates the advantages of Tailwind CSS and grows compiled CSS unimaginably.**

Adding custom styles

Only by providing a set of a rich number of utility classes to create any kind of styles Tailwind CSS couldn't be so popular. It is allowing developers to customize as, and they require for their needs. Let's look into how to make customization.

All the customizations will be added using the configuration file of the Tailwind CSS. Customization of styles is called customization of themes.

Open **`tailwind.config.js`**.

You can find this block. This is the place where you can make your customization. More specifically you are extending a **theme**:

```
theme: {
    extend: {},
}
```

In this extended block, we can define all our customization related to *screen resolution breakpoints*, *color variants*, and *font families* that need to be added. Let's see some of them:

```
module.exports = {
  theme: {
      extend: {
              colors: {
                   'silver': '#C0C0C0',
                   'bronze': '#CD7F32'
              },
      },
   }
 }
```

Now you can use these custom classes similar to default classes:

```
<div class="flex justify-center gap-2">
    <div class="h-20 w-20 bg-bronze"></div>
    <div class="h-20 w-20 bg-silver"></div>
    <div class="h-20 w-20 bg-green-100 text-silver">Silver Text</div>
    <div class="h-20 w-20 bg-green-100 text-bronze">Bronze Text</div>
</div>
```

This will render the following output:

***Figure 2.19**: Custom colors in utility classes*

Those custom colors cannot be limited to use only with background or text, you are free to use this color wherever **color** property has a possibility.

Defining customization like colors and other properties outside the extended block within the theme block creates new rules itself. Further, you cannot use Tailwind CSS default classes in your HTML document.

Similarly, we can extend **spacing** property, add the following definition within the **extend** block, these are the styles that are not there in Tailwind CSS by default:

```
spacing: {
        '101': '32rem',
        '102': '36rem',
}
```

Now you are free to use **101** and **102** digits with any spacing-related utility class as default possibilities. **101** and **102** can be used with *margin*, *padding*, *height*, *width*, and so on.

For example, m-101, pl-101, pt-102, h-101.

You can customize these spacing-related properties to extend blocks separately as well.

Arbitrary variants

Yes, Tailwind CSS provides a rich number of utility classes, by using them we can craft any kind of design. But at some moment we need a very perfect design for our website instead of adjusting with existing classes. There is no need to keep writing/extending custom classes for all of them.

Tailwind CSS supports usage of **arbitrary values** for utility classes wherever it is possible. That's a very useful feature where we can customize style more quickly and easily.

For example, there are certain values provided by Tailwind CSS for padding like **1**,**2**,**3**,**4**,**5**,**6**, and so on, these are the most used variants, but if we need a different variant than these then we just need to pass the expected value as an arbitrary value for padding class in place of those numbers but within square brackets **[]**. The expected value can be anything that CSS supports.

Possible arbitrary classes	Explanation of arbitrary value
`p-[15px]`	Adds padding of **15px**, relative to the viewing device.
`p-[4rem]`	It is relative to the font size of the root element.
`p-[3em]`	It is relative to the font size of the element.
`p-[2in]`	It adds padding in inches – (1in = 96px).
`p-[10cm]`	It adds padding in centimeters.

Possible arbitrary classes	Explanation of arbitrary value
`p-[15px]`	Adds padding of **15px**, relative to the viewing device.
`p-[4rem]`	It is relative to the font size of the root element.
`p-[80mm]`	It adds padding in millimeters.
`p-[5pt]`	It adds padding in points (*1pt* = *1/72* of *1in*).
`p-[10pc]`	It adds padding in picas (*1pc* = *12 pt*).
`p-[2ex]`	It is relative to the *x-height* of the current font.
`p-[5ch]`	It is relative to the width of the '0' (*zero*).
`p-[10vw]`	It is relative to *1% of the width* of the browser viewport. (If the viewport is 50 *cm wide*, *1 vw* = *0.5cm*)
`p-[2vmin]`	It is relative to *1% of browser* viewport's smaller dimension.
`p-[4vmax]`	It is relative to *1% of browser* viewport's smaller dimension.
`p-[10%]`	Adds padding in percentage, which is relative to the parent element.

Table 2.4*: Possibility of arbitrary values with padding property*

You can use the same kind of arbitrary values on any of those utility classes which can hold measurement-related values. For example, *height*, *width*, *margin*, and so on.

There are no restrictions to pass arbitrary values for utility classes with *states*, *events*, or *breakpoint*-related logics in your HTML document. For example, **top-[117px] lg:top-[344px]**.

Arbitrary value can be used with background property as well. Let's have some examples:

Possible arbitrary classes	Explanation of arbitrary value
`bg-[#ededed]`	Renders `#ededed` hex color as background-color.
`bg-[url(' https://shorturl.at/owDEW')]`	Render image as background- image.
`bg-['rgb(201, 76, 76)']`	Renders `rgb` color as background-color.
`bg-['rgba(201, 76, 76,1)']`	Render `rgb` with opacity as background-color.

Table 2.5*: Possibility of arbitrary values with background property*

Handling ambiguities

While adding arbitrary values, there are possibilities we may override some other property instead of the expected one or say pass the wrong value as an arbitrary value.

Tailwind CSS is built with automatic handling of ambiguity based on type arbitrary value that we pass and generates respective utility for it.

For example, we are trying to add an arbitrary value for text color, instead of passing a supported color value. If we pass a measurement value then by resolving this ambiguity it generates the respective class for text-size:

```
<div class="text-[5rem]">Hi TailwindCSS</div>
// This generates a class for text-size ( font-size - property)
<div class="text-[#d0d0d0]">I am gray text</div>
// This generates a class for text-color (color - property)
```

CSS and @layer

Whenever you want to add custom styles to your project then the easiest way is to add them in a stylesheet, where you are defining Tailwind CSS. Along with the usage of normal CSS rules, you can use the **@layer** directive of Tailwind CSS to gain more power.

Tailwind CSS identifies styles in *three* different ways:

- **base**: Styles of default HTML elements.
- **components**: Component styles.
- **utilities**: Utility styles.

We can customize each one of these using the **@layer** directive, we already see a glance at this approach before itself to create a customized generic component.

Let's look into the simple examples of each style section, before that make sure you added these three statements in your **input.css** file:

```
@tailwind base;
@tailwind components;
@tailwind utilities;
```

Customizing base styles

```
@layer base {
  p {
    font-size: 1.5rem ;
  }
  span {
    @apply bg-green-200;
  }
}
```

The preceding definition says that the **p** element should be rendered with **font-size 1.5rem** (CSS rule) and the span element should be with **green** as its background (utility class with **@apply**):

```
<p>this is paragraph </p>
<br />
<span>span text</span>
```

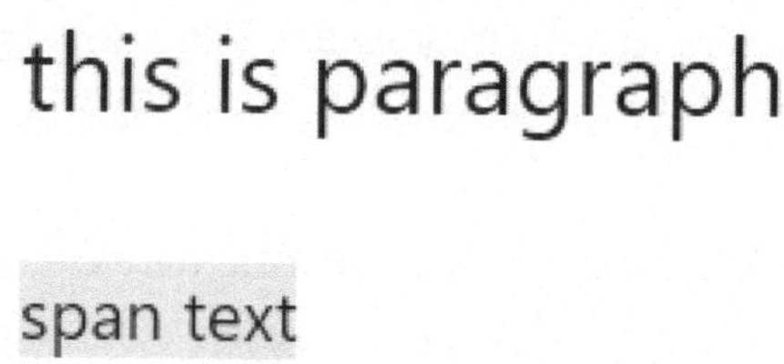

***Figure 2.20**: Custom base styles*

On browsers, you can get respected styles added to default elements.

Customizing component classes

Along with **@layer** directive we need to use the **components** keyword to customize component styles:

```
@layer components {
      .box {
            border: 2px solid black;
            border-radius:20px ;
            margin: theme('spacing.2');
```

```
    }
}
```

Here, we are defining style rules for a component called **box**, you can observe that the first *two* rules are normal CSS rules, and the last one is using the **theme()** function of Tailwind CSS to refer to style from the theme (either default style of Tailwind CSS or those we defined at the configuration file) to add **spacing-2** utility value for the component's **margin** property.

Just add the class name of the component in an HTML document:

```
<div class="box h-20 w-20 bg-green-400"></div>
```

You can observe the following result, referring to styles from custom component classes along with default utility classes:

Figure 2.21: *Custom component styles*

Customizing utility styles

Along with **@layer** directive, we need to use the **utilities** keyword to customize utility classes:

```
@layer utilities {
    .text-xl {
        color: '#0e0e0e';
        font-size: 5rem;
    }
}
```

Here, we are overriding default styles of **text-xl** class to custom styles, where we are adding **text-color** as hex **#0e0e0e** and **text-size** as **5rem**.

Add this class to the HTML element to observe custom styles added:

```
<p class="text-xl">I am xl text</p>
```

Figure 2.22: *Custom utility styles*

The default behavior of **text-xl** utility class has been overridden by custom styles.

Function and directives

From previous sections, you already saw some keywords of Tailwind CSS like **@layer**, **@tailwind**, **@appy**, and so on. Now let's look into them and what they mean.

Directives

These are tailwind-specific at-rule functionalities. Provides a special way of using Tailwind CSS in our CSS.

@tailwind

This directive is used to add Tailwind's base, components, and utilities in our CSS file:

Example: **`@tailwind base ;`**

@layer

This directive is used to mention customized classes belong to which set of styles.

Example: Custom classes belongs to base styles:

```
@layer base {
      //custom classes
}
```

@apply

This directive is used to add utility classes as a style rule for custom classes instead of *property-value* pairs.

Example: This definition should be present in your **input.css** file:

```
p {
      @apply bg-green-400 text-xl ;
}
```

@apply approach of defining styles will not work with internal CSS definitions (within **<style></style>** element of HTML document). As CSS and HTML files are processed separately.

It is not possible to add !important keywords along with @apply. If you add then Tailwind CSS removes it automatically in an output version of CSS.

@config

This directive is used to specify which config file of tailwind should be used while compiling our CSS file (**input.css**). Sometimes in projects, we need to refer to configuration from a different file than the actual **tailwind.config.js**.

Example: **@config "./tailwind.site.config.js";**

Functions

Tailwind provides some custom functions we can use in our CSS to access Tailwind-specific values. These functions are evaluated at build-time, and are replaced by static values in our output CSS.

theme()

This function is used to access Tailwind config values using (.) dot notation. From the example given in the previous section, you already got some hint of this.

Example: Here class **.greenery** gets background equal to **colors.green.600** utility class:

input.css

```
.greenery {
   background-color: theme(colors.green.600);
}
```

In our **output.css** file, we can observe that this class gets exactly the same style as **bg-green-500** style.

output.css

```
.greenery {
    background-color: #16a34a;
}
```

screen()

This function is used to get screen resolution values (breakpoint values) as defined in the configuration file. Using this, we can avoid mentioning resolution values directly while writing custom media queries.

Example: This shows how we can write custom media queries in our input.css and how it will be compiled into the **output.css** file:

input.css

```
@media screen(md) {
  /* ... */
}
```

output.css

```
@media (min-width: 768px) {
  /* ... */
}
```

Conclusion

This chapter provided brief information on core features that made Tailwind CSS popular for usability. Hope you gained a bit of knowledge on the pillars of the CSS framework – Tailwind CSS. A thorough understanding of these concepts makes it more convenient to use Tailwind CSS more powerfully.

In the next chapter, we are learning utility - classes in depth and applying them to HTML documents to analyze the results.

Points to remember

- Utility classes are the heart of the Tailwind CSS.
- State and events handling from utility classes itself made Tailwind CSS feel different from inline CSS.
- Utility classes with screen resolution breakpoints save lots of time we spend on writing media query.

- Dark mode development is easy; toggling keyword **dark** plays a key role.
- Reuse of classes has an efficient way to achieve this.
- Customization can be done easily with a configuration file.
- Tailwind-specific directive & function makes work easier.

Multiple choice questions

1. **Hover and focus are:**
    a. Events
    b. States
    c. Feature
    d. Functionality
2. **peer utility class affects:**
    a. Current element
    b. Root element
    c. Next element
    d. Previous element
3. **Mobile devices targeted with:**
    a. With **sm**
    b. With **md**
    c. No breakpoint
    d. With **lg**
4. **Dark mode toggled using:**
    a. HTML
    b. CSS
    c. JavaScript
    d. None of these

5. **@apply directive used for:**
    a. Define Tailwind CSS style
    b. Define components
    c. Apply utility classes as styles
    d. Define configuration file
6. **Extend block in the configuration file is meant for:**
    a. Utility classes
    b. Custom class definitions
    c. CSS rules
    d. JavaScript functions

Answers

1. **a**
2. **c**
3. **c**
4. **c**
5. **c**
6. **b**

CHAPTER 3

Utility-First Classes and Customization Options

Introduction

This chapter provides detailed information on resources available in Tailwind CSS: a set of utility-first classes. In the previous chapter, you already read that utility-first classes are the heart of Tailwind CSS. Yes, here we are explaining how they are formed and their various categories. Categories in the sense styling aspects of the webpage. We covered more information on the customization of the framework as well and you already had a glimpse of it in the previous chapter. Understanding the meaning of utility-first classes makes you fit to dive into the development of the website.

Structure

In this chapter, the following topics will be discussed:

- Customization
- Base style
- Layout
- Flexbox and Grid

- Spacing
- Sizing

Customization

Since Tailwind CSS comes with a rich number of built-in utility classes to create complex user interfaces, we are not able to stick with those default styles alone. Different projects require different sets of styles. That's where the customization concept arises and Tailwind CSS supports a very feasible way to achieve it.

In the previous chapter, you already understood what customization is and how Tailwind CSS supports it to make our custom style adapted to existing rules. Here, we are providing information on each concept involved in the *customization* process.

Before that, we suggest that you restore all the changes that we/you made on **tailwind.config.js** regarding customization. So that we can begin from scratch again:

```
module.exports = {
  content: [],
  theme: {
    extend: {},
  },
  plugins: [],
}
```

The preceding code block shows the default configuration code that will be generated after running the following command:

```
npx tailwindcss init
```

Also, remove anything apart from these three from the **input.css** file:

```
@tailwind base;
@tailwind utilities;
@tailwind components;
```

Let's look into the possible key-value pairs that **module.exports** can have.

Content

This section is where you provide those file paths in HTML, JS, or any other file where you are willing to use Tailwind CSS classnames:

```
content: [
    './pages/**/*.{html,js}',
    './components/**/*.{html,js}',
],
```

Tailwind CSS scans all sets of files that you mention within this content section for the existence of Tailwind CSS class names. It then generates the respective CSS styles in the output CSS file.

From the preceding code, you can see the usage of * that indicates that anything can come in the path (any number of intermediate folders except slashes and hidden folders), ** indicates zero or more possible folders named in the path. Remember that all file paths must be relative to the **`tailwind.config.js`** file.

Never include CSS in the content section as it is meant to scan class names within the template, not within the generated styles.

Scanning of classnames is nothing but Tailwind CSS uses regular expressions to match scanning strings with exact utility-first class names that might be available.

While adding a classname using a condition, you should provide a complete classname instead of adding part of the classname using a condition.

While styling those components from *third-party libraries*, we need not use **`@ layer`** directive to style as they are not a direct part of our project or Tailwind CSS environment.

Classes Safelisting

There is a feature in Tailwind CSS where you can provide class names that need to be added without scanning the files if you doubt encountering those classes from files, but you still need it for the safer side. It is safelisting of the classes.

You can add this within the **`module.exports`** object similar to the content section:

```
safelist: [
    'bg-red-500',
    'text-3xl',
    'lg:text-4xl',
]
```

This adds the mentioned classes' appropriate styles directly to output CSS even though scanning doesn't find them among any template files.

Theme

What you read in the previous chapter on customization is all about the theme section itself. It is a place purely meant for total customization. *Colors*, *fonts*, *spacing*, *breakpoints*, and so on are all defined here.

This theme section/object further contains sub-sections for *screens*, *colors*, *spacing*, *animation*, *float*, and so on, it can be a key or subpart which is among the core plugins of Tailwind CSS. Also, remember that not all plugins have a relative key within the theme object.

By using these objects, you can customize most of the styles as per your expectation. To make Tailwind CSS work seamlessly with your project. If you fail to mention custom styles for any of the objects, then they automatically inherit styles from the default theme. To disable a particular core plugin completely, mention that object with the **`corePlugins`** section within the **`module.exports`** object:

```
module.exports = {
  corePlugins: {
    container: false,
  }
}
```

This disables all styles of **container** objects with the default theme of Tailwind CSS.

Extend

This is the important object that comes under the theme object. By customizing supported core plugins using their objects you are overriding existing rules of the Tailwind CSS. By using this extended object, you can just add expected styles along with existing styles:

```
module.exports = {
  theme: {
      extend: {
            colors: {
                  'silver': '#C0C0C0',
```

```
                    'bronze': '#CD7F32'
                },
            },
        }
    }
```

In the previous chapter, you already saw this example of extending styles with existing themes.

Screens

This section under the **`module.exports`** object is used to define project-specific breakpoints which are different from default breakpoints. The classes you mention here can be used as responsive modifiers along with *utility* classes. This section elaborates on those things which we discussed in *Chapter 2, Design Principles for Tailwind* CSS with the title **Responsive Design**.

```
module.exports = {
  theme: {
    screens: {
      'sm': '640px',
      'md': '768px',
      'lg': '1024px',
      'xl': '1280px',
      '2xl': '1536px',
    }
  }
}
```

These are the default breakpoints of the Tailwind CSS, where each classname represents the minimum width they will target. If you wish to change this targeting width to your custom width then just mention that specific width with the respective classname. Then onwards that responsive modifier targets adding/removing styles with respect to the width you specify:

```
theme: {
    screens: {
      'sm': '500px',
      'md': '900px',
      'lg': '1500px'
```

```
    },
  }
```

It doesn't mean that you can only override those number of default breakpoints for breakpoint targeting, you are free to define new responsive modifiers as well:

```
screens: {
       '3xl': '1800px',
       '5xl': '2500px',
}
```

You can even name these responsive modifiers if you wish, but still, you are not restricted to that as well:

```
screens: {
       'mobile': '640px',
       'medium': '768px',
       'tablet': '1024px',
       'laptop': '1280px',
       'desktop': '1536px',
}
```

So, there is no change in the usage of these as a responsive modifier:

```
<div class=" mobile:bg-green-400
             medium:bg-gray-600
             laptop:bg-pink-400
             desktop:bg-red-600 ">
</div>
```

Feels awesome right?

Since, you targeted the devices based on **min-width**, its inverse is possible as well for breakpoint creation. You can define breakpoints by referring to the **max-width** that a breakpoint can have an effect on:

```
screens: {
       'lg': {
               'max': '1000px'
       },
}
```

Like media queries, you can even add **min** and **max** width for breakpoints as part of customization. So that style was added to this responsive modifier alone. It reverts with other bigger/smaller resolution breakpoints:

```
screens: {
     'md': {
      'max': '600px', // has no effect below this width (default behavior)
      'min': '900px' // has no effect after this width (added behavior)
      },
}
```

Colors

Right from the beginning of this book, we have provided lots of examples as you already read. We hope you might be curious about the usage of color names for *background*, *border*, and *text*. Along with the color name, we are mentioning some digits like 100, 200, 300, and so on.

As color is an important part of the aesthetics of the website, Tailwind CSS comes with enough varieties of utility classes by default. Those digits along with the color name indicate a variant of the same color with different transparency.

Starting from 50 to 900, the color variant's transparency increases gradually. This is the default set of colors that Tailwind CSS provides.

Slate, Gray, Zinc, Neutral, Stone, Red, Orange, Amber, Lime, Green, Emerald, Teal, Cyan, Sky, Blue, Indigo, Violet, Purple, Fuchsia, Pink, and Rose.

Each of these again has internal variants with 50 – 900 *range* transparency.

Feel free to override these default colors as per your project-specific requirements:

```
module.exports = {
        theme: {
                colors: {
                        'pale': '#fedfed',
                        'gum' : '#defdef',
                }
        }
}
```

These custom colors can be used similarly to other colors (except the transparency range).

For example, **bg-gum**, **text-pale**.

If you wish, you can define transparency values as well as an object parameter of color. These parameters can be anything relatable with color to group them with the color name, it is not mandatory to pass transparent values itself. Since you are passing the color hex code, you can pass any color of your wish:

```
colors: {
        'gum': {
                50: '#fefefd'
                100: '#ececef'
                200: '#adfe65'
        }
}
```

These can be used similarly to default color classes, for example, **bg-gum-50**, **text-gum-200**, and so on.

Apart from overriding the configuration you can even pass arbitrary values for the color along with expected utility classes.

bg-[#dbdb65] , text-[#456abc], border[#aabb77]

These are some examples of arbitrary classes for colors. You just need to pass the color code within square brackets.

You can use the existing colors to create new colors, and color objects provide access to the Tailwind CSS-supported color set. By importing it into the configuration file:

```
const colors = require('tailwindcss/colors');
module.exports = {
        theme: {
                colors: {
                        maroon: color.red
                }
        }
}
```

You are allowed to use any name for the color classes (*primary*, *secondary*, and so on) as per your needs. You can alias other colors to some other colors as well.

For example, **`green: colors.emerald`** - then onwards wherever you use the color **`green`** it will show color **`emerald`**. Simple, *isn't it*?

Instead of extending colors, if you directly mention colors under the theme object, it declines all other default colors and only those defined colors can be used in your templates.

`<div class=”bg-green-400”>` - This will add **`emerald`** color for the background instead of **`green`** as you mentioned **`emerald`** for **`green`** keyword.

It is not mandatory that you always need to use hex color codes for defining colors, you can use rgb (red, green, blue) colors and hsl (hue, saturation, lighness) colours.

```
        colors: {
            maroon : rgb(255, 87, 51),
            guava  : hsl(57°, 89%, 33%)
}
```

Spacing

While developing a user interface along with colors, the spacing parameter too has an important role. Simple design with a proper spacing mechanism can also create a good impact on user interfaces. Customization is like other sections, for this we need to use spacing objects to define our values.

This table shows the default values followed by Tailwind CSS for spacing scales:

0	px	0.5	1	1.5	2	2.5	3	3.5	4	5
0px	1px	2px	4px	6px	8px	10px	12px	14px	16px	20px

6	7	8	9	10	11	12	14	16	20	24
24px	28px	32px	36px	40px	44px	48px	56px	64px	80px	96px

28	32	36	40	44	48	52	56	60	64	72
112px	128px	144px	160px	176px	192px	208px	224px	240px	256px	288px

80	96
320px	384px

***Table 3.1**: Default spacing values*

These spacing values can be used with *border*, *margin*, *padding*, *height*, *width*, *gap* and other spacing-related utility classes.

For example, **m-1**, **p-5**, **w-24**, **h-36**.

Let's see an instance of customization of the spacing scale:

```
module.exports = {
  theme: {
    spacing: {
      '1': '10px',
      '2': '1.5rem'
    }
  }
}
```

Plugins

If you want to add some new features from an external source (pre-developed) to your project, you need to use plugins for that. Here, in our case, if we want to use external styles in our project, we can use plugins with Tailwind CSS, where JavaScript injects those styles directly into the project's stylesheet.

Let's look into some official plugins from Tailwind CSS, which are more useful while developing a website.

Typography - **`@tailwindcss/typography`**

This provides a set of prose classes that are useful to style typographic content blocks. This can override pre-styled content from CMS.

For example, **`prose md:prose-lg`**

Forms - **`@tailwindcss/forms`**

This plugin is used to style form elements along with utility classes. Enhances the look and feel of form elements of HTML documents.

Aspect ratio - **`@tailwindcss/aspect-ratio`**

This plugin provides classes to apply a *fixed height-width ratio* to the element, which is an aspect ratio of an element.

For example, **`aspect-w-3 aspect-h-2`** makes an element with an aspect ratio of **`3:2`**.

Prefix

While using Tailwind CSS along with other CSS libraries, there are chances that Tailwind CSS utility classes may face conflicts with classes in other libraries. In such scenarios, Tailwind CSS faces confusion about what to do with such class names. To resolve this, we can use a prefix object to add some prefixes for Tailwind CSS so that scanning captures suitable classnames for respected CSS rules generation.

For example:

```
module.exports = {
  prefix: 'tw-',
}
```

Furthermore, you need to use the **`tw-`** prefix for all utility-first classes of Tailwind CSS:

```
<div class="tw-bg-red-500 tw-m-2">
  <!-- -->
</div>
```

Tailwind CSS even provides an approach to create reusable configuration settings of our own that can be used across various projects – **preset configuration**.

The explanation of the creation of this reusable customization is beyond the context of this book.

Base styles

Tailwind CSS comes with a set of styles arranged for its projects – **Preflight.**

Preflight

Preflight is a set of base styles for Tailwind CSS which are crafted smoothly to overcome cross-browser inconsistencies and make the design system cleaner and easier.

These preflight styles are injected into the base styles of the **`@tailwind`** system. As these styles deal with HTML default tags so most of the time, they may go unnoticed while working with them. They are styled in a way that they behave as you would expect.

These are the modifications made for Tailwind CSS:

- Default margins removed:

  `blockquote`, **`dl`**, **`dd`**, **`h1`**, **`h2`**, **`h3`**, **`h4`**, **`h5`**, **`h6`**, **`hr`**, **`figure`**, **`p`**, **`pre`** for these tags margin kept as **`0`** (**`margin: 0px`**).

- Headings unstyled:

  `h1`, **`h2`**, **`h3`**, **`h4`**, **`h5`**, **`h6`** for these tags font size and font weight are just inherited, there are no specific styles defined.

- Lists unstyled:

  ```
  ol,
  ul {
    list-style: none;
    margin: 0;
    padding: 0;
  }
  ```

  While using lists in TailwindCSS you need to specify styles for them via utility classes.

- Images and other similar tags - block level and constrained with parent element width:

  ```
  img, svg, video, canvas, audio, iframe, embed, object
  {
    display: block;
    vertical-align: middle;
  }

   img, video {
        max-width: 100%;
        height: auto;
      }
  ```

- Border styles - reset globally:

  ```
  *, ::before, ::after {
  border-width: 0;
  ```

```
    border-style: solid;
    border-color: theme('borderColor.DEFAULT', currentColor);
  }
```

- Buttons - have a default outline:

```
button:focus {
        outline: 1px dotted;
        outline: 5px auto -webkit-focus-ring-color;
}
```

Extending Preflight

Feel free to add your own custom style on top of the preflight. Using the **`@layer`** directive we can define customization for preflight.

In your **`input.css`** of our project, you can try to add these and verify the changes:

```
@tailwind base;
@layer base {
  h1 {
    @apply text-2xl;
  }
  h2 {
    @apply text-xl;
  }
  h3 {
    @apply text-lg;
  }
  a {
    @apply text-blue-600 underline;
  }
}
```

Hope you remember doing this kind of customization on components and utilities that we discussed before.

Disabling Preflight

If you wish, you can disable the preflight that comes with Tailwind CSS. This restores the behavior of all tags to their default with different browsers:

```
module.exports = {
  corePlugins: {
    preflight: false,
  }
}
```

Further concepts from Tailwind CSS are purely about utility classes for various aspects, instead of explaining them in detail along with examples, we will explain respective classes while developing web pages for websites as and when they are required. Here you can get a glimpse of available utility classes. Again, we encourage you to apply and test the results of the reading utility class on your computer.

Layout

This is the set of utility classes that deals with the layout of a page, block, and so on.

Aspect ratio

This utility class is used to set the desired ratio for an element. There are three variants: **auto**, **square**, and **video**. The syntax will be **aspect-{ ratio } :**

Class name	Aspect ratio	Information
aspect-auto	auto	Auto sets aspect ratio.
aspect-square	1:1	Set equal height and width.
aspect-video	16:9	Sets aspect ratio to 16:9 as it's the default for videos.
aspect-[arbitrayvalue]	4:3, 6:4, 12:8	As an arbitrary value, you can pass your expected ratio. With the following syntax, for example: aspect-[4/3], aspect-[12/8]

Table 3.2: *Aspect ratio possibilities*

In some browsers (for example, Safari), this may behave inappropriately, in such scenarios utilizing Tailwind CSS's *aspect-ratio plugin* is a better approach.

Container

This utility class is used to fix the width of the element to the active breakpoint. This basically sets the **max-width** rule of an element to the active breakpoint. This enforces the design to have a static viewport.

container classes do not auto center the content and have no horizontal padding as well, you can either add suitable objects for this on configuration or add utility classes for them along with the container class.

The following table shows the width that the container sets for different breakpoints:

Breakpoint	Property
`none` (without container class)	width: 100%
`sm`	max-width: 640px
`md`	max-width: 768px
`lg`	max-width: 1024px
`xl`	max-width: 1280px
`2xl`	max-width: 1536px

***Table 3.3**: Default breakpoint values for container*

`max-width` property's value will be as per the default configuration, container will follow the same if you have already overridden breakpoint values in the configuration file.

Columns

These utility classes are used to control the number of columns needed to be created with the children of an element.

Based on column count

Controlling total columns by mentioning column count with **`column`** class. The width will be auto-adjusted based on mentioning count. The syntax looks like **`columns-{count}`**.

For example, **`columns-2`**, **`columns-3`**, **`columns-10`**.

The following table shows supported columns count classes by default:

1	2	3	4	5	6	7	8	9	10	11	12	auto
columns-1	columns-2	columns-3	columns-4	columns-5	columns-6	columns-7	columns-8	columns-9	columns-10	columns-11	columns-12	columns-auto

***Table 3.4**: column count default possibilities*

The following figure shows an example:

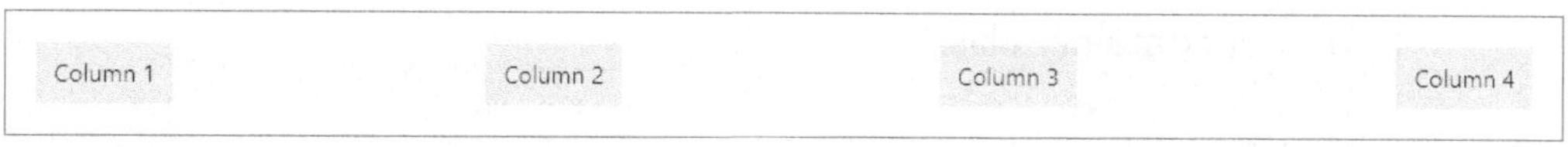

***Figure 3.1**: Example of column – 4 columns in a row*

Based on column width

This is a reverse operation of *column count*, here instead of mentioning column count we can mention the ideal width for the column and then the number of columns will be automatically adjusted to fit the total width value. The syntax looks like **`columns-{width}`**.

For example, **`columns-2xs`**, **`columns-lg`**, **`columns-xl`**.

The following table shows supported columns count classes by default.

3s	2s	xs	sm	md	lg	xl	2xl	3xl	4xl	5xl	6xl	7xl
columns: 16rem	columns: 18rem	columns: 20rem	columns: 24rem	columns: 28rem	columns: 32rem	columns: 36rem	columns: 42rem	columns: 48rem	columns: 56rem	columns: 64rem	columns: 72rem	columns: 80rem

***Table 3.5**: column width default possibilities*

You can even extend the theme with new column values by defining them in a configuration file. If you wish you can even pass arbitrary values as well for column width, where you need to pass the expected width.

For example, **`columns-[50px]`**, **`columns-[10rem]`**

Break After - Break Before - Break Inside

These utility classes are used to break a column or a page **after/break/inside** an element. The **Break After** class controls how a page or column should break after an element. Similarly, the **Break Before** class controls how a page or column should break **before** an element. The **Break Inside** class decides how a page or column should break within a particular element:

- break after syntax - **`break-after-{value}`**
- break before syntax - **`break-before-{value}`**
- break inside syntax - **`break-inside-{value}`**

Following are the possibilities of each breaking element class with equivalent CSS rules.

Variants of **break-after** class are given in the following table:

break-after-auto	break-after-avoid	break-after-all
break-after: auto;	break-after: avoid;	break-after: all;

break-after-avoid-page	break-after: avoid-page;	break-after-left
break-after: auto;	break-after: page;	break-after: left;

break-after-left	break-after-column
break-after: right;	break-after: column;

Table 3.6: *Break after default classes*

break-before

Variants of **break-before** class are given in the following table:

break-before-auto	break-before-avoid	break-before-all
break-before: auto;	break-before: avoid;	break-before: all;

break-before-avoid-page	break-before-page	break-before-left
break-before: avoid-page;	break-before: page;	break-before: left;

break-before-left	break-before-column
break-before: right;	break-before: column;

***Table 3.7**: Break before default classes*

break-inside

Variants of **break-after** class are given in the following table:

break-inside-auto	break- inside-avoid	break-inside-avoid-page	break-inside-avoid-page
break-before: auto;	break-before: avoid;	break-before: all;	break-before: all;

***Table 3.8**: Break inside default classes*

Box decoration break – box sizing

These utility classes are used to control how part of an element should be rendered across multiple pages, columns, or lines. Box-sizing utilities sway how the browser should calculate an element's total size.

Each of these concepts has two utility classes available for styling.

Box decoration break has the following variants:

- **`box-decoration-slice`**: Parts of the same element share the same styles that are applied to its parent.
- **`box-decoration-clone`**: All parts of the element get the same styles that are applied to its parent.

Box sizing has the following variants:

- **`box-border`**: This directs the browser to add margin and padding to the element when you mention height and width to it. The total area of the box includes **margin** and **padding**, which reduces the actual space of content.
- **`box-content`**: This directs the browser to the margin and padding on top of the mentioned height and width of the element. The total area of the content remains intact with mentioned height and width. The total box area grows accordingly with margin and padding values.

Display

This utility class section provides classes to handle the display type of the element.

The following table shows all the possibilities by default, each of them is the proper value for displaying CSS property.

Class	Explanation	Class	Explanation
`block`	Element fills to its parent width. The whole line gets blocked.	`inline-block`	It wraps the element to prevent its contents from extending beyond its parent.
`inline`	Contents wrap normally within the element.	`grid`	This creates a grid container.
`inline-grid`	This creates an inline grid container	`contents`	This creates a container where its children act like direct children of the parent element.
`hidden`	This utility class hides the element from the DOM (**`display:none; property`**).	`list-item`	This utility makes elements as a list item
`flex`	This creates a block level (**`width = parent width`**) flex container. Content can be displayed flexibly.	`inline-flex`	This creates an inline flex container that flows content.
`flow-root`	This creates a block-level element with its own block-formatting context.		

Table 3.9: *Display utility classes*

Apart from these, there are other display utility classes as well for table display:

table	inline-table	table-caption
table-cell	table-column	table-column-group
table-footer-group	table-header-group	table-row-group
table-row		

Table 3.10: *Table displays utility classes*

These table-related utility classes are used to style the respective properties of the table element.

Floats - clear - isolation

Float utility classes are used to wrap the content around the element, there are three possibilities. **Floating right**, **floating left**, and **floating none** (disabling float):

- `float-left` – This floats an element to the left of the container.
- `float-right` – This floats an element to the right of the container.
- `float-none` – This disables an element from floating.

Clear utility classes are used to position those elements which are below any preceding left/right floating elements. There are four possibilities: **clear right**, **clear left**, **clear both**, and **clear none**:

- `clear-left` – This positions elements below any preceding left-floated elements.
- `clear-right` – This positions elements below any preceding right-floated elements.
- `clear-both` – This positions elements below all preceding floated elements.
- `clear-none`- This resets any positioning applied to an element. (default behavior).

Isolation utility is used to explicitly create new stacking contexts with the element. There are two variants for it: **isolate** and **isolation-auto**:

- `isolate` – This creates a new stacking context for an element as we are mentioning.
- `isolation-auto` – Based on the status of an element in a browser, this class decides whether to isolate it or not.

Object Fit – Object Position

Object fit utility classes are used to determine how a replaced element's content should be resized

There are five possibilities for this: object-contain, object-cover, object-fill, object-none, and object-scale-down.

Table 3.11 explains the preceding classes:

Class	CSS Property-Value	Explanation
`object-contain`	`object-fit: contain;`	This resizes the element's content (object) to stay contained within the container of the element.
`object-cover`	`object-fit: cover;`	This resizes the element's content (object) to cover the container of the element.
`object-fill`	`object-fit: fill;`	This stretches the element's content (object) to fit the container of the element.
`object-none`	`object-fit: none;`	This displays the element's content (object) in its original size by ignoring the container size of the element.
`object-scale-down`	`object-fit: scale-down;`	This displays the element's content (object) in its original size but scales it down to fit within the container of the element. (Ratio remains the same)

Table 3.11: *Object fit classes*

Object position utility classes are used to decide what to show from an element's content (object) within the container. Positioning part of the object to the container of the element.

The following table shows all positioning possibilities:

Position class	CSS property – value	Explanation
`object-bottom`	`object-position: bottom ;`	This shows only the bottom part of the object within the container.
`object-center`	`object-position: center ;`	This shows only the center part of the object within the container.
`object-left`	`object-position: left ;`	This shows only the left part of the object within the container.

Position class	CSS property – value	Explanation
`object-left-bottom`	`object-position: left bottom ;`	This shows only the bottom left part of the object within the container.
`object-left-top`	`object-position: left top ;`	This only shows the top left part of the object within the container.
`object-right`	`object-position: right ;`	This shows only the right part of the object within the container.
`object-right-bottom`	`object-position: right bottom ;`	This only shows the bottom right part of the object within the container.
`object-right-top`	`object-position: right top ;`	This only shows the top right part of the object within the container.
`object-top`	`object-position: top ;`	This only shows the top part of the object within the container.

***Table 3.12**: Object position classes*

Overflow

These utility classes are used to handle the overflow behavior of an element within its container.

The following table explains different overflow scenarios:

Overflow class	CSS property - value	Explanation
`overflow-auto`	`overflow: auto ;`	It auto-decides what to do with overflowing content, and shows the scrollbar only if necessary.
`overflow-hidden`	`overflow: hidden ;`	It hides the overflowing content from the element.
`overflow-clip`	`overflow: clip ;`	This clips off the overflowing content of the element.
`overflow-visible`	`overflow: visible ;`	It shows an overflowing portion of the content completely.
`overflow-scroll`	`overflow: scroll ;`	It makes the element scrollable if the content is overflowing (always adds scrollbar)

Overflow class	CSS property - value	Explanation
`overflow-x-auto`	`overflow-x: auto ;`	It auto-decides what to do with overflowing content in the *x-axis*, and shows a scrollbar only if necessary.
`overflow-y-auto`	`overflow-y: auto ;`	It auto-decides what to do with overflowing content in the *y-axis*, and shows a scrollbar only if necessary.
`overflow-x-hidden`	`overflow-x: hidden ;`	It hides the overflowing content in the *x-axis* from the element.
`overflow-y-hidden`	`overflow-y: hidden ;`	It hides the overflowing content in the *y-axis* from the element.
`overflow-x-clip`	`overflow-x: clip ;`	It clips off the overflowing content in the *x-axis* from the element.
`overflow-y-clip`	`overflow-y: clip ;`	It clips off the overflowing content in the *y-axis* from the element.
`overflow-x-visible`	`overflow-x: visible ;`	It shows an overflowing portion of the content on the *x-axis* completely.
`overflow-y-visible`	`overflow-y: visible ;`	It shows an overflowing portion of the content on the *y-axis* completely.
`overflow-x-scroll`	`overflow-x: scroll ;`	It makes the element scrollable in the *x-axis* if the content is overflowing (always adds scrollbar).
`overflow-y-scroll`	`overflow-y: scroll ;`	It makes the element scrollable in the *y-axis* if the content is overflowing (always adds scrollbar).

Table 3.13: *Overflow classes*

Overscroll behavior

These utility classes are used to control browser behavior when reaching the end of the scrolling area.

The following table provides a brief explanation of each possibility:

Overscroll Class	CSS property – value	Explanation
`overscroll-auto`	`overscroll-behavior: auto ;`	It auto-decides if the child element is scrollable and if overscrolled then it scrolls the parent element as well.

Overscroll Class	CSS property - value	Explanation
`overscroll-contain`	`overscroll-behavior: contain ;`	It prevents the scrolling effect of the parent element that is coming from the child element (the parent element doesn't scroll when the child element gets over scrolled.) - but preserves the bounce effect (as per OS support).
`overscroll-none`	`overscroll-behavior: none;`	The same as **`overscroll-contains itself`** - but prevents the bounce effect as well.
`overscroll-y-auto`	`overscroll-behavior-y: auto ;`	It auto-decides if the child element is scrollable in the *y-axis* and if it is over-scrolled then it scrolls the parent element as well in the *y-axis*.
`overscroll-y-contain`	`overscroll-behavior-y: contain ;`	Prevents scrolling of the parent element in the *y-axis* but preserves bounce effect.
`overscroll-y-none`	`overscroll-behavior-y: none ;`	The same as **`overscroll-y-contains itself`** - but prevents the bounce effect as well.
`overscroll-x-auto`	`overscroll-behavior-x: auto ;`	It auto-decides if the child element is scrollable in the *x-axis*, and if over-scrolled, then it scrolls the parent element as well in the *x-axis*.
`overscroll-x-contain`	`overscroll-behavior-x: contain ;`	Prevents scrolling of the parent element in the *x-axis* but preserves bounce effect.
`overscroll-x-none`	`overscroll-behavior-x: none ;`	The same as **`overscroll-x-contains itself`** - but prevents the bounce effect as well.

Table 3.14: *Overscroll utility- classes*

Position

These are the element positioning utility classes that are useful to control the position of an element in a DOM. There are five possible position classes that Tailwind CSS provides:

- **static** - This positions an element to the normal flow of the document. Ignore any offsets added. Cannot be a position reference for absolutely positioned elements.

- **relative** - This positions an element to the normal flow of the document. Offsets are calculated relative to the normal position, and they will act as position references for absolutely positioned elements.
- **absolute** - This positions an element outside the normal flow of the document causes the neighboring element to act as if the element does not exist. Offsets are calculated relative to the nearest parent that has a position property except for static.
- **fixed** - This positions an element relative to the browser window. Offsets are calculated relative to the viewport of the browser.
- **sticky** - This positions an element as *relative* until it crosses a certain limit, then it changes to *fixed* until its parent moves off the screen. Offsets are calculated relative to the element's normal position.

Remember these classes as we use them frequently in our website development.

Top - Right - Bottom - Left

These utility classes are used for the placement of positioned elements. There are five main aspects of placements: **right**, **left**, **top**, **bottom**, and **inset**.

General syntax looks like `{ top | right | bottom | left | inset } - { size }.`

For example, **top-3**, **bottom-4**, **left-2**, **right-5**, **inset-0**, and so on.

- **top-{size}**: These classes are used to position the element from the top, for example, **top-0**, **top-1**, and so on. Ascending size can be any height or width.
- **bottom-{size}**:These classes are used to position the element from the bottom, for example, **bottom-0**, **bottom -1**, and so on.
- **left-{size}**: These classes are used to position the element from left, for example, **left-0**, **left -1**, and so on.
- **right-{size}**: These classes are used to position the element from right, for example, **right-0**, **right-1**, and so on.
- **inset-{size}**: These classes are used to position the element from all directions with equal distance, for example, **inset-0**, **inset-1**, and so on.
- **inset-x-{size}**: These classes are used to position the element from left and right with equal distance, for example, **inset-x-0**, **inset-x-1**, and so on.
- **inset-y-{size}**: These classes are used to position the element from top and bottom with equal distance, for example, **inset-y-0**, **inset-y-1**, and so on.

Negative value as a size

You can position the element with negative values as well, in such cases, the element positions from beyond the outside of its container as per mentioned size.

For example, **-top-4, -left-5, -inset-5,** and so on (observe - symbol added at the beginning of the classname).

Visibility

These utility classes are used to determine the visibility of the element. There are three possibilities: **visible**, **invisible**, and **collapse**:

- **visible**: This class is used to display the element.
- **invisible**: This class is used to make the element hidden from the browser window. This element stays within the DOM and affects other layouts within the layout.

  `(display:none;)`
- **collapse**: This class is used to hide the element from the browser window and from DOM as well. So, it will not affect other elements within the layout.

Z-Index

This class is used to decide the stacking order of the element. When you are adding elements one over the other, this class is required to set the priority of each element.

Its syntax looks like **`z-{size}`**.

Size decides priority, the higher the priority elements render over other elements with lower size:

z-0	z-10	z-20	z-30	z-40	z-50	z-auto

***Table 3.15**: Z-Index utility classes*

This table shows the size values available by default. Feel free to create more sizes for *Z-index* by extending the **`zIndex`** object on the configuration file. And you can even pass arbitrary values as well, for example, **z-[85]**, **z-[99]**, **z-[100]**, and so on.

Flexbox and Grid

As you already read, **Flexbox** and **Grid** are display types of an element. There are various detailing utility classes that come under these. Understand these classes perfectly because these are the important classes that make website development easier.

Flex-Basis

These utility classes are used to set the initial size of the flex items. These classes are added to the parent element that will affect the children element.

The general syntax is **`basis-{size}`**. Initial size increases as we increase the size value. Extended spacing utilities can be used for size as well. For example, **basis-1**, **basis-2**, **basis-1/2**, **basis-full**, and so on, as shown in *Figure* 3.2:

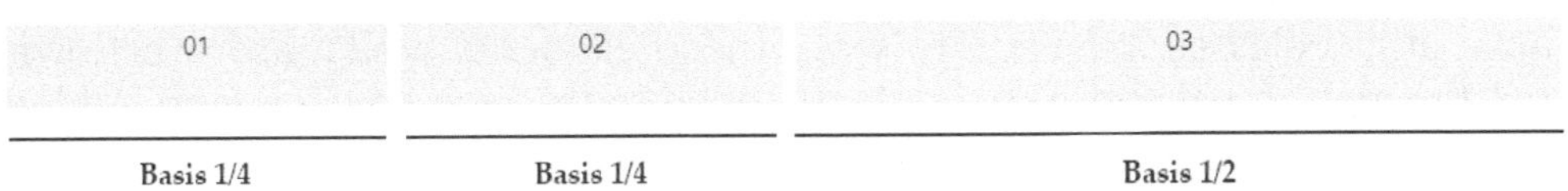

***Figure* 3.2**: *Example of flex-basis*

Flex Direction

These utility classes are used to define the direction of the flex items in the DOM. These classes are added to the parent element that handles the behavior of its children.

There are *four* ways to decide the direction of the elements:

- **`flex-row`**: This class shows children elements in the left to right direction in a single row.
- **`flex-row-reverse`**: This class shows children elements in the right to left direction in a single row.
- **`flex-col`**: This class shows children elements in the top to bottom direction in a single column.

- **`flex-col-reverse`**: This class shows children elements in the bottom to top direction in a single column.

(a) Example of flex-row

***Figure 3.3**: Example of flex direction*

Flex Wrap

These utility classes are used to wrap those elements which are overflowing from the mentioned width/height and added to the next row/column. Added a parent element that affects its children.

There are *three* possibilities for it:

- **`flex-wrap`**: This normally wraps the child elements to the next row/column if they do not fit within the same row/column.
- **`flex-wrap-reverse`**: This wraps the child elements to the next row/column if they do not fit within the same row/column but in reverse order.
- **`flex-nowrap`**: This disables any wrapping effect on the element cause overflowing of the child elements in a single row/column.

Flex

These utility classes are used to control the shrink and grow mechanism of flex items. These classes will be added to the children element itself. There are *four* possible states:

- **`flex-1`**: Ignoring the initial size of the element, this class allows an element to grow and shrink as needed.
- **`flex-auto`**: It is similar to **`flex-1`** but it auto decides either to grow or shrink an element by considering its initial size.
- **`flex-initial`**: This class allows to shrink an element but not grow beyond its initial size.

- **`flex-none`**: This class prevents either growing or shrinking of an element.

Flex Grow

These utility classes decide how an element can grow. This will be added to the children element itself. There are *two* variants for this:

- **`grow`**: This class allows an element to grow.
- **`grow-0`**: This class prevents an element from growing.

Flex Shrink

These utility classes decide how an element can shrink. These will be added to the children element itself. There are *two* variants for this:

- **`shrink`**: This class allows an element to grow.
- **`shrink-0`**: This class prevents an element from growing.

Order

These classes are used to decide the order of the element among its other elements. These will be added to the children element itself, lowering the order number of the element that comes first than other elements within its parent element. The general syntax is **`order-{order}`**.

The following table shows the default order available with Tailwind CSS:

order-0	order-1	order-2	order-3	order-4
order-5	order-6	order-7	order-8	order-9
order-10	order-11	order-12	order-first	order-last

***Table 3.16**: Flex order utility classes*

The following figure shows an example of ordering items:

***Figure 3.4**: Example of ordering items*

You can even add more order classes to the configuration file by extending a theme object.

Grid template columns

These utility classes are used to divide columns in a grid layout. These classes will be applied with a grid class and its children element will be differentiated from many columns.

The general syntax is, **`grid-column-{n}`**, **`n`** represents the number of columns to be created.

The following table shows the default classes available:

grid-cols-1	grid-cols-2	grid-cols-3
grid-cols-4	grid-cols-5	grid-cols-6
grid-cols-7	grid-cols-8	grid-cols-9
grid-cols-10	grid-cols-11	grid-cols-12
grid-cols-none		

***Table 3.17**: Grid template column classes*

If you wish, you can create utility classes for different numbers of columns by extending the theme object. You can even pass arbitrary values to the utility classes.

For example, **`grid grid-cols-[200px_minmax(700px,_1fr)_100px]`**

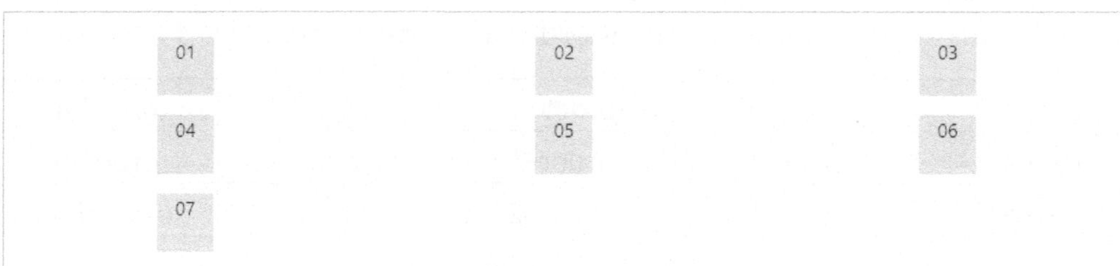

***Figure 3.5**: Example of grid columns - grid-columns-3*

Grid column start/end

These utility classes are used to determine how elements are sized and placed across grid columns. These classes are applied to children of grid elements. There are *three* main types of classes under this element: **column span**, **column start**, **column end**. The grid column begins with **index 1**, not **0**.

The general syntax of these looks like this:

- Current technology scenario
  - o It decides how many columns that element should span.
  - o For example, **`col-span-3`** – the same element occupies *three columns*.
- column start: **`col-start-{n}`**
  - o It decides at which column the element should begin.
  - o For example, **`col-start-2`** – element begins at *column* 2.
- column end: **`col-end-{n}`**
  - o It decides at which column the element should end.
  - o For example, **`col-end-5`** – element ends at *column* 5.

You can extend the theme object to create more size parameters. Arbitrary values can be passed as well for size parameters.

Grid template rows

These classes are used to create a number of rows in the grid layout. These will be applied along with the grid class. The general syntax looks like, **`grid-rows-{n}`** where `n` stands for the number of rows to be created.

The following table shows the row counts available by default in Tailwind CSS:

grid-rows-1	grid-rows-2	grid-rows-3
grid-rows-4	grid-rows-5	grid-rows-6
grid-rows-none		

Table 3.18: *Grid template rows classes*

If you wish, you can create utility classes for different numbers of rows by extending the theme object. You can even pass arbitrary values to the utility classes.

For example, **`grid grid-rows-[200px_minmax(700px,_1fr)_100px]`**.

Grid row start/end

These utility classes are used to determine how elements are sized and placed across grid rows. These classes are applied to children of grid elements. There are *three* main types of classes that exist under this: **row span**, **row start**, and **row end**. The grid row begins with **index 1**, not **0**.

The general syntax of these looks as follows:

- row span: **`row-span-{n}`**
  - It decides how many rows that element should span.
  - For example, **`row-span-3`** – the same element occupies *three rows*.
- row start- **`row-start-{n}`**
  - It decides at which row element should begin.
  - For example, **`row-start-2`** – element begins at *row* 2.
- row end – **`row-end-{n}`**
  - It decides at which row element should end.
  - For example, **`row-end-5`** – element ends at *row* 5.

You can extend the theme object to create more size parameters. Arbitrary values can be passed as well for size parameters.

Grid Auto Flow

These utility classes are used to determine how elements in a grid are auto-placed.

The general syntax is **`grid-flow-{keyword}`**. There are *five* possibilities:

- **`grid-flow-row`**: Items are placed by filling each row in turn, adding new rows as necessary. *Row* by default.
- **`grid-flow-col`**: Items are placed by filling each column in turn, adding new columns as necessary. *Column* By default.
- **`grid-flow-dense`**: This class attempts to fill in holes earlier in the grid if smaller items come up later. This may cause items to appear out-of-order when doing so would fill in holes left by larger items.
- **`grid-flow-row-dense`**: Same as **`grid-flow-dense`** but fills the holes by considering rows.
- **`grid-flow-col-dense`**: Same as **`grid-flow-dense`** but fills the holes by considering columns.

If none of these will be applied to the grid layout, it applies the *sparse* technique to place items, which ensures elements stay in order. Elements flow only in a forward direction, and there is no such backtracking to fill holes in between.

Grid Auto Columns

These utility classes are used to control the size of implicitly created grid columns. There are *four* possibilities for this. The general syntax looks like **`auto-cols-{size}`**:

- **`auto-cols-min`**: This class defines the largest minimal content contribution of the grid items occupying the grid element space.
- **`auto-cols-max`**: This class defines the largest maximal content contribution of the grid items occupying the grid element space.
- **`auto-cols-fr`**: **`fr`** is a fractional unit and *1fr* is for 1 *part* of the *available space.*
- **`auto-cols-auto`**: This class is identical to **`auto-cols-max`** if it's a maximum. As a minimum, it represents the largest minimum size of the grid items occupying the grid element space.

Arbitrary values can be passed to the utility class as well and you can define custom classes by extending the theme object with the **`gridAutoColumns`** key in a configuration file.

Grid Auto Rows

These utility classes are used to control the size of implicitly created grid rows. There are *four* possibilities for this. The general syntax looks like **`auto-rows-{size}`**:

- **`auto-rows-min`**: This class defines the largest minimal content contribution of the grid items occupying the grid element space.
- **`auto- rows-max`**: This class defines the largest maximal content contribution of the grid items occupying the grid element space.
- **`auto- rows-fr`**: **`fr`** is a fractional unit and *1fr* is for 1 *part* of the *available space.*
- **`auto- rows-auto`**: This class is identical to **`auto-cols-max`** if it's maximum. As a minimum, it represents the largest minimum size of the grid items occupying the grid element space.

Arbitrary values can be passed to utility classes as well and you can define custom classes by extending the theme object with the **`gridAutoRows`** key in a configuration file.

Gap

These are the utility classes used to define gutter space between child elements of grid and flex elements. These classes will be added to parent elements to create that much gutter between its children. The general syntax looks like **`gap-{size}`**.

Size represents the width that a gutter can occupy. Gaps can be added in both *vertical* and *horizontal* directions separately. If not specified, the direction then gutter space will be added in both directions.

For example, **`gap-4`**, **`gap-2`**, **`gap-x-6`**, **`gap-y-12`**, and so on.

You can define your custom gap width by extending the theme object and the gap follows what you defined for the spacing key in that theme object. Arbitrary values are supported as well, where you can pass width for the gap utility class.

For example, **`gap-[5rem]`**, **`gap-[12px]`**, and so on.

Justify - Align - Place

Justify-related utility classes are used to justify elements in a horizontal direction, **Align-related utilities** are used to align items in a vertical direction and **Place-related utility** classes are used to both justify and align the items within a flex or grid container.

Justify Content

These utilities are used to justify the flex and grid content along the container's total space (horizontally). There are *six* variants for this. These classes are added to the parent element and justification will be applied on its children. Consider all children as one content.

- **justify-start**: This class justifies the child elements from the start of the container element:

***Figure 3.6**: Example of flex –justify start*

- **justify-end**: This class justifies the child elements to the end of the container element:

Figure 3.7: *Example of flex –justify end*

- **justify-center**: This class justifies the child elements to the center of the container element:

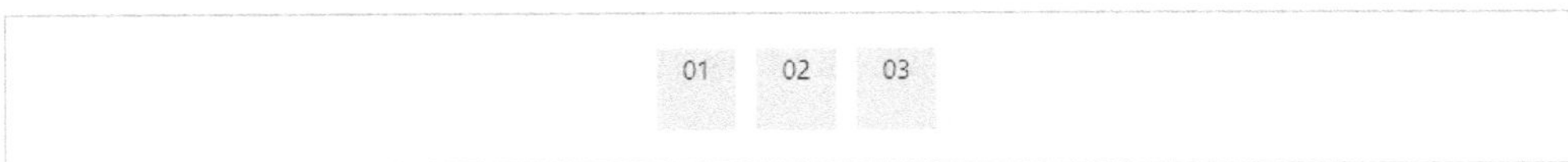

Figure 3.8: *Example of flex–justify center*

- **justify-between**: This class justifies even space between each child by taking the full width of the parent container.

Figure 3.9: *Example of flex –justify between*

- **justify-around**: This class adds equal amounts of space before and after each element by considering the full width of the parent.

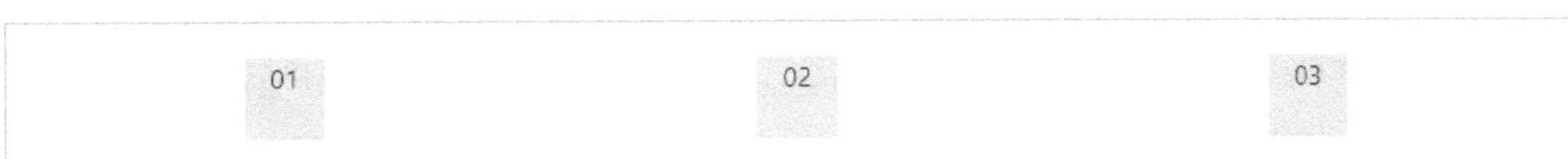

Figure 3.10: *Example of flex –justify around*

- **justify-evenly**: This class adds equal space between each child element, and at the beginning, and at the end of child elements. Similar to justify-around but the space width remains the same for each space within the parent:

Figure 3.11: *Example of flex –justify evenly*

Justify Items

These utility classes are used to control how grid items are aligned along their inline axis (horizontally). These classes are added to the parent element and justification will be applied on its children. There are *four* possibilities for this. Adds rules to each child:

- **`justify-items-start`**: This class is used to align elements to the start of their inline axis.
- **`justify-items-end`**: This class is used to align elements to the end of their inline axis.
- **`justify-items-center`**: This class is used to align elements to the center of their inline axis.
- **`justify-center-stretch`**: This class is used to stretch elements to their inline axis.

Justify Self

These utilities are used to decide how an individual grid item is aligned along its inline axis (horizontally). These classes are added to the child element itself. There are *five* possibilities for this. These classes on child element override justify items rule applied on its parent:

- **`justify-self-auto`**: This class auto-decides how to self-justify the element. Works as per justify items property on the parent element.
- **`justify-self-start`**: This class justifies an element to the start of its inline axis.
- **`justify-self-end`**: This class justifies an element to the end of its inline axis.
- **`justify-self-center`**: This class justifies an element to the center of its inline axis.
- **`justify-self-stretch`**: This class stretches an element to its full width.

Align content

These are the utility classes used to position rows in a container element which is a *multi-row flex* or *grid (vertically)*. These classes will be added on a parent element that will be affected on its children. This utility has seven possibilities. Consider all children as one content:

- **`content-start`**: This class aligns the row to the starting position of the container:

Figure 3.12: *Example of flex–align content start*

- **`content-end`**: This class aligns the row to the end position of the container.
- **`content-center`**: This class aligns the row to the center position of the container.

Figure 3.13: *Example of flex–align content center*

- **`content-between`:** This class aligns the elements from top to bottom with equal space between each row:

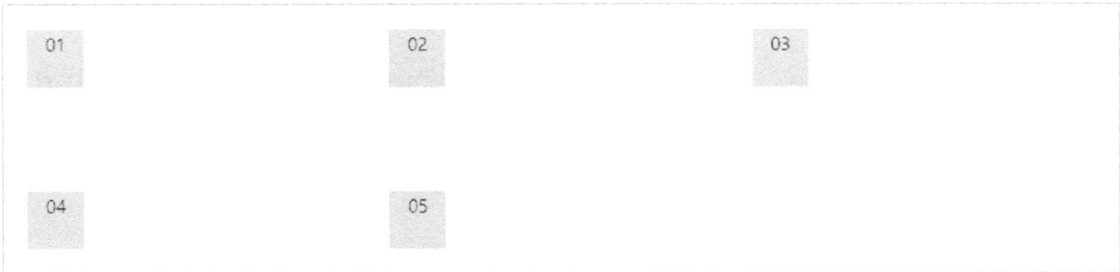

Figure 3.14: *Example of flex–align content between*

- **`content-around`**: This class aligns the elements from top to bottom by adding an equal amount of space above and below each row.
- **`content-baseline`**: This class aligns the rows to the baseline of the content present in the parent element.

- **`content-evenly`**: This class aligns the rows from top to bottom by adding an equal amount of space between each row. Also, the space width remains the same for the start and end positions of the parent:

***Figure 3.15**: Example of flex – align content evenly*

Align Items

These utility classes are used to align flex or grid items along the cross-axis of the parent element (vertical alignment). These classes will be applied to parents that will be affected by their children. There are *five* possibilities for this. Adds rules to each child:

- **`items-start`**: This class aligns the element to the start of the cross-axis of the parent.
- **`items-end`**: This class aligns the element to the end of the cross-axis of the parent.
- **`items-center`**: This class aligns the element to the center of the cross-axis of the parent.
- **`items-baseline`**: This class aligns the elements to their baseline and to the cross-axis of the parent.
- **`items-stretch`**: This class stretches the height elements to fill their parent element's cross-axis.

Align Self

This utility is used to align an element to the cross-axis of its parent element. It will be applied to child elements. These overrides align the item rule applied to its parent element. There are *six* possibilities for this class:

- **`self-auto`**: This class aligns an item based on the value of the parent element's align-items property.
- **`self-start`**: This class aligns an item to the start of the parent element's cross-axis.

- **`self-end`**: This class aligns an item to the end of the parent element's cross-axis.
- **`self-center`**: This class aligns an item to the center of the parent element's cross-axis.
- **`self-stretch`**: This class stretches an item to fill the parent element's cross-axis.
- **`self-baseline`**: This class aligns an item to its baseline in the parent element's cross-axis.

Place Content

These utilities control how content is justified and aligned at the same time. These classes will be added to parent elements that will affect its children. There are *eight* possibilities. Consider all children as one content:

- **`place-content-center`**: This class positions the elements to the center of the block axis of the parent element.
- **`place-content-start`**: This class positions the elements to the start of the block axis.
- **`place-content-end`**: This class positions the elements to the end of the block axis.
- **`place-content-between`**: This class positions the elements to the start of the block axis.
- **`place-content-around`**: This class is used to distribute grid items along the block axis so that there is an equal amount of space between each row on the block axis.
- **`place-content-evenly`**: This class is used to distribute grid items such that there is an equal amount of space around each row on the block axis.
- **`place-content-baseline`**: This class is used to distribute grid items such that there is an equal amount of space around each row on the block axis.
- **`place-content-stretch`**: This class is used to stretch grid items along their grid areas on the block axis.

Place Items

These utilities control how items are justified and aligned at the same time. These classes will be added to parent elements that will be affected on its children. There are *five* possibilities. This class adds CSS rules to each child:

- **`place-items-start`**: This class is used to place grid items at the start of their grid areas on both axis.
- **`place-items-end`**: This class is used to place grid items on the end of their grid areas on both axis.
- **`place-items-center`**: This class is used to place grid items in the center of their grid areas on both axis.
- **`place-items-baseline`**: This class is used to place grid items on their baseline in the grid areas on both axis.
- **`place-items-stretch`**: This class is used to stretch the grid items along their grid areas on both axis.

Place Self

These utility classes are used to determine how an individual item is justified and aligned at the same time. There are *five* possibilities for this. These classes will be applied to child elements directly. This overrides the place items rule applied to the parent element:

- **`place-self-auto`**: This class is used to align an item based on the value of the container's **`place-items`** property.
- **`place-self-start`**: This class is used to align an item to the start on both axis.
- **`place-self-end`**: This class is used to align an item to the end on both axis.
- **`place-self-center`**: This class is used to align an item to the center on both axis.
- **`place-self-stretch`**: This class is used to stretch an item on both axis.

Spacing

These utilities are for spacing functionality. There are *three* categories: *padding*, *margin*, and *space-between.*

Padding

Padding is a space created between the border and an actual content element. Spacing width will be applied inwards to the element.

Padding will be applied to all the directions of the element. Its general syntax looks like:

```
p{ t | b | l | r }-{ size }
```

`t`, `b`, `l`, `r` represents the **top**, **bottom**, **left**, and **right** respectively and **size** represents a number that adds a certain width. By default, Tailwind CSS provides a rich set of spacing values that can be used here as size parameters.

For example, **pt-2**, **pb-3**, **pr-4**, **pl-6**, and so on.

Padding can be applied in vertical and horizontal directions as well. **Horizontal padding** applies padding in left and right directions and **vertical padding** applies padding to the top and bottom direction of the element. Its general syntax looks like `p{ x | y }-{ size }`.

For example, **px-2**, **py-4**, and so on.

If you mention padding only with size, then the padding will be added to all the directions:

For example, **p-4**, **p-12**, and so on.

By extending the spacing object of the theme, we can use those values for padding as well.

Feel free to pass arbitrary values as well for the utility classes.

For example, **p-[5px]**, **px-[2rem]**, **pt-[3em**], and so on.

Margin

Margin is a space created outside the border of an element. **Spacing** width will be applied outwards to the element.

Margins will be applied to all directions of the element. Its general syntax looks like:

`m{ t | b | l | r }-{ size }`

`t`, `b`, `l`, `r` represent **top**, **bottom**, **left**, and **right** respectively and **size** represents a number that adds a certain width. By default, Tailwind CSS provides a rich set of spacing values that can be used here as size parameters.

For example, **mt-2**, mb-3, **mr-4**, **ml-6**, and so on.

Margin can be applied in *vertical* and *horizontal* directions as well. Horizontal margin applies margin to the left and right directions and vertical margin applies margin to the top and bottom directions of the element. Its general syntax looks like `m{ x | y }-{ size }`.

For example, **mx-2**, **my-4**, and so on.

If you mention margin only with size then the margin will be added to all the directions.

For example, **m-4**, **m-12**, and so on.

By extending the spacing object of the theme, we can use those values for the margin as well.

You are free to pass arbitrary values as well for the utility classes.

For example, **m-[5px]**, **mx-[2rem]**, **mt-[3em]**, and so on.

Space between

These utility classes are used to control the space between child elements. You can add space in *horizontal* and *vertical* directions. These classes will be added to parent elements that will add space between its children.

The general syntax looks like **`space-x-{amount}`** and **`space-y-{amount}`** respectively for horizontal and vertical directions.

For example, space-x-3, space-x-5, space-y-6, space-y-10, and so on.

You can even use negative spaces between elements like **-space-x-10**, **-space-y-3**, and so on.

Extended spacing object values of the theme object can be used as the amount parameter of space between classes. You are allowed to pass arbitrary values for the **`amount`** parameter.

For example, **space-y-[5px]**, **space-x-[1rem]**, and so on.

> **The space between utility classes is not designed to handle complex cases of grid and flex. In those situations, gap utilities perform better.**
>
> **Cannot use this space between utility classes with divided utilities. The scenario margin and padding classes on elements are suitable options.**

Sizing

These are the utility classes that are meant for the sizing of the elements.

Width

These utility classes are used to set the width of an element:

- Width using size, these are fixed width - **`w-{number}`** - for example, **w-0.5**, **w-4**, **w-12**, **w-16**, and so on.

- Width using fraction, these are percentage-based width - **`w-{fraction}`** - for example, **w-3/6**, **w-1/2**, **w-4/12**, and so on.

Width using size follows the spacing parameter defined or those that come with Tailwind CSS by default. Width using fraction is a way of occupying part of the complete width by referring to the complete width by a number. *w-/2* indicates *1 part among 2 total parts* of full width. *w-5/12* indicates *5 parts among 12 parts* of full width.

Additionally, you can extend width objects as well to use them as a number with width class.

The width can be set with its rendering viewport using the **`w-screen`** class. The width can be reset or auto-set using **`w-auto`** class.

The following table shows some other different width-specifying classes available:

`w-full`	`w-screen`	`w-min`	`w-max`	`w-fit`
width: 100%	width :100vh	width: min-content	width: max-content	width: fit-content

***Table 3.19**: Other utility classes for width*

You can even pass arbitrary values for fixed width classes. For example, **w-[20px]**, **w-[2rem]**, and so on.

Min-width

These are the utilities used to set the minimum width of an element. There are five possibilities by default. The general syntax looks like **`min-w-{width}`**:

- **`min-w-0`**: This class sets the minimum width of the element to **`0px`**.
- **`min-w-full`**: This class sets the minimum width of the content to the full width of its parent.
- **`min-w-min`**: This class sets the minimum width of the content to a possible minimum width of the content.
- **`max-w-max`**: This class sets the minimum width of the content to a possible maximum width of the content.
- **`min-w-fit`**: This class uses the fit-content formula with the available space replaced by the specified argument.

Custom `min-width` can be extended using the `minWidth` key on the theme object. You can even pass arbitrary values for the `min-width` utility, for example, **min-w-[40%]**, **min-w-[2rem]**, and so on.

Max-width

These are the utilities used to set the maximum width of an element. The general syntax looks like `max-w-{size}`. There are various ways to mention the maximum width for an element:

- By mentioning the number provided by Tailwind CSS by default. For example, **max-w-0, max-w-2xl**, **max-w-6xl**, and so on.
- By mentioning the width of the content itself, for example, **max-w-min**, **max-w-max**, **max-w-fit**.
- By mentioning the screen width. For example, **max-w-screen-sm**, **max-w-screen-xl**, **max-w-screen-lg**, and so on.

The `max-w-full` class considers the full width of the element for setting the maximum width of the element. The `max-w-prose` utility gives an element `max-width` optimized for readability and adapts based on the font size.

You can define the expected custom `max-width` class using `maxWidth` key by extending it to the `theme` object. Arbitrary values can be passed as well for width. For example, **max-w-[2rem]**, **max-w-[100px]**, and so on.

Height

These utility classes are used to set the height of an element:

- Height using size, these are fixed width - `h-{number}` –; for example, **h-0.5**, **h-4**, **h-12**, **h-16**, and so on.
- Height using fraction, these are percentage-based height - `h-{fraction}` –; for example, h-3/6, h-1/2, h-4/12, and so on.

Height using size follows the spacing parameters defined or those that come with Tailwind CSS by default. Height using fraction is a way of occupying part of complete height by referring to complete height by a number. *h-1/2 indicates 1 part among 2 total parts of full height. h-5/6 indicates 5 parts among the 6 parts of full height.*

Additionally, you can extend height objects as well to use them as a number with height class. Height can be set with its rendering viewport using **`h-screen`** class. Height can be reset or auto-set using **`h-auto`** class.

Table 3.20 shows some other different height-specifying classes available:

h-full	h-screen	h-min	h-max	w-fit
height: 100%	height: 100vh	height: min-content	height: max-content	height: fit-content

***Table 3.20**: Other utility classes for height*

You can even pass arbitrary values for fixed height classes. For example, **h-[20px]**, **h-[2rem]**, and so on.

Min-height

These are the utilities used to set the minimum height of an element. There are six possibilities by default. The general syntax looks like **`min-h-{height}`**:

- **`min-h-0`**: This class sets the minimum height of the element to **0px**.
- **`min-h-full`**: This class sets the minimum height of the content to the full width of its parent.
- **`min-h-min`**: This class sets the minimum height of the content to a possible minimum height of the content.
- **`max-h-max`**: This class sets the minimum height of the content to a possible maximum height of the content.
- **`min-h-fit`**: This class uses the fit-content formula with the available space replaced by the specified argument.
- **`min-h-screen`**: This class is used to set the minimum height of the element to visible screen height.

Custom min-height can be extended using the **`minHeight`** key within the theme object. You can even pass arbitrary values for the min-height utility, for example, **min-h-[40%]**, **min-h-[2rem]**, and so on.

Max-height

These are the utilities used to set the maximum height of an element. The general syntax looks like **`max-h-{size}`**. There are various ways to mention the maximum height for an element:

- By mentioning a number provided by Tailwind CSS by default; for example, **max-h-0**, **max-h-44**, **max-h-96**, and so on.
- By mentioning the height of the content itself. For example, **max-h-min**, **max-h-max**, **max-h-fit**.

The **`max-h-full`** class considers the full height of the element for setting the maximum height of the element.

You can define the expected custom max-height class using the **`maxHeight`** key by extending it to the theme object. Arbitrary value can be passed as well for height. For example, **max-h-[20rem]**, **max-h-[150px]**, and so on.

Conclusion

This chapter provided brief information on a different set of styling entities provided by Tailwind CSS by default to frame the layout of the webpage (an HTML document). Understanding these sections and remembering respective utility classes makes you ready to code an HTML layout that is said to be fully responsive. Hope you learned it and applied it for visual understanding.

In the next chapter, we are looking into the utilities provided by Tailwind CSS to style specific elements like text, images, and so on.

Points to remember

- Custom utility classes can be created by extending the theme object within the configuration.
- Colors and spacing utilities are used by many other utilities.
- Flex and grid utilities are important to design page layouts.
- Breakpoint prefixes are required to create a responsive page design.
- Arbitrary values for utilities are only for rare scenarios, do not follow multiple usages of the same arbitrary value instead create a specific class for it under the theme object.
- Official plugins are used along with the current environment that works out of the box for respective features.
- Sizing spacing and layout utilities play an important role in the development of web pages.

Multiple choice questions

1. **Customization is dependent on which object?**
    a. theme
    b. custom
    c. style
    d. config
2. **The default width for md viewport:**
    a. 640px
    b. 1024
    c. 768px
    d. none of the above
3. **Among these which is not a default color available in Tailwind CSS?**
    a. Slate
    b. Copper
    c. Gray
    d. Zinc
4. **The preflight theme adds the following style to 'Button':**
    a. a blue color
    b. a border of 1px
    c. a default outline
    d. rounded corner
5. **Among these which is not a positioning utility-class:**
    a. static
    b. absolute
    c. super
    d. fixed

6. **Z-index styling is used for:**
    a. To decide stacking order of an element
    b. To place the element in the corner
    c. To align the element to end
    d. To determine the opacity of the element
7. **The 'flex' utility class displays elements in:**
    a. a row
    b. a column
    c. a box
    d. none of the above
8. **The general syntax of `max-width` utility is:**
    a. `max-w-{size}`
    b. `max-width-{size}`
    c. `max-w-{amount}`
    d. `max-width-{arbitrary}`

Answers

1. **a**
2. **c**
3. **b**
4. **c**
5. **c**
6. **a**
7. **a**
8. **a**

CHAPTER 4

Element-Specific Styling with Utility-First Classes

Introduction

This chapter provides information on more utility-first classes available in Tailwind CSS. In the previous chapter, you read the information on utility-first classes available for layout and other sizing-spacing operations. This chapter provides information on more utility-first classes available in Tailwind CSS. We are explaining here those utilities available for element-specific styling. Elements can be **text-content**, **box**, **button**, **image**, and so on. Learning these element specific styling utilities makes you feel confident on styling elements, a building block of the website.

Structure

In this chapter, the following topics will be discussed:

- Typography
- Backgrounds
- Borders
- Effects
- Filters

- Tables
- Transitions and animations
- Transforms
- Interactivity
- SVG
- Accessibility

Typography

These are the utility classes related to *font*, *color*, *alignment*, *spacing*, and other aspects of text content.

Font

In this section of utilities, font-related styles are handled. Like *family*, *size*, *style*, and so on.

Font family

These utility classes are used to set the *font-family* of the text content. We can download and refer to the fonts of our wish and we need to create a class for those fonts in our configuration under the **`theme`** object:

```
module.exports = {
	theme: {
		fontFamily: {
			'montserrat': ['montserrat', 'system-ui']
		}
	}
}
```

Font **`montserrat`** makes text load with **`montserrat`** font, you can add these font-family utility classes similar to other utility classes.

There are some built-in fonts by Tailwind CSS, for example, **font-sans**, **font-serif**, **font-mono**.

Font size

These are the utilities used for controlling font size of the text content of the element. Tailwind CSS provides some font sizes by default.

Further, we can define our font sizes by using the `fontSize` key inside the `theme` object of the configuration.

The following table shows default availability:

text-xs	text-sm	text-base	text-lg
font-size: 0.75rem; line-height: 1rem;	font-size: 0.875rem; line-height:1.25rem;	font-size: 1rem; line-height: 1.5rem;	font-size: 1.125rem; line-height: 1.75rem;

text-xl	text-2xl	text-3xl	text-4xl
font-size: 1.25rem; line-height: 1.75rem;	font-size: 1.5rem; line-height: 2rem;	font-size: 1.875rem; line-height: 2.25rem;	font-size: 2.25rem; line-height: 2.5rem;

text-5xl	text-6xl	text-7xl	text-8xl
font-size: 3rem; line-height: 1rem;	font-size: 3.75rem; line-height: 1rem;	font-size: 4.5rem; line-height: 1rem;	font-size: 6rem; line-height: 1rem;

text-9xl
font-size: 8rem; line-height: 1rem;

Table 4.1: *Utility classes for font size*

Arbitrary values can be passed for font size as well, for example, **text-[14px]**, **text-[1.2rem]**, and so on:

Figure 4.1*: Examples of different font sizes*

Font smoothing

These utilities are used to control smoothness of the text content of an element. There are *two* possibilities:

- **antialiased**: To render text using *grayscale* antialiasing.
- **subpixel-antialiased**: To render text using *subpixel* antialiasing.

Font style

These utilities are used to control the style of the text content of the element. There are *two* possibilities:

- **italic**: Utility can be used to make text *italic*.
- **non-italic**: Utility can be used to display text *normally*.

Font weight

These utilities are used to control the style of the text content of the element. The syntax is **`font-{weight}`**.

The following table shows utility classes available by default:

font-thin	font-extralight	font-light
font-weight: 100;	font-weight: 200;	font-weight: 300;

font-normal	font-medium	font-semibold
font-weight: 400;	font-weight: 500;	font-weight: 600;

font-bold	font-extrabold	font-black
font-weight: 700;	font-weight: 800;	font-weight: 900;

***Table 4.2**: Utility classes for font weight*

Arbitrary value weight parameters can also be passed, for example, **font-[1200]**. You can define your own class for font weight by adding values for **`fontWeight`** key in a **`theme`** object of configuration:

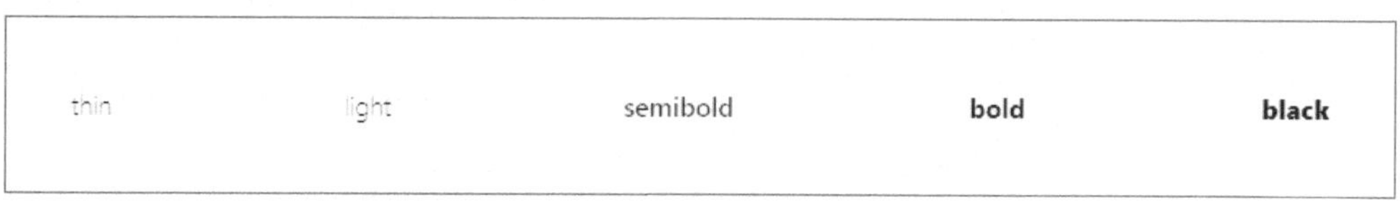

***Figure 4.2**: Examples of different font weights*

Font variant numeric

These utility classes are used to decide variant designs of a number. This enables additional glyphs for **numbers**, **fractions**, and **ordinal markers**. There are nine variants provided by Tailwind CSS.

The following table gives information on it:

Classname	Information
`normal-nums`	This class is used to display number sin normal style (default).
`ordinal`	This class is used to enable special glyphs for the ordinal markers, for example, **1st** (this will make *st* as superscript).
`slashed-zero`	This class is used to force a **0** with a *slash*; this is useful when a clear distinction between **O** and **0** is needed.
`lining-nums`	This class is used to use the numeric glyphs that are all aligned by their baseline. (default for most fonts)
`oldstyle-nums`	This class is used to use numeric glyphs where some numbers have descenders.
`proportional-nums`	This class is used to use numeric glyphs that have proportional widths. (rather than uniform/tabular).
`tabular-nums`	This class is used to use numeric glyphs that have uniform/ tabular widths. (rather than proportional)
`diagonal-fractions`	This class is used to replace numbers separated by a slash with common diagonal fractions.
`stacked-fractions`	This class is used to replace numbers separated by a slash with common stacked fractions. (very few fonts supports this)

***Table 4.3**: Utility classes for font variant numeric*

Letter spacing

These utilities are used for controlling the letter spacing (tracking) of text content of an element. The syntax is **`tracking-{size}`**. There are *six* possibilities by default as given in *Table* 4.4:

classname	CSS rule
`tracking-tighter`	letter-spacing: -0.05em;
`tracking-tight`	letter-spacing: -0.025em;
`tracking-normal`	letter-spacing: 0em;
`tracking-wide`	letter-spacing: 0.025em;
`tracking-wider`	letter-spacing: 0.05em;
`tracking-widest`	letter-spacing: 0.1em;

***Table 4.4**: Utility classes for letter spacing*

You can use *negative* values as well for letter spacing provided that you already need to define that spacing width inside the theme object of configuration using key **`letterSpacing`**. For example, **tracking-5**.

You can pass arbitrary values as well for letter spacing. For example, **tracking-[0.5rem]**, **tracking-[10px]**.

Line clamp

These utilities are used for clamping text to a specific number of lines. This will truncate a block of text after a specific number of lines. The syntax is **`line-clamp-{lines_count}`**. There are *seven* possibilities by default.

`line-clamp-1`, `line-clamp-2`, `line-clamp-3`, `line-clamp-4`, `line-clamp-5`, `line-clamp-6`

These will do line clamp as per mentioned lines count and there is another utility class that removes line clamp, that is, **line-clamp-none**.

Line height

These utilities are used for controlling the line height (leading) of an element. There are *two* ways of adding line-height:

- Relative line height
- Fixed line height

Relative line height

These utilities are used to give an element a relative line-height based on its current font-size. Possibilities available by default are:

- **`leading-none`**
- **`leading-tight`**
- **`leading-snug`**
- **`leading-normal`**
- **`leading-relaxed`**
- **`leading-loose`**

Fixed line height

These utilities are used to give an element a fixed line-height, irrespective of the current font-size. Size represents a *height*. Provides very precise control over an element's final size. Possibilities available by default are:

`leading-3`, **`leading-4`**, **`leading-5`**, **`leading-6`**, **`leading-7`**, **`leading-8`**, **`leading-9`**, **`leading-10`**

List style

These sets of utilities are used to control the type and position of list items.

List style type

These utilities are used for controlling the bullet or numbering style of a list item. There are *three* variants by default:

- **`list-none`**: Adds *no* styles for list items.
- **`list-disc`**: Adds *disc* styles for list items.
- **`list-decimal`**: Adds *decimal* numbering to list items.

You can define your list style by adding values to the key **`listStyleType`** key under the **`theme`** object. Arbitrary values can be passed to style parameters. For example, **`list-[lower-roman]`**.

List style position

These utilities are used for deciding the position of bullets or numbering in lists. There are *two* possibilities:

- **`list-inside`**: This class positions the markers *inside* the indentation of the list items.
- **`list-outside`**: This class positions the marker *outside* the indentation of the list items.

Text

The following set of utility classes explained here are used to control the styling of text content.

Text align

These utilities are used to decide the alignment of text content within its element/container. There are *six* default alignment classes available as follows:

- **`text-left`**: This class is used to align text to the *left* edge of the element (default).

- **`text-center`**: This class is used to align text to the *center* of the element.
- **`text-right`**: This class is used to align text to the *right* edge of the element.
- **`text-justify`**: This class is used to *justify* the text to the available width of the element.
- **`text-start`**: The same as *left* if the direction is *left-to-right* and *right* if the direction is *right-to-left*.
- **`text-end`**: The same as *right* if the direction is *left-to-right* and *left* if the direction is *right-to-left*.

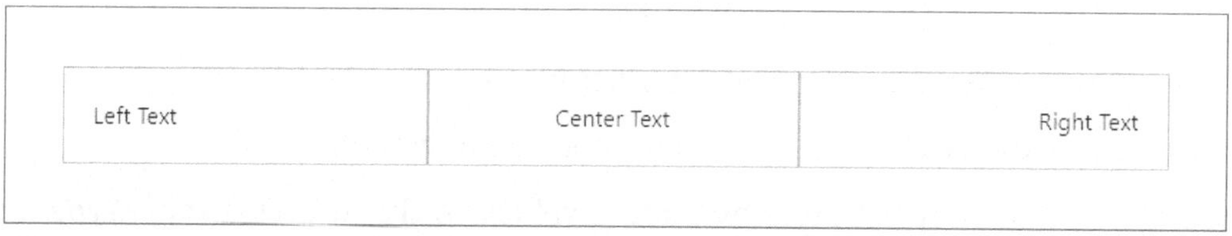

Figure 4.3: *Examples of text alignment*

Text color

These utilities are used for adding the color for the text content of an element. Those default colors with their variants are available for text coloring as well. When you extend colors in configuration those will be available to text coloring as well.

Passing arbitrary values for the color is as simple as passing a *hex* code of color for color value. Example: **text-[#44DD22]**.

Text decoration

These are the utilities used to add decorations to the text content. There are *four* default variants for this:

- **`underline`**: This class adds *underline* to the text content.
- **`overline`**: This class adds *overline* to the text content.
- **`line-through`**: This class adds *lines* on a text content.
- **`no-underline`**: This class removes *underline* from the text content.

Text decoration color

Similar to text color these utilities are used to add color to the decoration made on texts. All the default colors and their variants are supported for coloring text decoration, for example, *green underline*, *blue overline*, and so on.

Arbitrary colors are as simple as passing a *hex color* code to **decoration** class. Example: **decoration-[#55CC66]**.

Text decoration style

These are the utility classes used to style the text decoration. There are *five* possibilities by default, which should be used with suitable text decoration classes. The syntax is **decoration-{style}**.

- **decoration-solid**: This class adds a solid pattern for text decoration like solid *underline*, *solid overline*, and so on.
- **decoration-double**: This class adds a double pattern for text decoration like *double underline*, *double line through*, and so on.
- **decoration-dotted**: This class adds dotted patterns for text decoration like *dotted underline*.
- **decoration-dashed**: This class adds a dashed pattern for text decoration like *dashed overline*.
- **decoration-wavy**: This class adds wavy patterns for text decoration like *wavy underline*.

Text decoration thickness

These utilities are used for controlling the thickness of text decorations. The general syntax is **decoration-{width}**. Should be used along with suitable text decoration. There are *seven* default possibilities:

- **decoration-auto**
- **decoration-from-font**
- **decoration-0**
- **decoration-1**
- **decoration-2**
- **decoration-4**
- **decoration-8**

You are allowed to define your own decoration style thickness by adding value for key **textDecorationThickness** under the **theme** object.

Arbitrary values can be passed as well, for example, **decoration-[5px]**, **decoration-[1rem]**, and so on.

Text underline offset

These are the utility classes used to add offset for the underline decoration. Underline class should be present to get the effect of this class.

The general syntax is **`underline-offset-{width}`**. As *width* increases, *offset* space increases.

There are *six* variants for this class:

- **`underline-offset-auto`**
- **`underline-offset-0`**
- **`underline-offset-1`**
- **`underline-offset-2`**
- **`underline-offset-4`**
- **`underline-offset-8`**

You are allowed to define your underline offset by adding value for key **`textUnderlineOffset`** under **`theme`** object. Arbitrary values can be passed as well, for example, **underline-offset-[5px]**, **underline-offset-[1rem]**, and so on.

Text transform

These are the utility classes used for the transformation of text content. There are *four* default possibilities:

- **`uppercase`**: This class transforms all characters of the text content to *uppercase* letters.
- **`lowercase`**: This class transforms all the characters of the text content into *lowercase* letters.
- **`capitalize`**: This class transforms the first characters of each word to the *capital* letter.
- **`normal-case`**: This class shows texts as we enter, there is *no* added transformation on it.

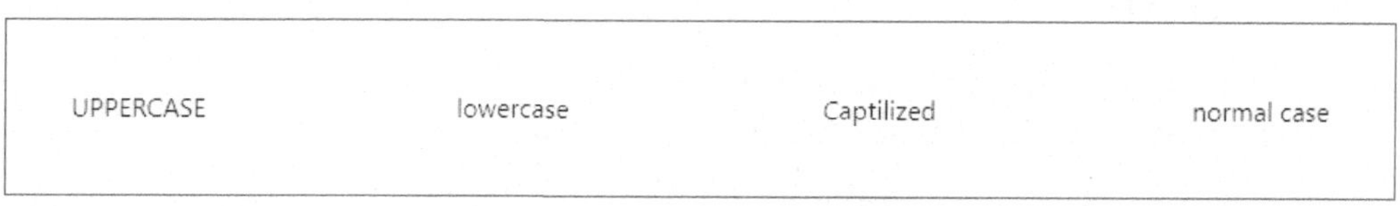

***Figure 4.4**: Examples of Text transform*

Text overflow

These are the utility classes used for controlling overflow of text elements in its container. There are *three* variants for it:

- **truncate**: This class truncates the overflow text and adds ... symbol if necessary along with whitespace as *nowrap* and *overflow-hidden* properties.
- **text-ellipsis**: This class truncates the overflow text and adds ... symbol if necessary.
- **text-clip**: This class truncates the text at the limit of the content area.

Text indent

These are the utility classes used to mention the amount of empty space shown before text in a block. As this empty space indicates empty width, you are allowed to pass spacing values provided by Tailwind CSS or your extended values from the configuration. The syntax looks like **indent-{width}**.

Examples of indent classes: **indent-2**, **indent-4**, and so on.

Negative indentation is also allowed, for example, **-indent-4**, **-indent-6**.

Arbitrary values can be any valid width parameter. For example, **indent-[5rem]**, **indent-[40%]**, and so on.

Vertical align

These are the utilities for controlling the vertical alignment of an *inline* or *table-cell* box. There are *eight* default possibilities.

The following table shows information about those:

Classname	Information
align-baseline	Used to align the baseline of an element with the baseline of its parent.
align-top	Used to align the top of an element and its descendants with the top of the entire line.
align-middle	Used to align the middle of an element with the baseline plus half the x-height of the parent.
align-bottom	Used to align the bottom of an element and its descendants with the bottom of the entire line.

Classname	Information
`align-text-top`	Used to align the top of an element with the top of the parent element's font.
`align-text-bottom`	Used to align the bottom of an element with the bottom of the parent element's font.
`align-sub`	Used to align the baseline of the element with the superscript-baseline of its parent.
`align-super`	Used to align the baseline of the element with the subscript-baseline of its parent.

Table 4.5: *Utility classes for vertical align*

You can pass arbitrary value for vertical align, for example, **align-[6px]**, **align-[0.5rem]**.

Whitespace

These are the utility classes used for controlling an element's white-space property. There are *five* default variants. The syntax looks like **`whitespace-{style}`**.

- **`whitespace-normal`**: This class keeps normal white spacing between texts (default).
- **`whitespace-nowrap`**: This class is used to prevent text from wrapping within an element. Newlines and spaces will be collapsed.
- **`whitespace-pre`**: This class is used to preserve newlines and spaces within an element. Text will not be wrapped.
- **`whitespace-pre-line`**: This class is used to preserve newlines but not spaces within an element. Text will be wrapped normally.
- **`whitespace-pre-wrap`**: This class is used to preserve newlines and spaces within an element. Text will be wrapped normally.

Word break

These are the utility classes used to handle word break patterns in an element. There are *four* possibilities. The syntax looks like **`break-{type}`**.

- **`break-normal`**: This class is used to only add line breaks at *normal* word break points.
- **`break-words`**: This class is used to add line breaks mid-word if needed.

- `break-all`: This class is used to add line breaks whenever necessary, without trying to preserve whole words.
- `break-keep`: This class is used for avoiding word breaks for **Chinese/ Japanese/Korean** (**CJK**) text.

Content

These utilities are for controlling the content of the *before* and *after* pseudo-elements.

`content-none` this class is used for removing content data added using content class.

For example, `content-none` removes `before:content-['here'] after: content-['go']` kind of classes from element.

Backgrounds

The following sections are the utility classes for the background styling of the element.

Background attachment

These utilities are for controlling how a background image behaves when a scrolling event happens on an element. There are *three* variants available:

- `bg-fixed`: This class is used to *fix* the background image relative to the viewport.
- `bg-local`: This class is used to *scroll* the background image with the container and the viewport.
- `bg-scroll`: This class is used to *scroll* the background image with the viewport, but not with the container.

Background clip

This utility is used for controlling the bounding box of an element's background. There are *four* possibilities. Syntax is `bg-clip-{keyword}`.

- `bg-clip-border`: By using this class the background extends to the outside edge of the border (but underneath the border in z-ordering).
- `bg-clip-padding`: By using this class the background extends to the outside edge of the padding. No background is drawn beneath the border.

- **`bg-clip-content`**: By using this class the background is painted within (clipped to) the content box.
- **`bg-clip-text`**: This class is used to crop an element's background to match the shape of the text. Useful for effects where you want a background image to be visible through the text.

Background color

This utility is used to decide the color of the background of an element. You are free to use any color and its variants that are provided by Tailwind CSS by default or those classes you have defined or extended in the theme object of configuration.

Syntax: **`bg-{color}`**

You can even control the opacity of the color with the opacity value.

For example, **bg-green-500/40** – adds **bg-green-500** color with 40% *opacity*.

You are free to use any color of your wish as a background color as an arbitrary value. Color can be a *hex code*, *rgb value*, and so on, for example, **bg-[#33BB22]**, **bg-[#5522AA]**, and so on.

Background origin

These utilities are used for controlling how an element's background is positioned relative to *borders*, *padding*, and *content*. There are *three* possibilities by default.

- **`bg-origin-border`**: This class makes the background positioned relative to the border box.
- **`bg-origin-padding`**: This class makes the background positioned relative to the padding box.
- **`bg-origin-content`**: This class makes the background be positioned relative to the content box.

Background position

These utilities are used for controlling the position of an element's background image. It decides what to focus on from the background with the viewing space of an element. The syntax is **`bg-{side}`**. There are *nine* possibilities for this.

The following table gives information about this.

Classname	CSS rule	Information
`bg-bottom`	background-position: bottom;	This focuses on the *bottom* portion of the background in an element space.
`bg-center`	background-position: center;	This focuses on the *center* portion of the background in an element space.
`bg-left`	background-position: left;	This focuses on the *left* portion of the background in an element space.
`bg-left-bottom`	background-position: left bottom;	This focuses on the *left* bottom portion of the background in an element space.
`bg-left-top`	background-position: left top;	This focuses on the *left* top portion of the background in an element space.
`bg-right`	background-position: right;	This focuses on the *right* portion of the background in an element space.
`bg-right-bottom`	background-position: right bottom;	This focuses on the *right* bottom portion of the background in an element space.
`bg-right-top`	background-position: right top;	This focuses the *right* top portion of the background in an element space.
`bg-top`	background-position: top;	This focuses the *top* portion of the background in an element space.

***Table 4.6**: Utility classes for background position*

You can define your custom position within a theme object with a key **`backgroundPosition`**. You are allowed to pass arbitrary values as well for background position.

For example, bg-[center_bottom_2rem].

Background repeat

These utilities are used for controlling the repetition of an element's background image. There are *six* possibilities. The syntax is **`bg-repeat-{type}`**.

- **`bg-repeat`**: This class is used to repeat the background image both *vertically* and *horizontally*.

- **`bg-no-repeat`**: This class is used when you don't want to repeat the background image.
- **`bg-repeat-x`**: This class is used to repeat the background image only *horizontally*.
- **`bg-repeat-y`**: This class is used to repeat the background image only *vertically*.
- **`bg-repeat-round`**: When this class is used, background images will stretch (leaving no gaps) until there is space (*space left >= half of the image width*) for another one to be added. When the next image is added, all the current ones compress to allow space.
- **`bg-repeat-space`**: When this class is used the image is repeated as much as possible without clipping. The first and last images are pinned to either side of the element, and whitespace is distributed evenly between the images.

Background size

These utilities for controlling the background size of an element's background image. There are *three* possibilities for this:

- **`bg-auto`**: This class is to display the background image at its *default* size.
- **`bg-cover`**: This class is to scale the background image until it fills the *background* layer.
- **`bg-contain`**: This class is to scale the background image to the *outer edges* without cropping or stretching.

You can define your custom background sizes within the theme object with a key **`backgroundSize`**. Arbitrary values can be passed with expected height and width in it.

For example, bg-[length:300px_150px].

Background image

These utilities are for adding images as a background for an element. You can even pass color gradients as a background image. Tailwind CSS provides *nine* default approaches to add gradients. **Syntax**: **`bg-gradient-{direction}`**.

- **`bg-none`**: This class removes the background *image* of an element.
- **`bg-gradient-to-t`**: This class adds gradients towards the *top* direction.

- `bg-gradient-to-tr`: This class adds gradients towards the *top-right* direction.
- `bg-gradient-to-br`: This class adds gradients towards the *bottom right.*
- `bg-gradient-to-b`: This class adds gradients towards the *bottom* direction.
- `bg-gradient-to-bl`: This class adds gradient towards the *bottom left* direction.
- `bg-gradient-to-l`: This class adds gradients towards the *left* direction.
- `bg-gradient-to-tl`: This class adds gradients towards the *top-left* direction.

Examples of gradient coloring for background:

bg-gradient-to-r from-cyan-500 to-blue-500 – gradient begins with *cyan*-500 color and ends at right with *blue*-500 color.

By extending the theme with a key `backgroundImage` you can define a custom background gradient or image. Arbitrary values can be passed for background image, the values can be an image URL as well. For example, **bg-[url('/img/live-image.png)]**.

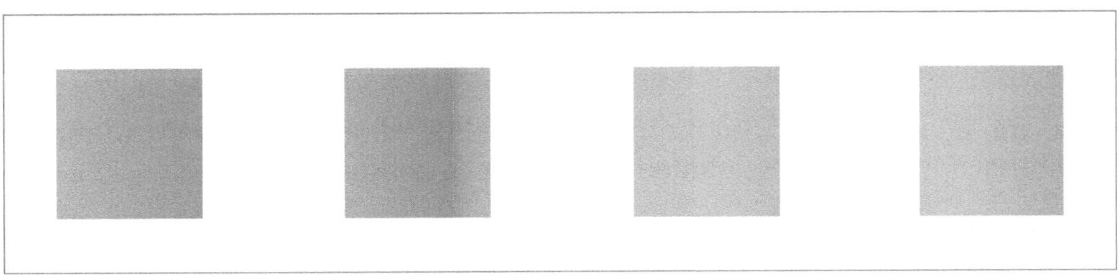

***Figure 4.5**: Examples of gradient backgrounds*

Gradient color stops

These are the utilities used for controlling the color stops in background gradients. There are *two* stops: **starting color** and **ending color** and **middle color**.

General syntax looks like `from-{color} and end-{color} and via-{color}`.

Similar to background color you are free to use any color and its variants which are provided by Tailwind CSS by default or those classes you have defined or extended in the `theme` object of configuration.

Fading effect on gradient need not be mentioned explicitly here, transparent effect will be added automatically. All the extended color of **`theme`** object can be used for these classes. Arbitrary values can also be passed for color value:

For example, from-[#243c5a], to[#aa4455], via-[#556677].

Borders

Border-related utilities are explained in the following sections. There are *four* types, **border**, **divide**, **outline**, and **ring**.

Border radius

These utility classes are used to add a border radius for an element. You are allowed to add a radius to complete the border or to a specific side of the border. Border radius can be applied with different sizing parameters.

- **`rounded`**: This class adds radius to all *sides* of the border.
- **`rounded-none`**: This class *removes* radius from all sides.
- **`rounded-full`**: This class makes a border look like a *complete* circle.

Along with the **`radius`** keyword, we can pass sizing parameters. Following is the list of default sizes available:

rounded-sm, rounded-md, rounded-lg, rounded-xl, rounded-2xl, rounded-3xl.

These **sm**, **lg**, **xl**, **2xl**, and **3xl** increase the radius value respectively, to make it relatable sizing parameters named with respect to breakpoints.

You can add border radius to only specific sides as well, only the *top side*, *bottom side*, and so on.

Mention these sides between rounded and size parameter, for example, **rounded-t-xl**, **rounded-l-sm**, and so on.

Following are the keys for border radius for different sides:

t	b	l	r
top	bottom	left	Right

tr	tl	br	bl
top right	top left	bottom right	bottom left

Table 4.7: *Sides available for border radius*

Custom border radius can be created by passing values for **borderRadius** within the **theme** object. Arbitrary values can be passed for size, for example, **rounded-[1rem]**, **rounded-t-[5px]**, and so on.

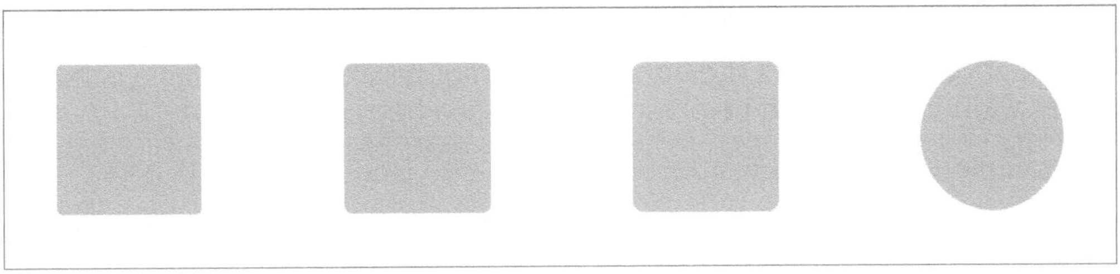

***Figure 4.6**: Examples of border radius*

Border width

These utilities are for controlling the width of an element's borders. There are *five* variants provided by Tailwind CSS by default:

- **border**: This adds *normal* border width.
- border-0: This *removes* border width.
- **border-2**, **border-4**, **border-8** are for *thicker* border width respectively.

You are allowed to add thickness to only specific sides of the total border as well. Between the border and the size, you can mention which side of the border to be thickened.

- t: for top side
- b: for bottom side
- l: left side
- r: right side.

For example, **border-t-2**, **border-l-8**, and so on.

You can thicken the border by the mentioned axis as well:

- x: Make the top and bottom side thicker and
- y: Make the left and right side thicker.

For example, border-x-2, border-y-4.

You can define more border width under the theme with a key **borderWidth**. Arbitrary values can be passed as well for width, for example, **border-[2px]**, **border-t-[1rem]**, **border-x-[2px]**, and so on.

Border color

These utility classes are for controlling the color of an element's borders. You are free to use any color and its variants which are provided by Tailwind CSS by default or those classes you have defined or extended in the object of configuration for coloring the border. The general syntax is **`border-{color}`**. A border width class should be present to get the effect of this class.

For example, border-green-400, border-red-600, and so on.

Similar to border width to specific sides and axis, color can also be applied to specific sides and axis as well.

For example, border-t-green-700, border-r-blue-400, border-x-gray-600, and so on.

Arbitrary values can be passed for color value. For example, **border-[#556688]**.

Border style

These are the utilities for controlling the style of an element's borders. There are *six* variants available for this. This class requires border width to be present to create a visual effect. The general syntax is **`border-{style}`**:

- **`border-solid`**: This class adds a *solid* border to the element(default).
- **`border-dashed`**: This class adds a *dashed* border to the element.
- **`border-double`**: This class adds *double normal* borders to the element.
- **`border-dotted`**: This class adds *dotted* borders to the element.
- **`border-hidden`**: This class hides the *border* style.
- **`border-none`**: This class removes all styles from the border.

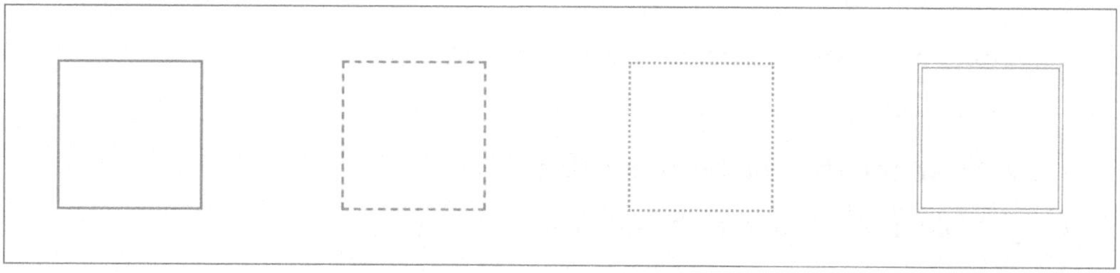

Figure 4.7: *Examples of border style*

Divide width

There are utilities for controlling the border width between elements. The general syntax is **`divide-x-{width}`**. **`divide`** width will be added either in *x-axis* or in *y-axis*. Based on the thickness of the width, Tailwind CSS provides *eight* default classes for it:

- **`divide-x`** is for adding width from normally ordered elements in *x-axis* and **`divide-x-reverse`** is for adding width from reversely ordered elements in *x-axis*.
- **`divide-y`** and **`divide-y-reverse`** works similarly but with respect to *y-axis*.

For *x-axis*, **divide-x-2**, **divide-x-4**, **divide-x-8**. For *y-axis*, **divide-y-2**, **divide-y-4**, **divide-y-**8 as width *parameter* increases *thickness* of border increases.

You can define expected divide width values under theme width with key **`borderWidth`**. And arbitrary values can be passed for width parameters.

For example, **divide-[5px]**, **divide-[1rem]**, and so on.

Divide color

These utility classes are for controlling the border color between elements. You are free to use any color and its variants which are provided by Tailwind CSS by default or those classes you have defined or extended in theme object of configuration for coloring the divide border. The general syntax is **`divide-{color}`**. **`divide-width`** should be present for this utility.

For example, divide-green-500, divide-blue-400, and so on.

Arbitrary values can be passed for color parameter, for example, **divide-[#CC5511]**, and so on.

Divide style

These are the utilities for controlling the border style between elements. There are *five* variants available for this. This class requires a divide width to be present to create a visual effect. The syntax is **`border-{style}`**:

- **`divide-solid`**: This class adds a *normal* border to divide between elements.
- **`divide-dashed`**: This class adds a *dashed* border to divide between elements.

- **`divide-dotted`**: This class adds a *dotted* border to divide between elements.
- **`divide-double`**: This class adds a *double solid* border for dividing between elements.
- **`divide-none`**: This removes styles added for divide width.

Outline width

These utilities are used for controlling the width of an element's outline. The syntax is **`outline-{width}`**. Based on the thickness of the outline there are *five* possibilities by default.

outline-0, outline-1, outline-2, outline-4, outline-8 greater width for thicker outline.

You can define your outline widths under the theme object using key **`outlineWidth`**. Arbitrary values can be passed for width as well. For example, **outline-[10px]**, **outline-[1rem]**.

Outline color

These utility classes are for controlling the color of an element's outline. You are free to use any color and its variants that are provided by Tailwind CSS by default or those classes you have defined or extended in the theme object of configuration for coloring of the outline. General syntax looks like **`divide-{color}`**. This utility requires a divide-width class to be present.

For example, divide-green-500, divide-blue-400, and so on.

Arbitrary values can be passed for color parameter, for example, **outline-[#EE4511]**, and so on.

Outline style

These are the utilities for controlling the border style of an element's outline. There are *five* variants available for this. This class requires outline width to be present to create a visual effect. General syntax looks like **`outline-{style}`**:

- **`outline`**: This class adds *normal* outline to the elements.
- **`outline-dashed`**: This class adds a *dashed* outline to the elements.
- **`outline-dotted`**: This class adds *dotted* outline to the elements.
- **`outline-double`**: This class adds *double normal* outline to the elements.
- **`outline-none`**: This removes styles added for *outline* of the elements.

Outline offset

These utilities are used to change the offset of an element's outline. This indicates a gap between outline and an actual content area. There are *five* variants by default based on offset value:

outline-offset-0	outline-offset-1	outline-offset-2	outline-offset-4
outline-offset-8			

***Table 4.8**: Outline offset utility classes*

Ring width

These utility classes are used for creating outline rings with box-shadows. There are *seven* possibilities by default for adding width. The general syntax will be **`ring-{width}`**.

ring, ring-0, ring-1, ring-2, ring-4, ring-8, ring-inset

`ring-inset` utility class is used to force a ring to render on the inside of an element instead of the outside. This prevents the hiding of the ring when the element presents at the edge of the screen.

You can define the ring width class of your wish under the theme object with a key **`ringWidth`**. Arbitrary values can be passed for width parameters. For example, **ring-[5px]**, **ring-[2rem]**, and so on.

Ring color

These utility classes are for controlling the color of outline rings. You are free to use any color and its variants which are provided by Tailwind CSS by default or those classes you have defined or extended in theme object of configuration for coloring of the ring. General syntax looks like **`ring-{color}`**. This utility requires a ring-width class to be present.

For example, **ring-green-500**, **ring-blue-400**, and so on.

Arbitrary values can be passed for color parameter, for example, **ring-[#EE4511]**, and so on.

Ring offset width

These utilities are used for simulating an offset when adding outline rings. There are *five* default classes available by default. General syntax looks like **`ring-`**

`offset-{width}`. This adds solid white box-shadow and increases the thickness of the accompanying outline ring to accommodate the offset.

ring-offset-0	ring-offset-1	ring-offset-2	ring-offset-4	ring-offset-8

***Table 4.9**: Ring offset width utility classes*

Custom utilities can be defined under the **`theme`** object with a key **`ringOffsetWidth`**. Arbitrary values can be passed as well with parameters.

For example, ring-offset-[5px], ring-offset-[1rem].

Ring offset color

These utility classes are for controlling the color of outline ring offsets. You are free to use any color and its variants which are provided by Tailwind CSS by default or those classes you have defined or extended in the theme object of configuration for coloring of the ring-offset. General syntax looks like **`ring-offset-{color}`**. This utility requires a ring-width class to be present.

For example, ring-offset-orange-500, ring-offset-sky-400, and so on.

Arbitrary values can be passed for color parameter, for example, **ring-offset-[#AA11CC]**, and so on.

Effects

The following sections explain different effects that can be added on elements utility classes.

Box shadow

This utility class is used to decide the box shadow of an element. There are *eight* utility classes provided by Tailwind CSS based on shadow width:

shadow	shadow-sm	shadow-md	shadow-lg
shadow-xl	shadow-2xl	shadow-inner	shadow-none

***Table 4.10**: Box shadow utility classes*

Width parameters named similar to breakpoints that represent respective width.

`shadow-inner` creates shadows inside the element, **`shadow-none`** removes box shadows added.

By extending the theme with key **`boxShadow`** you can define the box shadow width of your wish. Arbitrary values can be passed as well.

For example, shadow-[0_50px_30px_-20px_rgba(100,200,50,0.3)].

Figure 4.8: *Examples of box shadow*

Box shadow color

These utility classes are for controlling the color of a box shadow. You are free to use any color and its variants that are provided by Tailwind CSS by default or those classes you have defined or extended in the object of configuration for coloring of the box shadow. The syntax will be **`shadow-{color}`**. This utility requires a box shadow class to be present.

For example, shadow-gray-500, shadow-pink-400, and so on.

Arbitrary values can be passed for color parameters, for example, **shadow--[#22BB77]**, and so on.

Opacity

These utilities are for controlling the opacity of an element. There are *fifteen* default classes available by default based on different opacity values.

Syntax: **`opacity-{amount}`**

opacity-0, opacity-5, opacity-10, opacity-20, opacity-25, opacity-30, opacity-40, opacity-50, opacity-60, opacity-70, opacity-75, opacity-80, opacity-90, opacity-95, opacity-100

Extend them with key opacity to define your custom opacity classes. Arbitrary values can be passed to the amount parameter, for example, **opacity-[.55]**, **opacity-[.30]**, and so on.

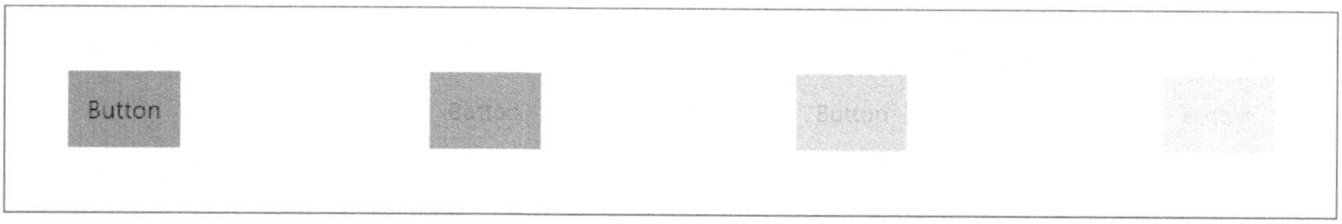

***Figure 4.9**: Examples of opacity effects*

Mix blend mode

These are the utilities for controlling how an element should blend with the background. General syntax looks like **`mix-blend-{mode}`**. There are *seventeen* default variants for this:

mix-blend-normal	mix-blend-multiply	mix-blend-screen	mix-blend-overlay
mix-blend-darken	mix-blend-lighten	mix-blend-color-burn	mix-blend- hard-light
mix-blend-soft-light	mix-blend-color-dodge	mix-blend-difference	mix-blend-exclusion
mix-blend-hue	mix-blend-saturation	mix-blend-color	mix-blend-luminosity
mix-blend-plus-lighter			

***Table 4.11:** Mix blend mode utility classes*

Background blend mode

These utilities for controlling how an element's background image should blend with its background color. There are *sixteen* default variants for this:

mix-blend-normal	mix-blend-multiply	mix-blend-screen	mix-blend-overlay
mix-blend-darken	mix-blend-lighten	mix-blend-color-burn	mix-blend- hard-light
mix-blend-soft-light	mix-blend-color-dodge	mix-blend-difference	mix-blend-exclusion
mix-blend-hue	mix-blend-saturation	mix-blend-color	mix-blend-luminosity

***Table 4.12**: Background blend mode utility classes*

Normal filters

These utilities are the filter adding attributes on elements. The following sections are the type of filters:

Blur

These utilities are for applying blur filters to an element. There are *eight* variants based on the amount of blur needed to apply. The naming of these utilities follows breakpoint sizing to convey it easier.

General syntax looks like **`blur-{amount}`**.

- **Blur**: This class adds normal blur to the element, **`blur-none`** – this class removes *blur* from the element.
- **blur-sm**, **blur-md**, **blur-lg**, **blur-xl**, **blur-2xl**, **blur-3xl**: As the amount parameter increases, the blurring effect increases.

By extending the themes object with *key blur*, you can define your blur utility classes. Arbitrary values can be passed as well. For example, **blur-[5px]**, **blur-[2rem]**, and so on:

***Figure* 4.10**: *Examples of blur effect*

Brightness

These utility classes are for applying brightness filters to an element. There are *eleven* default classes provided by Tailwind CSS. The syntax is **`brightness-{amount}`**.

The amount parameter follows the brightness level, as it increases the *brightness effect* from the normal level:

brightness-0, brightness-50, brightness-75, brightness-90, brightness-95, brightness-100,

brightness-105, brightness-110, brightness-125, brightness-150, brightness-200

By extending themes objects with key brightness, you can define your own brightness utility classes. Arbitrary values can be passed as well. For example, **brightness-[1.25]**.

Contrast

These utility classes are for applying contrast filters to an element. There are *seven* default classes provided by Tailwind CSS. The syntax is **`contrast-{amount}`**.

Amount parameter follows the contrast level, as it increases the *contrast effect* from the normal level:

contrast-0, contrast-50, contrast-75, contrast-100, contrast-125, contrast -150, contrast-200

By extending the **`themes`** object with **`key`** contrast, you can define your brightness utility classes. Arbitrary values can be passed as well. For example, **contrast-[.35]**.

Drop shadow

These utility classes are for applying drop-shadow filters to an element. There are *seven* default classes provided by Tailwind CSS. General syntax looks like **`drop-shadow-{amount}`**.

Amount parameter follows drop shadow level, as it increases *drop shadow effect* increases from normal level. Naming of these follows breakpoint sizing to convey it easier.

- **`drop-shadow`**: This class adds normal drop shadow to the element.
- **`drop-shadow-none`**: This class removes drop shadows from the element.
- **`drop-shadow-sm`**, **`drop-shadow-md`**, **`drop-shadow-lg`**, **`drop-shadow-xl`**, **`drop-shadow-2xl`**

By extending the themes object with key **`dropShadow`**, you can define your own drop shadow utility classes. Arbitrary values can be passed as well.

For example, drop-shadow-[0_25px_35px_rgba(0,0,0,0.5)].

Grayscale

These utilities are used for applying grayscale filters to an element. There are *two* utilities for this one to add grayscale and one to remove it:

- **`grayscale`**: This class adds the grayscale to the element.
- **`grayscale-0`**: This class removes the grayscale from the element.

By extending **`themes`** objects with **`key`** grayscale, you can define your own grayscale utility classes. Arbitrary values can be passed as well.

For example, grayscale-[60%].

Hue rotate

These utilities are used for applying hue-rotate filters to an element. There are *six* variants by default based on the amount of *hue-rotate* added to the element.

Syntax: **`hue-rotate-{amount}`**

hue-rotate-0, hue-rotate-15, hue-rotate-30, hue-rotate-60, hue-rotate-90, hue-rotate-100

By extending the theme object with key **`hueRotate`**, you can define your own hue-rotate utility classes. Arbitrary values can be passed as well.

For example, hue-rotate-[145deg].

Invert

These utilities are used for applying invert filters to an element. There are *two* utilities for this one to add invert and one to remove it.

- **`invert`**: This class adds the invert filter to the element.
- **`invert-0`**: This class removes the invert filter from the element.

By extending the theme object with key **`invert`**, you can define your own invert utility classes. Arbitrary values can be passed as well. For example, **invert -[.35]**.

Saturate

These utilities are used for applying saturation filters to an element. There are *five* variants by default based on the saturation amount to be added. The general syntax is **`saturate-{amount}`**.

As the amount *parameter* increases, *saturation* increases.

saturate-0, saturate-50, saturate-100, saturate-150, saturate-200

By extending themes object with key **`saturate`**, you can define your own saturate utility classes. Arbitrary values can be passed as well. For example, **saturate-[.75]**.

Sepia

These utilities are used for applying sepia filters to an element. There are *two* utilities for this one to add sepia and one to remove it:

- **`sepia`**: This class adds the sepia filter to the element.
- **`sepia-0`**: This class removes the sepia filter from the element.

By extending themes object with key **`sepia`**, you can define your own sepia utility classes. Arbitrary values can be passed as well. For example, **invert-[.35]**.

Backdrop filters

Those all filters you already read just before this can be applied to backdrops as well. When multiple elements have been placed into full screen mode, the backdrop is drawn immediately beneath the front most such element, and on top of the older full screen elements. The next section explains the set of available filters on backdrops.

Backdrop blur

These utilities are for applying backdrop blur filters to an element. There are *eight* variants based on the amount of blur needed to apply. Naming of these follows breakpoint sizing to convey it easier. The syntax will be **`backdrop-blur-{amount}`**.

- **`backdrop-blur`**: This class adds normal blur to the element, **`backdrop-blur-none`** – this class removes backdrop blur from the element.
- **`backdrop-blur-sm`**, **`backdrop-blur-md`**, **`backdrop-blur-lg`**, **`backdrop-blur-xl`**, **`backdrop-blur-2xl`**, **`backdrop-blur-3xl`**: As the amount parameter increases blurring effect increases.

By extending themes object with key **`backdropBlur`**, you can define your own backdrop blur utility classes. Arbitrary values can be passed as well.

For example, backdrop-blur-[5px].

Backdrop brightness

These utility classes are for applying backdrop brightness filters to an element. There are *eleven* default classes provided by Tailwind CSS.

Syntax: **`backdrop-brightness-{amount}`**

The amount parameter follows the brightness level, as it increases *brightness effect* from the normal level.

backdrop-brightness-0, backdrop-brightness-50, backdrop-brightness-75,

backdrop-brightness-90, backdrop-brightness-95, backdrop-brightness-100,

backdrop-brightness-105, backdrop-brightness-110, backdrop-brightness-125,

backdrop-brightness-150, backdrop-brightness-200

By extending **themes** object with key **backdropBrightness**, you can define your own backdrop brightness utility classes. Arbitrary values can be passed as well.

For example, backdrop-brightness-[1.25].

Backdrop contrast

These utility classes are for applying backdrop contrast filters to an element. There are *seven* default classes provided by Tailwind CSS.

Syntax: **backdrop-contrast-{amount}**

The amount parameter follows the contrast level, as it increases *the contrast effect* increases from the normal level.

backdrop-contrast-0, backdrop-contrast-50, backdrop-contrast-75, backdrop-contrast-100, backdrop-contrast-125, backdrop-contrast -150, backdrop-contrast-200

By extending **themes** object with key **backdropContrast**, you can define your own brightness utility classes. Arbitrary values can be passed as well.

For example, backdrop-contrast-[.35].

Backdrop grayscale

These utilities are used for applying backdrop grayscale filters to an element. There are *two* utilities for this one to add grayscale and one to remove it:

- **backdrop-grayscale**: This class *adds* the backdrop grayscale to the element.
- **backdrop-grayscale-0**: This class *removes* the backdrop grayscale from the element.

By extending **themes** object with key **backdropGrayscale**, you can define your own backdrop grayscale utility classes. Arbitrary values can be passed as well.

For example, backdrop-grayscale-[0.9].

Backdrop hue rotate

These utilities are used for applying backdrop **hue-rotate filters** to an element. There are *six* variants by default based on the amount of hue-rotate added on the element.

Syntax: **backdrop-hue-rotate-{amount}**

hue-rotate-0, hue-rotate-15, hue-rotate-30, hue-rotate-60, hue-rotate-90, hue-rotate-100

By extending **`themes`** objects with key **`backdropHueRotate`**, you can define your own backdrop hue-rotate utility classes. Arbitrary values can be passed as well.

For example, backdrop-hue-rotate-[300deg].

Backdrop invert

These utilities are used for applying backdrop invert filters to an element. There are *two* utilities for this: one to add invert and one to remove it:

- **`backdrop-invert`**: This class *adds* the backdrop invert filter to the element.
- `backdrop-invert-0`: This class *removes* the backdrop invert filter from the element.

By extending **`themes`** object with key **`backdropInvert`**, you can define your own backdrop invert utility classes. Arbitrary values can be passed as well.

For example, backdrop-invert-[.55].

Backdrop opacity

These utilities are for controlling the backdrop opacity of an element. There are *fifteen* default classes available by default based on different opacity values.

The general syntax is **`backdrop-opacity-{amount}`**.

backdrop-opacity-0, backdrop-opacity-5, backdrop-opacity-10, backdrop-opacity-20, backdrop-opacity-25, backdrop-opacity-30, backdrop-opacity-40, backdrop-opacity-50, backdrop-opacity-60, backdrop-opacity-70, backdrop-opacity-75, backdrop-opacity-80, backdrop-opacity-90, backdrop-opacity-95, backdrop-opacity-100

Extend **`theme`** object with key **`backdropOpacity`** to define your custom opacity classes. Arbitrary values can be passed to amount parameter, for example, **backdrop-opacity-[.70]**.

Backdrop saturate

These utilities are used for applying backdrop saturation filters to an element. There are *five* variants by default based on the saturation amount to be added.

General syntax is **`backdrop-saturate-{amount}`**.

As the amount *parameter* increases, *saturation* increases.

backdrop-saturate-0, backdrop-saturate-50, backdrop-saturate-100, backdrop-saturate-150, backdrop-saturate-200

By extending **`theme`** object with key `backdropSaturate`, you can define your own saturate utility classes. Arbitrary values can be passed as well.

For example, backdrop-saturate-[.75].

Backdrop sepia

These utilities are used for applying backdrop sepia filters to an element. There are *two* utilities for this one to add sepia and one to remove it:

- **`backdrop-sepia`**: This class *adds* the backdrop-sepia filter to the element.
- **`backdrop-sepia-0`**: This class *removes* the backdrop-sepia filter from the element.

By extending **`themes`** object with key **`backdropSepia`**, you can define your own sepia utility classes. Arbitrary values can be passed as well. For example, **backdrop-invert-[.35]**.

Any kind of normal filter or backdrop filter can be removed from elements using **`filter-none`** and **`backdrop-filter-none`** classes respectively.

Tables

Tailwind CSS provides some utilities for table elements to control styles applied to it. The forthcoming sections give information about it.

Border collapse

These utilities are for controlling whether table borders should collapse or be separated. There are *two* classes available for this to be used with table elements:

- **`border-collapse`**: This class is used to combine adjacent cell borders into a single border when possible. Note that this includes collapsing borders on the top-level **`<table>`** tag.
- **`border-separate`**: This class is used to force each cell to display its own separate borders.

Border spacing

These utilities for controlling the spacing between table borders. You can use all those Tailwind CSS's default or your extended spacing utilities as a border spacing utility's spacing parameter. Spacing can be added in both the **x** and **y** axis separately.

For example, border-spacing-4, border-spacing-2, border-spacing-x-3.

You can even extend **borderSpacing** under the **theme** object to define your custom border spacing utilities. You can even pass arbitrary values for spacing width.

For example, border-spacing-[10px], border-spacing-[1rem], and so on.

Table layout

These are the utilities for controlling the table layout algorithm. There are *two* possibilities:

- **table-auto**: This class is used to allow the table to automatically size columns to fit the contents of the cell.
- **table-fixed**: This class is used to allow the table to ignore the content and use fixed widths for columns. The width of the first row will set the column widths for the whole table.

Transitions and animations

To create transitions and animations of elements Tailwind CSS provides the following utility classes.

Transition property

These are the utilities required to control properties of the transition. There are *seven* variants by default. General syntax is **transition-{properties}**:

- **transition**: This class adds transition to the element.
- **transition-none**: This class removes transition from the element.
- **transition-colors**: This class adds transition with the color styling of the element.
- **transition-opacity**: This class adds transitions with the *opacity* styling of the element.
- **transition-shadow**: This class adds transitions with the *shadow* styling of the element.
- **transition-transform**: This class adds transition with the *transform* styling of the element.

Transition duration

These are the utility classes for mentioning transition duration for the CSS transition. General syntax looks like **`duration-{amount}`**. There are *eight* duration-related classes by default based on duration span:

duration-75, duration-100, duration-150, duration-200, duration-300, duration-500, duration-700, duration-1000

Here, the duration amount represents total milliseconds that a transition can take. By extending a theme with a key **`transitionDuration`**, you can define your own duration utilities. Arbitrary values can also be applied. For example, **duration-[2000ms]**, **duration-[5000ms]**, and so on.

Transition timing function

These are the utilities used for controlling the easing of CSS transition. There are *four* default classes available by default. The general syntax is **`ease-{timing}`**.

ease-linear, ease-in, ease-out, ease-in-out

Custom values can be defined under the theme object with a key **`transitionTimingFunction`**. Arbitrary values can be passed as well.

For example, ease-[cubic-bezier(0.80,0.03,0.450,0.050)].

Transition delay

These utilities are for controlling the delay of the CSS transition. There are *eight* variants for it. Like transition duration these classes are also based on the amount of delay in milliseconds. The general syntax is **`delay-{amount}`**.

delay-75, delay-100, delay-150, delay-200, delay-300, delay-500, delay-700, delay-1000

By extending a theme with a key **`transitionDelay`**, you can define your own delay utilities. Arbitrary values can also be passed for duration value.

For example, delay-[2000ms], delay-[5000ms], and so on.

Animation

These are the utility classes available for creating an animation effect of an element. Tailwind CSS provides *five* animation classes by default.

- **`animate-none`**: This class removes the animation property from the element.

- `animate-spin`: This class adds spinning animation for an infinite number of times that happens every second on an element.
- `animate-ping`: This class adds pinging animation for an infinite number of times that happens every second on an element.
- `animate-pulse`: This class adds pulsing animation for an infinite number of times that happens every second on an element.
- `animate-bounce`: This class adds pulsing animation for an infinite number of times that happens every second on an element.

You can define your own animation utilities by extending the theme with a key `animation`. Arbitrary values can be passed as well.

For example, **animate-[wiggle_3s_ease-in _infinite]**, provided wiggle animation should be defined prior in the configuration.

Transforms

The next sections give information about transform utilities available in Tailwind CSS.

Scale

These are the utility class for scaling elements with transform. Scaling can be done in *three* ways. Scaling in both axis, scaling in *x-axis* and scaling in *y-axis*. There are *ten* variants available by default based on percentage of scale. General syntax is `scale-{percentage}`.

scale-0, scale-50, scale-75, scale-90, scale-95, scale-100, scale-105, scale-110, scale-125, scale-150

These scale class's percentage values can be applied for *scale-x* and *scale-y* classes as well. For example, **scale-x-75**, **scale-x-110**, **scale-y-125**, **scale-y-10**, and so on.

Custom scaling classes can be defined under the `theme` object with a key scale. Arbitrary values can be passed as well. For example, **scale-[1.85]**, **scale-[0.7]**, and so on.

Rotate

These are the utility class for rotating elements with transform. There are *nine* variants available for rotation based on the angle of the rotation. The general syntax is `rotate-{angle}`.

rotate-0, rotate-1, rotate-2, rotate-3, rotate-6, rotate-12, rotate-45, rotate-90, rotate-180

Negative rotation can be added as well using these default classes just by mentioning the minus symbol before the class. For example, **-rotate-12**, **-rotate-180**, and so on.

Custom rotation values can be defined by extending the theme object with a key **`rotate`**. Arbitrary values can be passed for the angle parameter. For example, **rotate-[75deg].**

***Figure 4.11**: Examples of Rotate transform*

Translate

These are the utility class for translating elements with transform. Translating can be done in *two* ways. One in the *x-axis* and in the *y-axis*.

The syntaxes will be **`translate-x-{amount} and translate-y-{amount}`**.

Amount parameter can take those values of spacing utilities provided by Tailwind CSS or those extended by you.

For example, translate-x-3, translate-x-56, translate-y-44, translate-y-60, and so on.

You can enable GPU instead of CPU to render this by adding class **`transform-gpu`**.

You are still allowed to create custom classes for translate by extending the theme object with the `translate` key. Arbitrary values can be passed for the translate amount.

For example, translate-y-[10rem], translate-x-[50px], and so on.

Skew

These are the utility class for skewing elements with transform. Skewing can also be done in both the axes. There are *five* variants for each available by default in Tailwind CSS.

The general syntax is **`skew-x-{amount}`** and **`skew-y-{amount}`**. **`skew`** amount represents a degree to be skewed.

skew-x-0, skew-x-1, skew-x-2, skew-x-3, skew-x-6, skew-x-12

skew-y-0, skew-y-1, skew-y-2, skew-y-3, skew-y-6, skew-y-12

By extending the **`theme`** object with a key `skew` you are allowed to define your own skew classes. Arbitrary values can be passed for skew amount.

For example, skew-x-[20deg], skew-y-[10deg], and so on.

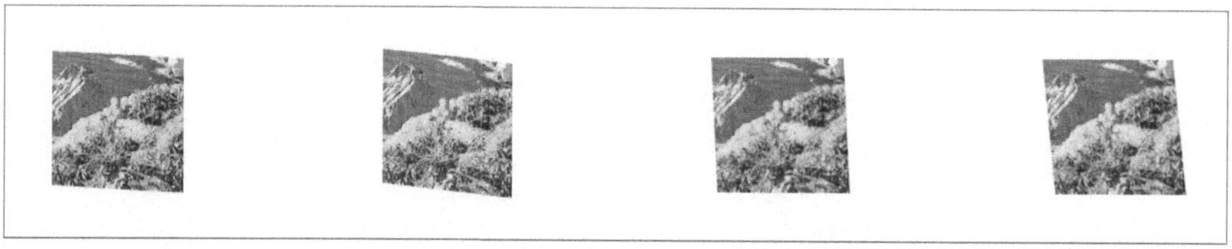

***Figure 4.12**: Examples of skew transform*

Transform origin

These are the utilities for specifying the origin of an element for its transformations. There are *nine* variants available based on the position of the element (see *Table* 4.13). General syntax looks like **`origin-{keyword}`**:

Class name	Information
`origin-center`	Transformation origin will be at the center of the element.
`origin-top`	Transformation origin will be at the top of the element.
`origin-top-right`	Transformation origin will be at the top right of the element.
`origin-right`	Transformation origin will be at the right of the element.
`origin-bottom-right`	Transformation origin will be at the bottom right of the element.
`origin-bottom`	Transformation origin will be at the bottom of the element.
`origin-bottom-left`	Transformation origin will be at the bottom left of the element.
`origin-left`	Transformation origin will be at the left of the element.
`origin-top-left`	Transformation origin will be at the top left of the element.

***Table 4.13**: Transform origin utility classes*

Custom utility classes can be created by extending a theme object with a key **transformOrigin**. Arbitrary values can be passed for keyword parameters.

For example, origin-[66%_66%], origin-[50%_20%], and so on.

Interactivity

The following sections are the interactivity-related classes provided by Tailwind CSS by default.

Accent color

These utilities are for controlling the accent color of a form control. Like **checkbox**, **radio button**, and so on which overrides default behavior added by browser. You are free to use any color and its variants which are provided by Tailwind CSS by default or those classes you have defined or extended inside a **theme** object of configuration for coloring of the accent. The general syntax is **accent-{color}**.

For example, accent-gray-500, accent-green-800, and so on.

Arbitrary values can be passed for color parameters. For example, **accent-[#56ABCD]**.

Appearance

These utility classes are used for suppressing native form control styling. There is a class available for this called **appearance-none.** This removes those styling's added by browser on a form element.

Cursor

These utilities are for controlling the cursor style when hovering over an element. General syntax looks like **cursor-{style}**.

cursor-auto	cursor-default	cursor-pointer	cursor-wait
cursor-text	cursor-move	cursor-help	cursor-not-allowed
cursor-none	cursor-cell	cursor-progress	cursor-context-menu
cursor-crosshair	cursor-alias	cursor-copy	cursor-vertical-text
cursor-no-drop	cursor-grab	cursor-grabbing	cursor-all-scroll
cursor-col-resize	cursor-n-resize	cursor-row-resize	cursor-e-resize

cursor-sw-resize	cursor-sw-resize	cursor-ew-resize	cursor-ns-resize
cursor-ns-resize	cursor-w-resize	cursor-ne-resize	cursor-nwse-resize
cursor-zoom-in	cursor-nw-resize	cursor-sw-resize	cursor-nesw-resize

Table 4.14: *Cursor interactivity utility classes*

Caret color

These are the utilities for controlling the color of the text input cursor. You are free to use any color and its variants which are provided by Tailwind CSS by default or those classes you have defined or extended inside a theme object of configuration for coloring of the caret. The general syntax looks like **`caret-{color}`**. For example, **caret-green-600**, **caret-red-400**, and so on.

Arbitrary values can be passed for color parameters. For example, **caret-[#56ABCD]**.

Pointer events

These are the utilities for controlling whether an element responds to pointer events. There are *two* classes:

- **`pointer-events-none`**: This class reverts the default browser behavior for pointer events (like :hover and click).
- **`pointer-events-auto`**: This class is to make an element ignore pointer events.

Resize

These utilities for controlling how an element can be resized. There are *four* variants for this:

- **resize**: This class is to make an element *horizontally* and *vertically* resizable.
- **resize-none**: This class is to prevent an element from being resizable.
- **resize-x**: This class is to make an element *horizontally* resizable.
- **resize-y**: This class is to make an element *vertically* resizable.

Scroll behavior

These are the utilities for controlling the scroll behavior of an element. There are *two* classes:

- `scroll-auto`: This class is to flag auto scrolling behavior within an element.
- `scroll-smooth`: This class is to enable smooth scrolling within an element.

Scroll margin

These utilities for controlling the scroll offset around items in a snap container. General syntax looks like `scroll-m{side}-{size}`. Size parameters can take those values of spacing utilities provided by Tailwind CSS or those extended by you. Side parameter can be any side or axis.

Still, you are allowed to use custom classes by extending the `theme` object with a key `scrollMargin`. You can also pass arbitrary values. For example, **scroll-m-[24rem]**.

Scroll padding

These utilities for controlling an element's scroll offset within a snap container. General syntax looks like `scroll-p{side}-{size}`. Size parameters can take those values of spacing utilities provided by Tailwind CSS or those extended by you. Side parameter can be any side or axis.

Still, you are allowed to use custom classes by extending the `theme` object with a key `scrollPadding`. Arbitrary values can be passed as well. For example, **scroll-p-[24rem]**.

Scroll snap align

These utilities for controlling the scroll snap alignment of an element. There are *four* variants for this:

- `snap-start`: This utility to snap an element to its start when being scrolled inside a snap container.
- `snap-end`: This utility is to snap an element to its end when being scrolled inside a snap container.
- `snap-center`: This utility to snap an element to its center when being scrolled inside a snap container.

- **`snap-align-none`**: This utility removes snap alignment applied on elements.

Scroll snap stop

These utilities for controlling whether you can skip past possible snap positions. There are *two* possibilities:

- **`snap-normal`**: This class is to allow a snap container to skip past possible scroll snap positions.
- **`snap-always`**: Use the snap-always utility together with the snap-mandatory utility to force a snap container to always stop on an element before the user can continue scrolling to the next item.

Scroll snap type

These utilities for controlling how strictly snap points are enforced in a snap container. There are *six* possibilities as follows:

- **`snap-x`**: This class is to enable horizontal scroll snapping within an element.
- **`snap-y`**: This class is to enable vertical scroll snapping within an element.
- **`snap-both`**: This class is to enable horizontal vertical scroll snapping within an element.
- **`snap-mandatory`**: This class is to force a snap container to always come to rest on a snap point.
- **`snap-proximity`**: This class is to make a snap container come to rest on snap points that are close in proximity. This is the browser default.
- **`snap-none`**: This class is to disable scroll snapping within an element.

Touch action

These utilities for controlling how an element can be scrolled and zoomed on touchscreens. General syntax looks like **`touch-{action}`**. There are ten variants available as shown in *Table* 4.15:

Classname	Information
`touch-auto`	This class auto decides touch *interaction* with an element.
`touch-none`	This class removes touch *interactivity* with an element.

Classname	Information
`touch-pan-x`	This class is to enable touch interaction only in *x-axis* with an element.
`touch-pan-left`	This class is to enable touch only in the *left* direction with an element.
`touch-pan-right`	This class is to enable touch only in the *right* direction with an element.
`touch-pan-y`	This class is to enable touch interaction only in the *y-axis* with an element.
`touch-pan-up`	This class is to enable touch only in *up* direction with an element.
`touch-pan-down`	This class is to enable touch only in *down* direction with an element.
`touch-pinch-zoom`	This class is to enable multi-finger panning and zooming with an element.
`touch-manipulation`	This class enables panning and pinch zoom gestures, but disables additional non-standard gestures such as double-tap to zoom.

***Table 4.15**: Touch action interactivity utility classes*

User select

These utilities for controlling whether the user can select text in an element. There are *four* variants for this:

- **`select-none`**: This class is to prevent selecting text in an element and its children.
- **`select-text`**: This class is to allow selecting text in an element and its children.
- **`select-all`**: This class is to select automatically all the text in an element when a user clicks.
- **`select-auto`**: This class is to use the default browser behavior for selecting text.

Will change

These utilities for optimizing upcoming animations of elements that are expected to change. There are *four* variants by default:

- `will-change-auto`: This class auto decides the changing of elements for the browser.
- `will-change-scroll`: This class flags scrolling behavior will change.
- `will-change-contents`: This class flags content will change.
- `will-change-transforms`: This class flags transforms will change.

The last three classes optimize an element that's expected to change in the near future by instructing the browser to prepare the necessary animation before it begins.

You are allowed to extend the **`theme`** object with a key `willChange` to define more will-change classes of your wish. Arbitrary values can be passed as well.

For example, will-change-[right,bottom].

SVG

Scalable Vector Graphics. SVG is used to define graphics for the web. It is a W3C recommendation. It is defined within **`<svg> </svg>`** in an HTML document. SVG can contain **shapes**, **gradients**, **images**, and so on. It has *three* main properties:

- `fill`: Defines color to be filled for **`svg`**.
- `stroke`: Defines color to be filled for stroke or border of **`svg`**.
- `stroke-width`: Defines width for stroke or border of **`svg`**.

Tailwind CSS provides utilities to handle these more efficiently. As fill and stroke expect color values, you are free to use any color and its variants that are provided by Tailwind CSS by default or those classes you have defined or extended inside a theme object of configuration for coloring them.

General syntax for **fill** is **`fill-{color}`**.

General syntax for **stroke** is **`stroke-{color}`**.

Examples of fill and stroke, fill-green-500, fill-gray-200, stroke-blue-700, stroke-pink-400, and so on.

Arbitrary value can also be passed to color parameter, for example, **fill-[#446688]**, **stroke-[#113355]**, and so on.

For stroke width Tailwind CSS provides three default variants based on width thickness. General syntax looks like **`stroke-{width}`**.

By extending the **`theme`** object with key **`strokeWidth`** you can define custom classes for stroke width. Arbitrary values can be passed for width, for example, **stroke-[5px]**, **stroke-[1rem]**, and so on.

Accessibility: Screen readers

These utilities are used for improving accessibility with screen readers. There are *two* classes by default:

- `sr-only`: To hide an element visually without hiding it from screen readers and
- `not-sr-only`: To make an element visible to sighted users as well as screen readers.

Conclusion

This chapter provided brief information on different categories of styling entities provided by Tailwind CSS by default. Understanding these sections and remembering respective utility classes makes you ready to begin with the development of the website that begins from the next chapter. Hope you learned it and applied for visual understanding.

In the next chapter, we are understanding the meaning of the website and the development of some pages of it.

Points to remember

- Background image can be a gradient value or an URL of image.
- Gradient coloring has three parts: **from color**, **to color** and optionally **stop color**.
- Three attributes of SVG elements are **fill**, **stroke**, and **stroke-width**.
- Accent color is used to override default color of browser for form elements like **radio**, **checkbox**.

Multiple choice questions

1. **Object for extending font family is:**
    a. font-family
    b. font
    c. fontFamily
    d. FontFamily

2. **'italic' utility class is a:**
    a. font family
    b. font decoration
    c. font style
    d. font weight
3. **Which of the following is not a background attachment class?**
    a. `bg-fixed`
    b. `bg-flow`
    c. `bg-local`
    d. `bg-scroll`
4. **utility-class to create circular div element:**
    a. `rounded-div`
    b. `rounded-corner`
    c. `rounded-full`
    d. `rounded-xl`
5. **Which of the following is not a transform property?**
    a. scale
    b. draw
    c. skew
    d. rotate

Answers

1. c
2. c
3. b
4. c
5. b

CHAPTER 5

Developing a Website with Tailwind CSS

Introduction

This chapter provides a detailed explanation of the developer aspect of the website. We will learn the way a developer can analyze a website. We will explain HTML Doc and features of the webpage that we are developing. As the website comprises a set of webpages, we are providing a plan which we are following to build a web page in a Tailwind CSS way. Then we are building three web pages as well

Structure

In this chapter, the following topics will be discussed:

- Website – the developer's viewpoint
- Building a Restaurant website
- Parts of website
- Plan of each page
- Think in a Tailwind Way
- Webpage 1 – Home page

- Webpage 2 – Menu page
- Webpage 3 – Gallery page

Website

A **website** is an URL where we can find information on a place, person, company, and so on, they are meant for providing information to its visitors. There are different pages for different sets of information that come under the same context, for example, *contact us*, *about us*, *feedback page*, and so on. There are links to travel between different pages. It all conveys *What* is a website.

In simple terms, you are representing data or information digitally by entering a specific URL which can be accessed using the internet on various sets of devices.

Categories of websites

Based on the data, we are displaying we can say there are *two* types of websites:

- Static website
- Dynamic website

Static website

These websites contain data that is static on each of its pages, and we are convinced that the information on its pages are defined there. This information may not change, or it may change less frequently. As information is merged along with the code, we cannot alter them without direct intervention on its code.

Technically, these websites don't require any other programming tool or database which decides what to be shown, as all data and visual representation will be decided on HTML, and CSS itself.

For example, a website on an event, a website on a historical place, and so on.

Dynamic website

These are the websites where data can be dynamically changed. Information present on web pages changes as and when they get new information or as they get controlled from another end. Information present on a specific page is not written there along with a code. Either manually or automatically new data can be arrived at without intervention of its code directly.

Technically, these websites require an external source of data and a programming tool that decides what information will be shown at which part of the webpage.

That handles all the logic of data and HTML, and CSS are responsible for visual representation.

For example, social media websites, News websites, and so on.

Types of websites

Based on the data or information, we are displaying on the website following are the types of websites:

- **E-commerce website**: A website that is made for shopping.
- **Blogs website**: Shows a set of blogs (information on different subjects).
- **Business website**: Provides information on business.
- **Portfolio website**: Introduces a person, place, and so on.
- **Social media websites**: Connects peoples digitally.
- **Membership websites**: Provides data based on membership. For example, YouTube, Netflix, and so on.

Requirement of website

As we know, a **website** is a medium that shows information on the respective context for what it is built. When they are built with more precise and user convenience they act as an effective way of reaching the world about the context. Blogs provide user traffic to the website, e-commerce websites create virtual shops for business, social media creates connections between people, and so on.

Following are some of the reasons for the existence of the website:

- Websites on business, person, and place create a positive impression on people before they experience them physically – enhancing the brand.
- Websites convey more about what companies, people, and so on will do; it creates social proof that they are connected to the world.
- Perfectly built websites bring more business to the companies – act as a medium for competition.
- E-commerce websites make their users know about their huge set of products at their fingertips (quality, reviews, prices, and so on) which saves time for its user and eliminates the requirement of physical shop setup for vendors.
- User-friendly websites create good credibility for a company or a person with a first impression.

- Websites built for growing businesses to reach more people within a shorter period can make a good return on investment for companies - act as an advertising medium.
- Portfolio websites provide insight for its user about the experience of a company or a person in a concerned field. As a website has a way to reach out, it can bring more leads for the business.
- **Search Engine Optimization** (**SEO**) tool on websites, a business can identify the type of peoples visiting their website - analyzes the target audience for their product.
- Making websites properly listed using search engines will bring more people to visit a company's website which may create awareness of it in the people.
- Blog websites provide various sets of knowledge to their visitors that they can get by reading. This engages people with the website, and it creates a positive belief factor about the company or a person.

Website – the developer's viewpoint

Being a developer, you should think of it as *How* rather than just *What*. A website is an HTML document, where the layout is defined using HTML blocks, the aesthetic is defined using CSS and interactivity is defined using JavaScript. The simplest observation as a developer! *Isn't it?*

Being a normal user or website visitor, you always expect that content should be easily accessible and important information should be nicely represented. These are dependent on how you design your website. It talks about the visiting experience of the user. There are a set of separate minds who can think like a common man, or who can inquire, analyze, and study on those colors, image sizes, and length of data that can cause convenience for most of the visitors with respect to the interface of the website. These may or may not know how developers can develop a piece of such a user interface.

Similarly, being a developer it is not mandatory that you should know about what the taste of the user with respect to the user interface of the website is, rather you must concentrate on what needs to be done from the code level to achieve the provided design within the system.

The working way of website

Whenever you develop a website, it will be loaded on a browser or browser engine to its visitors. Here, the website in the context simply thinks in the sense that it will be an entity loaded on a browser window. Website is an entity that has a specific **Uniform Resource Locator** (**URL**) to view its contents. URL locates the live location of the files belonging to that website, then brings them to the browser of the visitor then renders them on its window. As you know, a static website has everything (visual representation and information) merged within the same files, when that file gets loaded on the browser it will display the data to the visitor.

In *Chapter 1, Getting Started with* HTML CSS *and Tailwind* CSS , we understood the responsibility of HTML, CSS, and JS with respect to an HTML document. These get downloaded into the browser before they get loaded on a window. It works the same for dynamic websites as well provided that dynamic data or its logic remains in the server, browsers cannot download them, it can listen to the data sent by them to update on HTML documents.

It is always true that a browser is a tool that loads the user interface of the webpage. Here in this book, we are developing a website that renders a simple user interface developed using Tailwind CSS. We are not concentrating on any data logic or any external data source that may drag the actual subject of this book.

Parts of the website

As a normal visitor, when you observe an ideal website you can identify some facts about the website. There is a common header for the pages which has links to traverse between different web pages of the website. There is a footer which remains the same for almost all the pages. And there is a main section in-between, which varies page to page.

When you observe it as a developer, you need to keep in mind what is the effort that you need to invest to achieve it. An effort can be the level of understanding required; lines of code to be written, step-by-step approach that need to be followed, and so on.

The development expects a concept called **DRY – Don't Repeat Yourself**, where you must try to reduce the repetition of work you are doing for the same kind of work that arises repeatedly in the context. Repetition can be developing a piece of user interface from scratch even though you already made it before with full effort, writing logic again that you already identified before, and so on. Repetition yields an obvious result at an end, but it violates a way of proper approach to resolving. For-loops, functions, classes, and so on, are there in programming languages to make work easier.

As we will develop a static website, there is no way of controlling data between different web pages, it is accepted in the learning stage of the website (as here we are concentrating on user interface only) that we can rewrite common parts among all the webpages. But while developing dynamic websites (while using any frameworks) where you have control over repetitive sections you must follow the DRY approach for development.

Building a restaurant website

Here as a part of applying knowledge gained from learning Tailwind CSS from previous chapters, we are building a simple website to understand the way of applying it to create a design parameter for it. We are developing a responsive website that has different web pages. Then we are hosting it in the GitHub pages as well.

Here we are building a restaurant website where we are showcasing food and drinks available in it along with the various details that customers can have about the restaurant.

Let's look into the list of webpages we are developing that in combination build a full website:

- **Home page or landing page**: It is the starting point of the website. When you enter the URL of the website and soon it loads on the browser this page will be shown. Developing this page with a neat design and highlighting content will create a good impression on the visitor.
- **Menu page**: This page showcases a set of different foods and drinks available in the restaurant. The clean design creates a good feel to the visitor.
- **Gallery page**: This is for showcasing the ambiance of the restaurant. Images of different corners of the restaurant in a well-arranged manner may create a positive feel for the visitor.
- **Blogs**: This page shows a set of blogs written on various foods, about the place, and different occasions. These kinds of pages make visitors engage with the website as it will provide some unique information.
- **Contact us page**: This page is for form activity where visitors interact with the restaurant person for their enquiries, orders, and so on.
- **FAQ Page - Frequently Asked Questions**: This page provides a set of questions and answers, where the visitor may find an answer to his doubt.

Parts of our website

Following are the parts we are building for a complete website; you can understand what each page contains in it:

- **Header**: In this section, we are showing hyperlinks to all the web pages and a logo of the website. We are repeating/rewriting this section on all our websites, as it remains common for all.
- **Footer**: In this section, we are showing some important links to the website, address, and contact details of the restaurant. Similar to the header section this section too remains the same for all the pages.
- **Home page**: This is the landing page of the website, which gives a glimpse of what the restaurant has in it.
- **Menu page**: This has a combination of image and text where you can find detailed information on special and popular recipes of the restaurant.
- **Gallery page**: This page showcases a set of images arranged in a systematic way to convey images of the restaurant.
- **Blogs page**: This page shows a list of blogs written on events in a restaurant. Title, short description, and an image are displayed for each blog item.
- **Contact us page**: This is a page which has a form in it, where website visitors can fill it and submit to contact individuals of the restaurant regarding their expected information.
- **FAQ Page**: It is a page where visitors can find a set of questions and answers, which are frequently doubts of the other visitors.

Think in Tailwind way

We are developing a static website by concentrating on the rapid development of user interface using Tailwind CSS. Here, whenever you are starting into the development of a piece of user interface you must analyze and identify the set of Tailwind CSS utility classes required to achieve it. Then you should begin with adding them really into the code. Classnames should keep on flashing in your mind whenever you look into the piece of user interface that you need to begin with development.

Let's begin development

In this section, we will develop a website that comprises the pages mentioned before.

We are keeping the design of the website as simple as possible purposefully because explaining the parts of the component (part of the user interface) will be easier. Also, as and how the complexity of the interface increases we need to use a greater number of utility classes for an HTML element that makes you feel complicated about the overall result classes set and its effect. Even though here we are developing a simple website, we will try to utilize most of the utility classes that we have learnt in the previous chapters.

At the end, you will agree to the point without writing the single line of CSS code we successfully developed a website that too with a considerably shorter period.

Are you ready?

As we are explaining ways to develop the user interfaces, which are parts of a webpage. We usually provide a piece of the code base for its brief information throughout the upcoming pages, and we may repeat the same piece of code-block to explain other aspects. So do not rush to begin development as and when we mention code blocks here. It will create confusion for sure. Instead, look carefully classname we mentioned and read the brief note we provided with it and try to understand the context. At the end of the development of each webpage, we will provide the complete HTML code of that page, and at the end of the development of all the webpages we are deploying it under GitHub pages and providing complete source code access to the public users. So again, make sure you will understand the usage of classes and digest the note provided on that code instead of code block itself.

Webpages

As we are developing our website from scratch, we prefer you to follow the TailwindCSS installation process again with a different folder apart from that you already used while learning, those are described in our previous chapters. (Avoid direct CDN usage as of now)

As we said before, we are trying to practicalize concepts and different types of the utility classes we learned. If you still feel you haven't done enough with learning utility classes do read previous chapters again then start from.

Further reading comprises lots of code and a brief explanation. Codes are written as per their syntax as we follow while writing them on IDE. Have patience while reading and understanding the code-blocks.

As we are developing a static website, we need to keep the same piece of code for the **header** and the **footer** of the website on all our web pages. So, we are developing it only once and we add it to all our web pages. We have our navigation bar of the website in the header section itself, we need to add one more utility class to highlight the active page's link to make it distinguish from other links.

As we have *two* modes of themes (**dark** and **light**) we need JavaScript interference here, we kept it as simple as possible so that it can be explained to you briefly.

The usage of prebuilt open-source libraries that makes our run shorter is a key for an enhancement of the pace of development. We are utilizing this advantage as well. Here, we are using a couple of *Google fonts*, *lord-icons*, *ionicons* JS libraries via CDN and a set of copyright-free images (stored under **`src/images`** folder).

CDNs of the fonts and icons will be added to the **`<head></head>`** section of the HTML Document:

- CDN resources added for **ionicons**:

```
<script
      type="module"
      src="https://unpkg.com/ionicons@5.5.2/dist/ionicons/
ionicons.esm.js">
</script>
```

- CDN resources added for **Google fonts**:

```
<link rel="preconnect" href="https://fonts.googleapis.com">
<link      rel="preconnect"      href="https://fonts.gstatic.com"
crossorigin>
<link href="https://fonts.googleapis.com/css2?family=Domine:w-
ght@500&family=Jost:wght@500&display=swap" rel="stylesheet">
```

- CDN resources added for **lord-icons**:

```
<script src="https://cdn.lordicon.com/fudrjiwc.js"></script>
```

Let's begin with things that need to be added in the config file, (**`tailwind.config.js`**).

Here, we are providing you those changes we made on the config file for our home page of the website. As we develop further, we may add more changes to the config and we will provide them before developing that page:

```
/** @type {import('tailwindcss').Config} */
module.exports = {
  darkMode: 'class',

  content: ["./src/**/*.{html,js}"],

  theme: {
```

```
extend: {
  colors: {
    'primary':'#BEAA2F',
    'secondary':'#FB4F29',
    'tertiary':'#AF4462',
    'quaternary':'#C53773',
    'quinary':'#452F70'
  },

  fontFamily: {
    domine: ['Domine', 'sans-serif'],
    jost: ['Jost', 'sans-serif'],
  },

  keyframes: {
    wave: {
      '0%': { transform: 'rotate(0.0deg)' },
      '10%': { transform: 'rotate(14deg)' },
      '20%': { transform: 'rotate(-8deg)' },
      '30%': { transform: 'rotate(14deg)' },
      '40%': { transform: 'rotate(-4deg)' },
      '50%': { transform: 'rotate(10.0deg)' },
      '60%': { transform: 'rotate(0.0deg)' },
      '100%': { transform: 'rotate(0.0deg)' },
    },
    rotating : {
      '0%': { transform: 'rotate(0.0deg)' },
      '25%': { transform: 'rotate(90deg)' },
      '50%': { transform: 'rotate(180deg)' },
      '75%': { transform: 'rotate(270deg)' },
      '100%': { transform: 'rotate(360deg)' },
    }
  },
```

```
animation: {
        'waving': 'wave 2s linear infinite',
        'rotating':'rotating 5s linear infinite',
      },
    },
  },
  plugins: [],
}
```

Observations on the preceding code-block:

- Added **darkMode** key with value **class** – it says dark mode can be toggled using class property. **dark** class will be toggled with **<html>** element (**root** element of the HTML document) so that we can get effects of dark mode on adding it.
- Extended five more colors (**primary**, **secondary**, **tertiary**, **quaternary**, **quinary**) with their respective hex-codes, so that they will be available along with the default colors of the Tailwind CSS.
- After adding CDNs of the Google fonts we need to declare class names for those fonts, it will be done by extending **fontFamily**, where we define font class name and expected font followed by fallback font of it.
- For animation effects, we need **keyframes** defined. These **keyframes** are defined with a specific name and their transition flow, under keyframes key.
- Animation classes are defined which may utilize keyframes that are already extended.
- Extended properties are used along with their parent key names,

For example, bg-primary, text-secondary, border-tertiary, font-jost, font-domine, animate-waving, and so on.

Now let's look into the HTML document which is modified to begin with development:

```
<!doctype html>
<html class="dark">

<head>
    <meta charset="UTF-8">
```

```
    <meta name="viewport" content="width=device-width, initial-
scale=1.0">
    <link href="/dist/output.css" rel="stylesheet">
    <script type="module"
src="https://unpkg.com/ionicons@5.5.2/dist/ionicons/ionicons.esm.js">
</script>
    <script src="https://cdn.lordicon.com/fudrjiwc.js"></script>
    <link rel="preconnect" href="https://fonts.googleapis.com">
    <link rel="preconnect" href="https://fonts.gstatic.com" crossorigin>
    <link
href="https://fonts.googleapis.com/
css2?family=Domine:wght@500&family=Jost:wght@500&display=swap"
rel="stylesheet">
</head>
<body></body>
</html>
```

Header and footer

These remain the same throughout all the web pages we are developing under this website. While using framework or any systematic DRY *approach* we do not write header and footer in all the pages, but here to keep the approach simple we are repeating it in all the pages.

These *two* sections are *starting* and *ending* sections of the visual part of the HTML document. Everything that arises in-between these will build an actual webpage.

Header section will be present within **<header></header>** element and **Footer** section will be present within **<footer></footer>** element of the HTML document within the **<body></body>** element.

The code for **Header** is given as follows:

```
<header
   class=" sticky top-0 z-20
           bg-purple-100 text-purple-800
           w-full h-12 md:h-auto
           dark:text-purple-100 dark:bg-slate-800 shadow-md dark:shadow-
zinc-700">
```

```
  <div class="  flex flex-row justify-between md:items-end
              px-5 md:px-10 py-2">
      <div class="md:hidden" onclick="toggleMenu('open')">
          <ion-icon size="large" name="menu-outline"></ion-icon>
      </div>
      <div class="relative">
                  <a href="index.html">
                  <div
                      class=" absolute top-0 z-10
                              h-16 w-16 md:h-24 md:w-24 rounded-full
                              outline-4 outline-dotted outline-purple-700
dark:outline-purple-300 animate-rotating
duration-500 ease-out hover:animate-none
cursor-pointer">
                  </div>
                  <img  src="/src/images/logo.png"
                      class="h-16 w-16 md:h-24 md:w-24 z-20 " />
            </a>
  </div>
        <div class="flex items-start md:items-center">
            <div class=" hidden md:grid grid-cols-6 gap-x-10
                          grow items-stretch place-content-center
                          justify-items-center px-5 max-w-7xl">
                  <a href="index.html">
                      <div class=" menu-item border-b-4 border-purple-400">
                          Home
                      </div>
                  </a>
                  <a href="menu.html">
<div class="menu-item">Menu</div>
</a>
                  <a href="gallery.html">
<div class="menu-item">Gallery</div>
```

```
</a>
                    <a href="blogs.html">
<div class="menu-item">Blogs</div>
</a>
                    <a href="contact_us.html">
<div class="menu-item">Contact us</div>
</a>
                    <a href="faq.html">
<div class="menu-item">FAQ</div>
</a>
</div>
             <div class="md:mb-1">
                   <div id="light"
                         class="hidden cursor-pointer place-self-center"
                         onclick="changeTheme('light')"
                         title="Normal mode">
                    <ion-icon name="sunny-outline"></ion-icon>
               </div>
               <div id="dark"
                    class="hidden cursor-pointer place-self-center"
                           onclick="changeTheme('dark')"
                           title="Dark mode">
                        <ion-icon name="moon"></ion-icon>
                </div>
           </div>
      </div>
   </div>
      <aside id="drawer"
          class="  absolute top-0 z-50 bg-purple-100 text-purple-800
md:hidden
                 min-h-screen min-w-full overflow-y-hidden
                 dark:text-purple-100 dark:bg-slate-800
                 -translate-x-[100%] duration-200 ease-in-out">
```

```
            <div class="flex flex-col py-10 px-5">
                <div class="w-full flex justify-end">
                    <div class="w-4/6 flex justify-between">
                        <div class="relative">
                            <div class=" absolute top-0 h-16 w-16 md:h-
24 md:w-24
  rounded-full outline-4 outline-dotted
  outline-purple-700
  dark:outline-purple-300
                                        animate-rotating duration-500
ease-out">
                            </div>
                            <img src="/src/images/logo.png"
 class="h-16 w-16 md:h-24 md:w-24 z-20" />
                        </div>
                        <div class="md:hidden"
onclick="toggleMenu('close')">
                            <ion-icon size="large" name="close-
outline">
         </ion-icon>
                        </div>
                    </div>
                </div>
                <ul class=" flex flex-col divide-y
                            divide-purple-200 font-jost gap-y-4 m-10 ">
                    <a href="index.html">
<li class="text-base font-bold py-3">Home</li>
</a>
                    <a href="menu.html">
<li class="text-base py-3">Menu</li>
</a>
                    <a href="gallery.html">
<li class="text-base py-3">Gallery</li>
</a>
```

```
                    <a href="blogs.html">
<li class="text-base py-3">Blogs</li>
</a>
                    <a href="contact_us.html">
<li class="text-base py-3">Contact us</li>
</a>
                    <a href="faq.html">
<li class="text-base py-3">FAQ</li>
</a>
                </ul>
            </div>
        </aside>
    </header>
```

The explanation is as follows:

- Make sure you are concentrating on the classenames we used with the HTML elements, HTML structure can be created in multiple ways for the same user interface. For ease of reading, we already marked class names with bold style.
- **Head** has a *sticky style*, which means it will always be stuck to the position mentioned – here we mentioned **`top-0`**, even the onscroll on page header part remains stuck to the top of the page.
- As we are developing a responsive website, there are two blocks of code present in the header for the navigation bar. One is for mobile devices, where it will be opened on click of menu button and the other will be for devices bigger than mobiles viewports – **`md:<utility-class>`** will add the same style on and above medium devices.
- Design of the header changes from the mobile viewport and other devices. On mobile devices, the navigation drawer will be opened on click of the menu button, whereas on desktop that button disappears. This **`on click`** logic will be handled from JavaScript.
- **`Onclick`** of menu button calls a function from JavaScript which opens a navigation menu on a screen. We have added a transition effect with delay for navigation menu opening, where it is like a drawer opening from the left side.

- For dark theme handling, classes with **`dark:`** prefix were mentioned along with normal theme classes. These classes with dark prefixes will be active only when we shift the website theme to dark.
- There is a function written in JavaScript to toggle between light and dark themes.
- There is a class mentioned called **`menu-item`** this is not a default class from Tailwind CSS, as all the menu items follow the same design pattern, instead of repeating all classes for all menu items, we made declaration of a classname which comprises all those classes of menu item, then we use that class name wherever we need same style pattern. (Defined under **`input.css`** file).
- On mobile devices, the logo of the restaurant will be displayed in the center of the row where it will be present at the left side of the screen in bigger devices.
- Following is the visually rendered status of the header in mobile devices:

5.1 (*a*) 5.1 (*b*)

Figure 5.1: *Header images in both light (a) and dark (b) themes in mobile devices*

- Following are the images of the header in the desktop viewport:

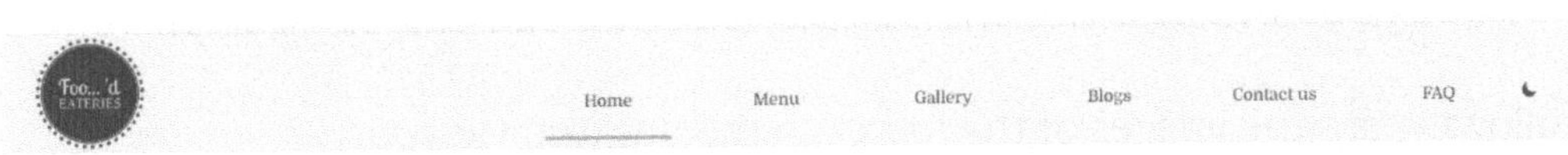

5.2(*a*)

5.2(*b*)

Figure 5.2: *Header images in both light (a) and dark (b) themes in desktop devices*

The code for **Footer** is given as follows:

```
<footer class=" static bottom-0 p-3
                flex justify-center bg-purple-100
                dark:bg-slate-800  dark:text-zinc-200">
        <div class="flex flex-col justify-center items-center">
            <img src="/src/images/logo.png" class="h-12 w-12" />
            <div>Copyrights 2023</div>
            <small>Contact +91 4458156974126</small>
        </div>
</footer>
```

Let's explain the preceding code:

- We have developed a simple form of footer, which shows a logo of the restaurant in the middle of the row in all find devices/viewports.
- Following is the visual rendered status of footer in mobile devices:

5.3(*a*)

5.3(*b*)

***Figure* 5.3**: *Footer images in both light (a) and dark (b) themes in mobile devices*

Following are the images of the footer in the desktop viewport:

5.4 (a): *Footer images in both light theme in desktop devices*

5.4(*b*)

***Figure* 5.4**: *Footer images in both dark theme in desktop devices*

Home page or Index page

This page is the landing page of the website which means when you hit the URL and when you see things loaded on the browser window that is nothing but an index page or landing page. This is the page that creates a positive impression on visitors about the business/person/place. In general visitors, judge their experience with the website by referring to this page itself. Developing a highly designed and properly informative landing page led to the success of a website. Here, we are keeping things simple from the design aspect, we are just eager to experiment more with utility class than in-depth design. We are developing simple information blocks for the homepage to make it feel like a homepage.

As we saw the code level design of header and footer before this section, we are not adding the same code in this webpage.

We made *four* parts on this homepage; each part represents different kinds of information. These parts are nothing but chunks of user interfaces. These are independent of each other. A set of these chunks makes a complete webpage:

- Banner block
- Features block
- Reviews block
- Numerical block

The following code represents the placement of each block along with the complete body of the HTML Document:

```
<body class="font-domine">
   // header code comes here
   <main>
      // Banner Block
      // Features Block
      // Reviews Block
      // Numerical Block
   </main>
   // footer code comes here
</body>
```

```
Banner block
<div class="  relative p-3 md:p-10 min-h-screen max-w-screen
```

```
              bg-[url('/src/images/bg1.jpg')]
              dark:contrast-125">
  <div class="  grid grid-cols-1 md:grid-cols-2 grid-rows-2
                items-stretch place-content-center min-h-screen
                text-white text-3xl">
      <div class="  border md:border-l-4 md:border-y-4 border-sky-400
 md:rounded-tl-xl
                    dark:border-stone-300">
         <div class=" h-full py-10
   flex flex-col justify-center items-center">
              South Indian
              <img src="/src/images/sf.png"
                   class="h-44 w-44 md:h-80 md:w-80" />
         </div>
      </div>
      <div class="  border md:border-t-4 md:border-x-4 border-amber-500
  md:rounded-tr-xl dark:border-stone-300">
         <div class=" h-full py-10
  flex flex-col justify-center items-center">
              North Indian
              <img  src="/src/images/nf.png"
class="h-44 w-44 md:h-80 md:w-80" />
         </div>
      </div>
      <div class="  border border-blue-60
 md:border-b-4 md:border-x-4 0 md:rounded-bl-xl
                    dark:border-stone-300">
         <div class=" h-full py-10
   flex flex-col justify-center items-center">
              Vegan
              <img  src="/src/images/vf.png"
class="h-44 w-44 md:h-80 md:w-80" />
         </div>
```

```
        </div>
        <div class=" border md:border-r-4 md:border-y-4 border-orange-600
md:rounded-br-xl dark:border-stone-300">
            <div class="h-full py-10 flex flex-col justify-center items-
center">
                Drinks and Juices
                <img src="/src/images/juices.png"
                    class="h-44 w-44 md:h-80 md:w-80" />
            </div>
        </div>
    </div>
    <div class=" hidden absolute top-0 h-full w-[95%] z-10
        md:flex items-center justify-center">
<img src="/src/images/logo.png"
     class=" h-44 w-44 drop-shadow-2xl cursor-pointer
            border-2 border-dashed border-zinc-200 rounded-full
            hover:animate-waving duration-900 ease-in-out" />
    </div>
</div>
```

Observations on the preceding code-block:

- We used an image as a background for the grid layout. We are increasing brightness on shift to dark mode.
- We are creating a grid block with 2 *rows* and 2 *columns*, where these *rows-columns* are reduced to 1 in the mobile viewport. Each block shows sample food items available in the restaurant.
- In the center of this *four-block layout*, there is a restaurant logo present that disappears on the mobile viewport.
- Logo has an absolute position with reference to the grid layout. This logo animates once as a hover effect.

- Following are the snapshots of these blocks on both mobile viewports:

5.5(*a*)

5.5(*b*)

Figure 5.5: *Banner block images in both light (a) and dark (b) themes in desktop devices*

Following are the images of *banner-block* on desktop devices:

5.6(*a*)

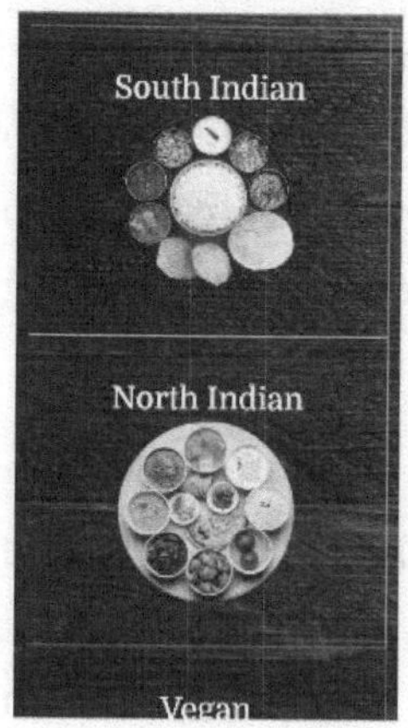

5.6(*b*)

Figure 5.6: *Banner block images in both light (a) and dark (b) themes in mobile devices*

Features block is given as follows:

```
<div class=" h-full w-full md:h-[20rem] p-10 font-jost
            bg-lime-200  flex justify-center
            dark:bg-slate-800/90 text-gray-800 dark:text-white">
    <div class="w-full flex flex-col md:flex-row justify-around text-2xl">
        <div class="px-20 flex flex-col items-center justify-center">
        <lord-icon src="https://cdn.lordicon.com/vukdchss.json"
trigger="loop" delay="2000"
```

```
                    class="h-36 w-36 md:h-[10rem] md:w-[10rem]">
            </lord-icon>
            <div class="font-semibold">Clean</div>
        </div>
        <div class=" px-20 flex flex-col items-center justify-center">
            <lord-icon  src="https://cdn.lordicon.com/ihyatngg.json"
                        trigger="loop" delay="2000"
                        class="h-36 w-36 md:h-[10rem] md:w-[10rem]">
            </lord-icon>
            <div class="font-semibold">Quality</div>
        </div>
        <div class="px-20 flex flex-col items-center justify-center">
            <lord-icon src="https://cdn.lordicon.com/efdhjqgx.json"
trigger="loop"
delay="2000"
                    class="h-36 w-36 md:h-[10rem] md:w-[10rem]">
            </lord-icon>
            <div class="font-semibold">Original</div>
        </div>
    </div>
</div>
```

- Here we are using a **flex box** to display live icons from *lord-icons*. By default, that is on mobile devices it will be in a *column direction* where three icons will be shown one below another and in desktop devices this flex will be displayed in a *row direction*, where icons will be displayed one aside from another.
- We are using another font family for this that we declared in our **config** file – **`font-jost`**.
- On shifting to *dark mode*, this flex-box's background color and text color will be changed.
- Following are the snapshots of these blocks on both mobile and desktop viewports:

5.7(*a*)

5.7(*b*)

Figure 5.7: *Feature block images in both light (a) and dark (b) themes in desktop devices*

- Following are the images of *features-block* in desktop devices:

5.8(*a*)

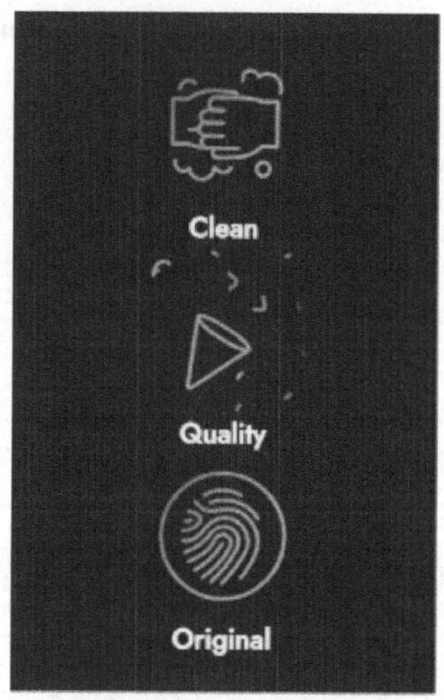

5.8(*b*)

Figure 5.8: *Feature block images in both light (a) and dark (b) themes in mobile devices*

Code for **Reviews Block** is given as follows:

```
<div class="  container min-w-full p-2 md:p-20
              bg-orange-200 dark:bg-slate-600 ">
      <div class="  flex justify-center text-4xl py-3 font-semibold
font-jost text-gray-700  dark:text-zinc-200">
                Reviews
      </div>
      <div class=" columns-1 px-4 text-xs p-5 space-y-3
                   md:columns-3 md:px-10 md:text-base
                   dark:text-zinc-200">
           <div class=" flex flex-col p-4
                        border border-secondary rounded-md
                        dark:bg-slate-800 ">
              <div class="flex space-x-2 items-center">
                  <img src="/src/images/profile.png"
                       class="w-12 h-12 rounded-full" />
                  <div class="text-md font-semibold">Person 1</div>
              </div>
              <div class="italic">
                   Nice ambience, good restaurant
              </div>
           </div>
           <div class=" flex flex-col p-4 border border-primary rounded-md
                       dark:bg-slate-800 ">
             <div class="flex space-x-2 items-center">
                 <img src="/src/images/profile.png"
                      class="w-12 h-12 rounded-full" />
                 <div class="text-md font-semibold">Person 2</div>
             </div>
             <div class="italic">
                  Good Taste :)
             </div>
         </div>
```

```
        <div class=" flex flex-col p-4
                    border border-tertiary rounded-md
                    dark:bg-slate-800 ">
            <div class="flex space-x-2 items-center">
<img src="/src/images/profile.png"
    class="w-12 h-12 rounded-full" />
                  <div class="text-md font-semibold">Person 3</div>
            </div>
            <div class="italic">
                Pocket friendly prices.. best offers
            </div>
        </div>
        <div class=" flex flex-col p-4
                    border border-quaternary rounded-md
                    dark:bg-slate-800 ">
            <div class="flex space-x-2 items-center">
                <img src="/src/images/profile.png"
   class="w-12 h-12 rounded-full" />
                <div class="text-md font-semibold">Person 4</div>
            </div>
            <div class="italic">
                 Decent Environment, lots of choices
            </div>
        </div>
        <div class="  flex flex-col p-4
                    border border-quinary rounded-md
                    dark:bg-slate-800 ">
            <div class="flex space-x-2 items-center">
                <img src="/src/images/profile.png"
  class="w-12 h-12 rounded-full" />
                <div class="text-md font-semibold">Person 5</div>
            </div>
            <div class="italic">
```

```
                Overall Good Experience
            </div>
        </div>
        <div class=" flex flex-col p-4
                   border border-secondary rounded-md
                   dark:bg-slate-800 ">
            <div class="flex space-x-2 items-center">
                <img src="/src/images/profile.png"
    class="w-12 h-12 rounded-full" />
                <div class="text-md font-semibold">Person 6</div>
            </div>
            <div class="italic">
                 Nice Restaurant with good, clean maintenance
            </div>
          </div>
    </div>
</div>
```

- Here in this block, we are using the columns utility class for arranging items within the element.
- On mobile devices, we can see all the items will be arranged in a single column and further, on bigger devices, it will be changed to *three columns.*
- Each item under this block is further aligned using *flexbox.*
- Following are the snapshots of these blocks on both mobile and desktop viewports:

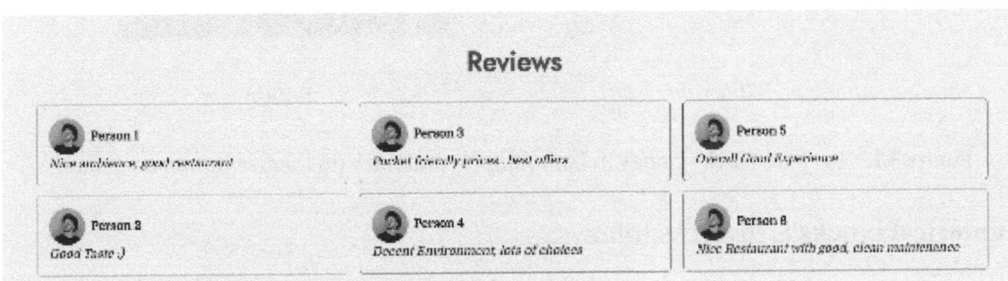

5.9(*a*)

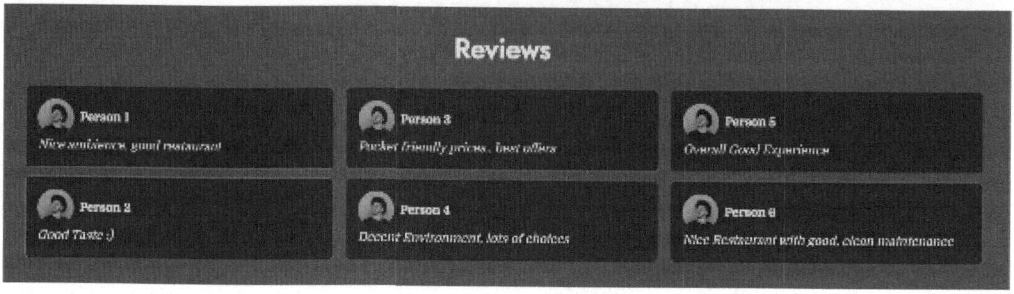

5.9(b)

***Figure 5.9**: Reviews block images in both light (a) and dark (b) themes in desktop devices*

- Following are the images of **reviews-block** in desktop devices:

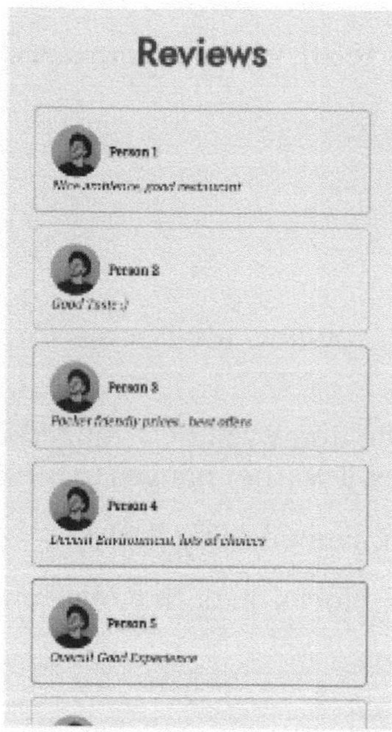

5.10(a)

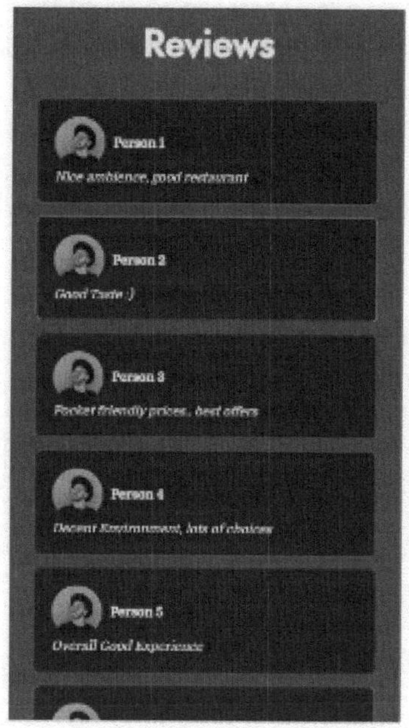

5.10(b)

***Figure 5.10**: Reviews block images in both light (a) and dark (b) themes in mobile devices*

Numerical blocks is given as follows:

```
<div class="  container min-w-full p-10
              bg-rose-200 dark:bg-gray-800">
  <div class="flex flex-col md:flex-row justify-around gap-y-6">
```

```
        <div class=" w-full md:w-44 lg:w-56 xl:w-72 2xl:w-80 flex flex-
col p-5
                          text-center text-gray-700 dark:text-gray-200
                          border border-rose-500 rounded-md shadow-xl
shadow-rose-400
                          dark:border-gray-100  dark:shadow-gray-100
   dark:hover:border-gray-50 hover:-translate-y-5 duration-150
   hover:border-rose-700 hover:shadow-2xl">
             <div class="text-2xl">400+</div>
             <div class="text-base">Tables</div>
        </div>
        <div class="  w-full md:w-44 lg:w-56 xl:w-72 2xl:w-80 flex flex-
col p-5
                          text-center text-gray-700 dark:text-gray-200
                          border border-rose-500 rounded-md shadow-xl
shadow-rose-400 dark:border-gray-100  dark:shadow-gray-100
dark:hover:border-gray-50 hover:-translate-y-5
duration-150 hover:border-rose-700 hover:shadow-2xl">
              <div class="text-2xl">500+</div>
              <div class="text-base">Dishes</div>
        </div>
        <div class=" w-full md:w-44 lg:w-56 xl:w-72 2xl:w-80 flex flex-
col p-5
                          text-center text-gray-700 dark:text-gray-200
                          border border-rose-500 rounded-md shadow-xl
shadow-rose-400
                             dark:border-gray-100  dark:shadow-gray-100
dark:hover:border-gray-50 hover:-translate-y-5
duration-150 hover:border-rose-700 hover:shadow-2xl">
               <div class="text-2xl">10-15 Mins</div>
               <div class="text-base">Prep. Time</div>
        </div>
        <div class=" w-full md:w-44 lg:w-56 xl:w-72 2xl:w-80 flex flex-
col p-5
                          text-center text-gray-700 dark:text-gray-200
```

```
                              border border-rose-500 rounded-md shadow-xl
shadow-rose-400
                              dark:border-gray-100  dark:shadow-gray-100
   dark:hover:border-gray-50 hover:-translate-y-5 duration-150
   hover:border-rose-700 hover:shadow-2xl">
                    <div class="text-2xl">25</div>
                    <div class="text-base">Total Kitchens</div>
              </div>
    </div>
</div>
```

- Here in this block, we are showing *four-card elements* that are having *border* and *shadows* effects. On hover interaction, they will slightly translate upwards within specific duration.
- We are using a *flexbox* to align these *four items* within its container. On mobile devices, they will be in a *single column* and on bigger devices they will be in a *single row*.
- Each of these items will take a different width on different viewport devices. On smaller or mobile devices, it will be a full width item and for *medium*, *large*, *extra-large*, and *double extra-large* devices it increases gradually.
- Following are the snapshots of these blocks on both mobile and desktop viewports:

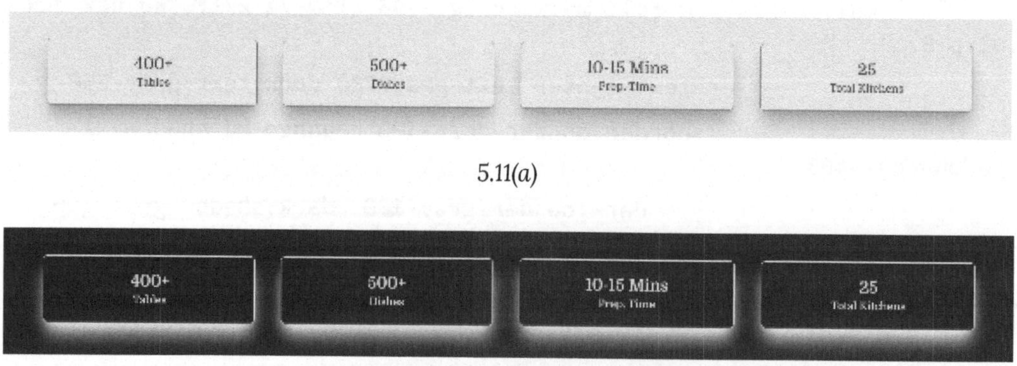

5.11(a)

5.11(b)

Figure 5.11: *Numerical block images in both light (a) and dark (b) themes in desktop devices*

- Following are the images of **numerical-block** in desktop devices:

5.12(*a*)

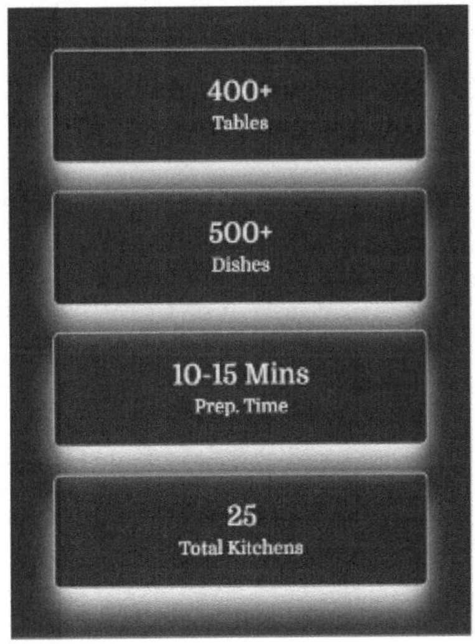

5.12(*b*)

***Figure* 5.12**: *Numerical block images in both light (a) and dark (b) themes in mobile devices*

Including *header*, *footer*, and these *four* blocks within the proper HTML layout completes the homepage. We name it as **`index.html`**, you can try following the HTML document in your browser to look into all the features we discussed earlier. Make sure the **`output.css`** file is added in the header and all images are exist.

JavaScript used for mobile navigation and *light-dark theme* shifting has been added here in the code. Have a look into those simple logic as well.

A complete HTML file can be found at this link:

https://github.com/iamkartikbhat23/tailwindCSSWebsite/blob/main/index.md

Gallery page

Gallery page is one where we are mainly focusing on image representation. There are many ways to represent images on a webpage; here, we follow a simple approach by making *three* sections of images in our gallery page:

- Our ambiance
- Clicks from kitchen
- Our food gallery

Our ambience

This section is to show the ambiance of the restaurant, where we show a set of images around the restaurant logo:

```
<div class=" mx-auto relative
          bg-teal-100 dark:bg-gray-800">
    <div class=" px-4 py-8 w-full dark:text-zinc-300
              text-right text-xl md:text-4xl text-slate-800">
          It's all about our ambiance...
    </div>
    <div class="  grid grid-cols-2 p-4
               md:grid-cols-4
               gap-3 place-content-stretch">
        <img class=" inset-0 h-full w-full object-cover rounded
                  dark:border dark:border-gray-500"
            src=" /src/gallery/image1.jpg"
            alt="image"/>
        <img class=" inset-0 h-full w-full object-cover rounded
                  dark:border dark:border-gray-500"
            src=" /src/gallery/image2.jpg"
            alt="image"/>
        <img class=" inset-0 h-full w-full object-cover rounded
                  dark:border dark:border-gray-500"
            src=" /src/gallery/image3.jpg"
            alt="image"/>
        <img class=" inset-0 h-full w-full object-cover rounded
                  dark:border dark:border-gray-500"
            src=" /src/gallery/image4.jpg"
            alt="image"/>
        <img class=" inset-0 h-full w-full object-cover rounded
                  dark:border dark:border-gray-500"
            src=" /src/gallery/image5.jpg"
            alt="image"/>
        <div class="w-full p-10 order-first col-span-2
                 md:order-none md:row-span-2 ">
           <img class=" p-10 md:m-auto shadow-2xl shadow-emerald-600
```

```
                rounded-full md:rounded"
                src="/src/images/logo.png"
                alt="image"/>
        </div>
        <img class=" inset-0 h-full w-full object-cover rounded
                     dark:border dark:border-gray-500"
             src=" /src/gallery/image6.jpg"
             alt="image"/>
         <img class="inset-0 h-full w-full object-cover rounded
                     dark:border dark:border-gray-500"
              src=" /src/gallery/image7.jpg"
              alt="image"/>
         <img class=" inset-0 h-full w-full object-cover rounded
                      dark:border dark:border-gray-500"
              src=" /src/gallery/image8.jpg"
              alt="image"/>
         <img class=" inset-0 h-full w-full object-cover rounded
                      dark:border dark:border-gray-500"
              src=" /src/gallery/image9.jpg"
              alt="image"/>
         <img class=" inset-0 h-full w-full object-cover rounded
                      dark:border dark:border-gray-500"
              src=" /src/gallery/image10.jpg"
              alt="image"/>
         <img class=" inset-0 h-full w-full object-cover rounded
                      dark:border dark:border-gray-500"
              src=" /src/gallery/image11.jpg"
              alt="image"/>
         <img class=" inset-0 h-full w-full object-cover
                      rounded dark:border dark:border-gray-500"
               src=" /src/gallery/image12.jpg"
               alt="image"/>
      </div>
</div>
```

- Here we are using a *grid layout* with *two columns* in the *mobile viewport* and *four columns* in the *desktop viewport*. In the case of the desktop viewport, the restaurant logo is there in the middle of the layout by spanning *two rows* and *two columns*.

- The same logo block will be moved to the top of the layout by using the order utility class.
- Following are the snaps of the rendered result of this code block:

5.13(*a*) 5.13(*b*)

Figure 5.13: *Ambience block images in both light (a) and dark (b) themes in desktop devices*

- Following are the images of **ambiance-block** in desktop devices:

5.14(*a*) 5.14(*b*)

Figure 5.14: *Ambience block images in both light (a) and dark (b) themes in mobile devices*

Clicks from kitchen

This block showcases images related to the kitchen of the restaurant. Here, we are using a simple *image-moving marquee* for image representation:

```
<div class=" relative py-20 flex flex-col space-y-8
            bg-sky-100 dark:bg-slate-700 overflow-hidden">
    <div class=" px-4 w-full dark:text-zinc-300
                text-left text-slate-800 text-xl md:text-4xl">
        Clicks from our kitchen...
    </div>
    <div class=" md:h-[18rem] grid grid-cols-2 gap-2
    md:flex md:justify-between
    md:items-center space-x-1 md:animate-marquee">
        <img class="inset-0 h-full w-full object-cover "
             src=" /src/kitchen/1.jpg"
             alt="image"/>
        <img class="inset-0 h-full w-full object-cover "
             src=" /src/kitchen/2.jpg"
             alt="image"/>
        <img class="inset-0 h-full w-full object-cover "
             src=" /src/kitchen/3.jpg"
             alt="image"/>
        <img class="inset-0 h-full w-full object-cover "
             src=" /src/kitchen/4.jpg"
             alt="image"/>
        <img class="inset-0 h-full w-full object-cover "
             src=" /src/kitchen/5.jpg"
             alt="image"/>
        <img class="inset-0 h-full w-full object-cover "
             src=" /src/kitchen/6.jpg"
             alt="image"/>
        <img class="inset-0 h-full w-full object-cover "
             src=" /src/kitchen/7.jpg"
             alt="image"/>
        <img class="inset-0 h-full w-full object-cover "
             src=" /src/kitchen/8.jpg"
```

```
            alt="image"/>
        <img class="inset-0 h-full w-full object-cover "
            src=" /src/kitchen/9.jpg"
            alt="image"/>
        <img class="inset-0 h-full w-full object-cover "
            src=" /src/kitchen/10.jpg"
            alt="image"/>
        <img class="inset-0 h-full w-full object-cover "
            src=" /src/kitchen/11.jpg"
            alt="image"/>
        <img class="inset-0 h-full w-full object-cover "
            src=" /src/kitchen/12.jpg"
            alt="image"/>
    </div>
</div>
```

- Here in this block, we are showing images in a *marquee pattern* by adding animation to the layout of the images.
- Each image will occupy the full space of the grid block - using the **`inset`** utility class.
- On mobile devices instead of a marquee it shows a grid of *two columns*.
- Following are the snapshots of rendered results from this code block:

5.15(*a*) 5.15(*b*)

***Figure 5.15**: Kitchen images block in desktop (a) and mobile (b) devices*

Our **food gallery** code-block is given here. This block showcases a set of images in a *masonry tile design:*

```
<div class="p-5 bg-amber-100 dark:bg-gray-700 ">
      <div class=" px-4 py-8 w-full dark:text-zinc-300
                 text-left text-gray-700 text-xl md:text-4xl">
Our food gallery...
 </div>
       <div class="columns-2 md:columns-5 space-y-3">
              <img src="/src/food/1.jpg"
                  class="rounded dark:border dark:border-amber-200">
              <img src="/src/food/2.jpg"
                  class="rounded dark:border dark:border-amber-200">
              <img src="/src/food/3.jpg"
                  class="rounded dark:border dark:border-amber-200">
              <img src="/src/food/4.jpg"
                  class="rounded dark:border dark:border-amber-200">
              <img src="/src/food/5.jpg"
                  class="rounded dark:border dark:border-amber-200">
              <img src="/src/food/6.jpg"
                  class="rounded dark:border dark:border-amber-200">
              <img src="/src/food/7.jpg"
                  class="rounded dark:border dark:border-amber-200">
              <img src="/src/food/8.jpg"
                  class="rounded dark:border dark:border-amber-200">
              <img src="/src/food/9.jpg"
                  class="rounded dark:border dark:border-amber-200">
              <img src="/src/food/10.jpg"
                  class="rounded dark:border dark:border-amber-200">
              <img src="/src/food/11.jpg"
                  class="rounded dark:border dark:border-amber-200">
              <img src="/src/food/12.jpg"
                  class="rounded dark:border dark:border-amber-200">
              <img src="/src/food/13.jpg"
```

```
        class="rounded dark:border dark:border-amber-200">
    <img src="/src/food/14.jpg"
        class="rounded dark:border dark:border-amber-200">
    <img src="/src/food/15.jpg"
        class="rounded dark:border dark:border-amber-200">
    <img src="/src/food/16.jpg"
        class="rounded dark:border dark:border-amber-200">
    <img src="/src/food/17.jpg"
        class="rounded dark:border dark:border-amber-200">
    <img src="/src/food/18.jpg"
        class="rounded dark:border dark:border-amber-200">
    <img src="/src/food/19.jpg"
        class="rounded dark:border dark:border-amber-200">
    <img src="/src/food/20.jpg"
        class="rounded dark:border dark:border-amber-200">
    <img src="/src/food/21.jpg"
        class="rounded dark:border dark:border-amber-200">
    <img src="/src/food/22.jpg"
        class="rounded dark:border dark:border-amber-200">
    <img src="/src/food/23.jpg"
        class="rounded dark:border dark:border-amber-200">
    <img src="/src/food/24.jpg"
        class="rounded dark:border dark:border-amber-200">
    <img src="/src/food/25.jpg"
        class="rounded dark:border dark:border-amber-200">
    <img src="/src/food/26.jpg"
        class="rounded dark:border dark:border-amber-200">
    <img src="/src/food/27.jpg"
        class="rounded dark:border dark:border-amber-200">
    <img src="/src/food/28.jpg"
        class="rounded dark:border dark:border-amber-200">
    <img src="/src/food/29.jpg"
        class="rounded dark:border dark:border-amber-200">
```

```
            <img src="/src/food/30.jpg"
                class="rounded dark:border dark:border-amber-200">
            <img src="/src/food/31.jpg"
                class="rounded dark:border dark:border-amber-200">
            <img src="/src/food/32.jpg"
                class="rounded dark:border dark:border-amber-200">
            <img src="/src/food/33.jpg"
                class="rounded dark:border dark:border-amber-200">
            <img src="/src/food/34.jpg"
                class="rounded dark:border dark:border-amber-200">
            <img src="/src/food/35.jpg"
                class="rounded dark:border dark:border-amber-200">
            <img src="/src/food/36.jpg"
                class="rounded dark:border dark:border-amber-200">
            <img src="/src/food/37.jpg"
                class="rounded dark:border dark:border-amber-200">
            <img src="/src/food/38.jpg"
                class="rounded dark:border dark:border-amber-200">
            <img src="/src/food/39.jpg"
                class="rounded dark:border dark:border-amber-200">
            <img src="/src/food/40.jpg"
                class="rounded dark:border dark:border-amber-200">
    </div>
</div>
```

- This block uses a *column layout* to display all the images in a masonry title pattern. As each image is having different height properties and when multiple such images are arranged under a column layout it will form an arrangement that looks similar to a masonry block arrangement.
- On the *mobile viewport*, all the images are arranged within *two columns*, and in the desktop viewport, it will be *five columns*.
- In *dark mode*, each image gets a border property to make them visible and highlighted with a dark background.

- Following are the snapshots of rendered results from this code block:

5.16(a) 5.16(b)

***Figure 5.16**: Food images block in both light (a) and dark (b) themes in desktop devices*

- Following are the images of food **images-block** in desktop devices:

5.17(a) 5.17(b)

***Figure 5.17**: Food images block in both light (a) and dark (b) themes in mobile devices*

Extended the following configurations Tailwind **config** file for gallery page:

```
animation: {
        'marquee':'marquee 30s linear infinite',
},
keyframes: {
       marquee : {
          '0%': { transform: 'translateX(1%)' },
          '100%': { transform: 'translateX(-100%)' },
        },
}
```

Complete HTML Document of gallery page that you can try in your browser. We saved it as **`gallery.html`**.

Complete HTML file can be found at this link:

https://github.com/iamkartikbhat23/tailwindCSSWebsite/blob/main/gallery.md

Menu page

This is a web page where we show brief information about the restaurant and a simple menu of items available in the restaurant.

For this page, we are using one of the official plugins from Tailwind CSS called **Line-clamp**. This plugin is used to clamp the exceeding line in the block.

Run the following command in the terminal within your **`project`** folder:

```
npm install -D @tailwindcss/line-clamp
```

Then add the following (**`require()`** line) in the **config** file within the plugin block, this enables installed plugins to the project:

```
plugins: [
   require('@tailwindcss/line-clamp')
 ]
```

There are two sections in this page:

- Text block
- Menu block

Text block

This block displays the dummy text along with the logo of the restaurant:

```
<div class="text-gray-900 text-xl md:text-3xl py-10 dark:text-
slate-100">

Foo...'d Eateries

</div>

<div class="w-full bg-slate-100 dark:bg-gray-800 ">

    <img class="float-left w-44 h-44 p-3" src="/src/images/logo.png">

    <p class="text-gray-700 dark:text-white clear-right

            first-letter:text-3xl md:first-letter:text-5xl">

                Contrary to popular belief, Lorem Ipsum is not simply
            random text. It has roots in a piece of classical Latin
            literature from 45 BC, making it over 2000 years old. Richard
            McClintock, a Latin professor at Hampden-Sydney College in
            Virginia, looked up one of the more obscure Latin words,
            consectetur, from a Lorem Ipsum passage, and going through
            the cites of the word in classical literature, discovered the
            undoubtable source. Lorem Ipsum comes from sections 1.10.32
            and 1.10.33 of "de Finibus Bonorum et Malorum" (The Extremes
            of Good and Evil) by Cicero, written in 45 BC. This book
            is a treatise on the theory of ethics, very popular during
            the Renaissance. The first line of Lorem Ipsum, "Lorem ipsum
            dolor sit amet..", comes from a line in section 1.10.32.

                The standard chunk of Lorem Ipsum used since the
            1500s is reproduced below for those interested. Sections
            1.10.32 and 1.10.33 from "de Finibus Bonorum et Malorum"
            by Cicero are also reproduced in their exact original form,
            accompanied by English versions from the 1914 translation by
            H. Rackham.

                Contrary to popular belief, Lorem Ipsum is not simply
            random text. It has roots in a piece of classical Latin
            literature from 45 BC, making it over 2000 years old. Richard
            McClintock, a Latin professor at Hampden-Sydney College in
            Virginia, looked up one of the more obscure Latin words,
            consectetur, from a Lorem Ipsum passage, and going through
            the cites of the word in classical literature, discovered the
            undoubtable source. Lorem Ipsum comes from sections 1.10.32
```

```
            and 1.10.33 of "de Finibus Bonorum et Malorum" (The Extremes
            of Good and Evil) by Cicero, written in 45 BC. This book
            is a treatise on the theory of ethics, very popular during
            the Renaissance. The first line of Lorem Ipsum, "Lorem ipsum
            dolor sit amet..", comes from a line in section 1.10.32.

    </p>
</div>
```

Here, we are showing an image that is immersed in a flow of text. The image is floating to the *left of the text* and the text has clear space for the image:

- The first character can be capitalized using the *first-letter modifier* available in the utility classes.
- On shift to *dark mode* text color and background color got toggled.
- Following are the snapshots of the block:

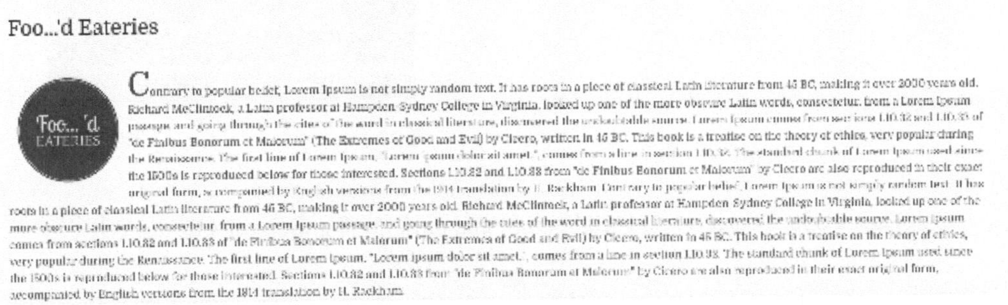

5.18(*a*)

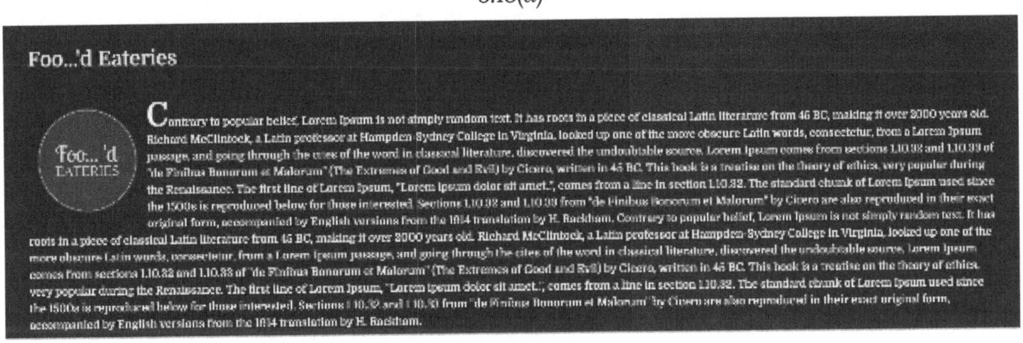

5.18(*b*)

Figure 5.18: *Text block in both light (a) and dark (b) themes in desktop devices*

- Following are the images of **text-block** in desktop devices.

5.19(a)

5.19(b)

***Figure* 5.19**: *Text block in both light (a) and dark (b) themes in mobile devices*

Menu Block

This block gives a list of available items for the restaurant. In a different category, we are showing different food item names:

```
<div class="relative">
     <div class=" z-50 inset-0 h-full w-full flex
                 flex-col md:flex-row font-jost py-5 space-y-4 md:space-y-0
                  md:space-x-5">
        <div class="w-full border border-dashed border-slate-800">
            <div class="relative">
               <div class="absolute -inset-0.5 blur-md opacity-75
                             bg-gradient-to-r from-pink-600 to-purple-600
                           ">
               </div>
               <div class="relative flex flex-col">
```

```
            <div class="border border-slate-900 py-4 px-3 text-center
                  text-2xl dark:bg-slate-200 dark:text-slate-800
                   bg-slate-800 text-slate-300 ">
                  South Indian
            </div>
            <div class="flex flex-col space-y-4 px-5 py-3
                  divide-y-2 divide-slate-200 dark:divide-slate-500
                   text-slate-800 dark:text-slate-200
                    bg-white dark:bg-gray-700 ">
               <div class="line-clamp-1 w-full pt-5">
                  Rava idly..................................
               </div>
               <div class="line-clamp-1 w-full pt-5">
                  Pulao........................
               </div>
               <div class="line-clamp-1 w-full pt-5">
                  Kesaribath............
               </div>
               <div class="line-clamp-1 w-full pt-5">
                  Masala Dosa.....................
               </div>
               <div class="line-clamp-1 w-full pt-5">
                  Set Dosa.........................
               </div>
            </div>
         </div>
      </div>
   </div>
<div class="w-full border border-dashed border-slate-800">
         <div class="relative">
            <div class="absolute -inset-0.5 blur-md opacity-75
                   bg-gradient-to-r from-pink-600 to-purple-600
                  ">
```

```
                    </div>
                    <div class="relative flex flex-col">
                    <div class="border border-slate-900 py-4 px-3 text-center
                             text-2xl dark:bg-slate-200 dark:text-slate-800
                              bg-slate-800 text-slate-300 ">
                             North Indian
                     </div>
                     <div class="flex flex-col space-y-4 px-5 py-3
                          divide-y-2 divide-slate-200 dark:divide-slate-500
                              text-slate-800 dark:text-slate-200
                               bg-white dark:bg-gray-700 ">
                         <div class="line-clamp-1 w-full pt-5">
                             Wheat Roti..................................
                          </div>
                          <div class="line-clamp-1 w-full pt-5">
                             Naan........................
                           </div>
                           <div class="line-clamp-1 w-full pt-5">
                             Veg Biriyani............
                           </div>
                           <div class="line-clamp-1 w-full pt-5">
                             Parota......................
                            </div>
                           <div class="line-clamp-1 w-full pt-5">
                             Samosa..........................
                            </div>
                      </div>
                </div>
            </div>
        </div>
<div class="w-full border border-dashed border-slate-800">
            <div class="relative">
                <div class="absolute -inset-0.5 blur-md opacity-75
```

```
                bg-gradient-to-r from-pink-600 to-purple-600
                ">
            </div>
            <div class="relative flex flex-col">
            <div class="border border-slate-900 py-4 px-3 text-center
                    text-2xl dark:bg-slate-200 dark:text-slate-800
                    bg-slate-800 text-slate-300 ">
                    Vegan
            </div>
            <div class="flex flex-col space-y-4 px-5 py-3
                divide-y-2 divide-slate-200 dark:divide-slate-500
                    text-slate-800 dark:text-slate-200
                    bg-white dark:bg-gray-700 ">
                <div class="line-clamp-1 w-full pt-5">
                    Fruit Mix.................................
                </div>
                <div class="line-clamp-1 w-full pt-5">
                    Coconuty........................
                </div>
                <div class="line-clamp-1 w-full pt-5">
                    Cashew Dosa............
                </div>
                <div class="line-clamp-1 w-full pt-5">
                    Veg Chops.....................
                </div>
                <div class="line-clamp-1 w-full pt-5">
                    Soy Paneer masala.........................
                </div>
            </div>
        </div>
    </div>
</div>
<div class="w-full border border-dashed border-slate-800">
```

```
        <div class="relative">
            <div class="absolute -inset-0.5 blur-md opacity-75
                    bg-gradient-to-r from-pink-600 to-purple-600
                   ">
            </div>
            <div class="relative flex flex-col">
            <div class="border border-slate-900 py-4 px-3 text-center
                    text-2xl dark:bg-slate-200 dark:text-slate-800
                    bg-slate-800 text-slate-300 ">
                    North Indian
            </div>
            <div class="flex flex-col space-y-4 px-5 py-3
                divide-y-2 divide-slate-200 dark:divide-slate-500
                    text-slate-800 dark:text-slate-200
                    bg-white dark:bg-gray-700 ">
                <div class="line-clamp-1 w-full pt-5">
                    Tea..................................
                </div>
                <div class="line-clamp-1 w-full pt-5">
                    Coffee........................
                </div>
                <div class="line-clamp-1 w-full pt-5">
                    Coco cola............
                </div>
                <div class="line-clamp-1 w-full pt-5">
                    Apple Juice.....................
                </div>
                <div class="line-clamp-1 w-full pt-5">
                    Soup........................
                </div>
            </div>
        </div>
    </div>
```

```
  </div>
</div>
```

Observations on the preceding code-block:

- Here, in this block, we are using **flexbox** to align four menu categories one beside another, on the *mobile viewport* they will be one below another.
- There is a **line-clamp-1** utility used from the installed plugin, which can take only one row, further data will be clamped.
- There is a background element for each menu category which has a gradient background and a blur effect added.
- The following shows snapshots of the code block:

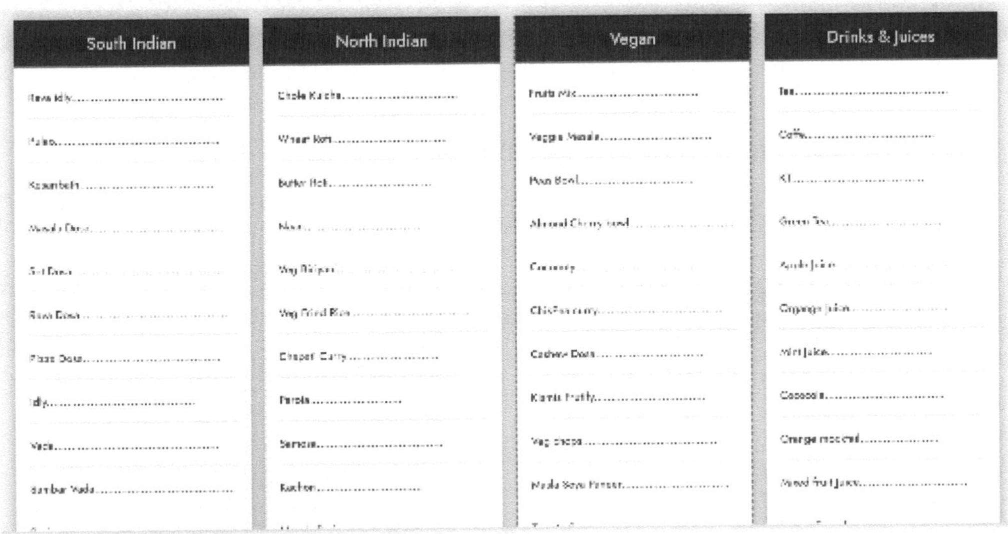

5.20(*a*)

5.20(b)

***Figure 5.20**: Menu block in both light (a) and dark (b) themes in desktop devices*

- Following are the images of **menu-block** in desktop devices:

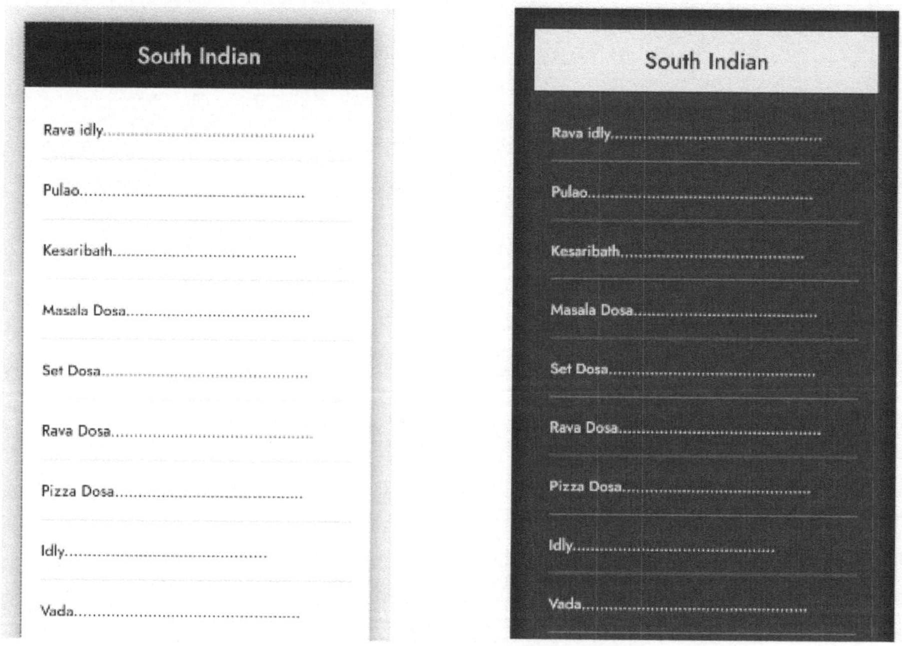

5.21(a) 5.21(b)

***Figure 5.21**: Menu block in both light (a) and dark (b) themes in mobile devices*

Complete HTML file can be found at this link:

https://github.com/iamkartikbhat23/tailwindCSSWebsite/blob/main/menu.md

Conclusion

This chapter provided information on different ways of web pages that can be created using Tailwind CSS utilities. Understanding the way we approached to develop Tailwind CSS can help you to create UI components on your own.

In the next chapter, we will see the development of some more web pages along with deploying this website into the GitHub pages.

CHAPTER 6

Advanced Website Development with Tailwind CSS

Introduction

In the previous chapter, we covered the development of the first three pages of the website we are building using Tailwind CSS. We hope it brought you at least some knowledge on the structure of web pages. This chapter is a continuation of the previous chapter, here presenting the other *three webpages* of the website. At the end, we are giving brief information on **GIT**, a code management platform. We will also explain a way to deploy a website that we are developing.

Structure

In this chapter, the following topics will be discussed:

- Webpage 4 – Blogs page
- Webpage 5 – Contact us page
- Webpage 6 – FAQ page
- GIT: a brief note
- GIT operations
- GitHub
- Deployment

Blogs page

This page is meant for providing information to the users, in real time, these kinds of pages make visitors engage with the website. Here in our development, we are focusing on blog listing pages, where you can see a set of blogs already published by restaurants on various topics that give a set of information to visitors. The same block of HTML that repeats multiple times with different data in it makes a blog page.

Here, our blog items consist of *two* main columns, one has an *image of the blog*, and the other shows the *title*, *brief description*, and *publish date*.

We are using a grid block to render similar HTML blocks systematically. It shows one blog item in a row for mobile devices and *three* items in a row for bigger screen resolutions.

Let's look into this repeating block as an HTML code:

```
<div class=" bg-slate-100 md:flex rounded-xl dark:bg-slate-600 min-h-max
            dark:border-2 dark:border-slate-50/25">
    <img class="h-48 w-full md:w-48 object-cover rounded-t-xl
                md:rounded-l-xl md:min-h-max"
         src="/src/blogs/blog1.jpg" />
    <div class="flex flex-col p-4 justify-between">
        <div class="flex flex-col">
            <div class="font-semibold text-lg dark:text-gray-100 line-
clamp-1">
                5 Best North Indian Recipes
            </div>
           <div class="text-sm text-gray-600 dark:text-gray-100 text-md
                       line-clamp-3 md:line-clamp-4">
                       Lorem Ipsum is simply dummy text of the printing
                       and typesetting industry. Lorem Ipsum has been
                       the industry's standard dummy text ever since
                       the 1500s, when an unknown printer took a galley
                       of type and scrambled it to
            </div>
```

```
            </div>
            <div class="flex flex-col text-sm">
                <div class="text-gray-400">21-08-2022</div>
            </div>
            <div class="flex justify-end text-sm cursor-pointer underline
                        text-blue-500 hover:text-blue-600">
                    Read more
            </div>
    </div>
</div>
```

Key highlights of this block of code:

- Blog items will be displayed vertically on the mobile aspect where blog image and description are displayed vertically . On bigger devices, image and information blocks will be shown one beside another.
- The *Information section* will be aligned using the *flex column*, where the *title*, *description*, and *publish date* will be displayed one below another.
- Multiple such items can be children of the following grid layout:

```
<div class="  grid grid-cols-1 p-4
              md:grid-cols-3
              gap-3 place-content-stretch">
        // blog blocks
</div>
```

- Following are the snaps of the rendered result of this code block in desktop devices:

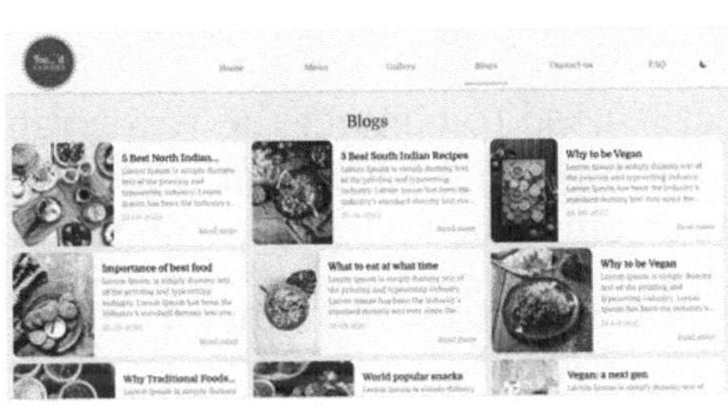

6.1 *(a)*

6.1 *(b)*

Figure 6.1: *Blogs list images in both light (a) and dark (b) themes in desktop devices*

- Blogs page on mobile devices:

6.2 (a)

6.2 (b)

***Figure 6.2**: Blogs list of images in both light (a) and dark (b) themes in mobile devices*

A complete HTML file can be found at this link:

https://github.com/iamkartikbhat23/tailwindCSSWebsite/blob/main/blogs.md

As you learned to create the user interface of web pages using Tailwind CSS utility classes, you can create a blog detail page for the blog list page that we just created. You can give it a try for the development user interface of that page.

Contact us page

This page represents the form structure that is used to contact the restaurant by filling the details in the form. Here, we are using TailwindCSS's official forms plugin. This makes the form's input elements attain basic styles by default.

To install this plugin, run the following command on the Command Prompt within the `project` folder:

```
npm install -D @tailwindcss/forms
```

After installing the plugin, you need to mention this plugin on the **config** file of the Tailwind CSS to enable its effects.

There is a plugin array present within **tailwind.config.js** file under **module.exports** object, add this form plugin as another array item:

```
plugins: [
    require('@tailwindcss/forms'),
    // other plugins if anything added before
]
```

The aim is to create a page with a form where it contains basic input fields that a common contact us form contains, for example, *first name*, *last name*, *email address*, and so on.

Both on Mobile and Desktop viewport devices form looks similar where we will show input fields one below another and a button to submit at the end. Similar to the *Blogs page*, here also we are reusing the design of the input field to all the elements of the form, so that form looks cleaner.

Let's look into the piece of HTML block that creates one form element:

```
<div class="relative">
    <input  type="text" name="fname" id="fname" autocomplete="off"
            class="px-4 py-2 peer w-full border border-purple-400 bg-
gray-50
                shadow-sm placeholder-transparent text-purple-600
                focus:outline-none rounded-md
              focus:border-purple-600 focus:ring focus:ring-purple-300
                  focus:ring-opacity-50 dark:bg-slate-800 dark:text-
        gray-50"
        placeholder="First Name" />
      <label for="fname"
            class=" bg-gray-50 px-2 absolute left-2 -top-3.5 text-
        gray-600
                text-sm transition-all peer-focus:-top-3 peer-
             focus:bg-
               gray-50 peer-focus:text-gray-600 peer-focus:text-
             sm
                peer-placeholder-shown:text-base
```

```
                    peer-placeholder-shown:text-gray-400
                    peer-placeholder-shown:top-2
                    dark:peer-focus:bg-slate-800
                    dark:bg-slate-800  dark:text-gray-50
                    dark:peer-focus:text-gray-100 ">
                First Name
        </label>
    </div>
```

Highlights we can observe from the preceding piece of code:

- Here, we are using the peer concept available in the utility classes that help us to control peer elements from another element.
- Input's placeholder will be transparent.
- Border color changes on focusing the input box and input gets different colors on *dark themes*.
- Input element holds peer class, on interacting with the input element associated label element reacts to it.
- On focusing the input element, the *label* element:
    - o Moves in the top direction for three points (that is, **`-top-3`** utility class).
    - o Changes its text color to **gray-600** (that is, **`text-gray-600`**).
    - o Changes its text size to **sm** (that is, **`text-sm`**).
- On the placeholder shown of the input element, the *label* element:
    - o Changes its text size to **base** (that is, **`text-base`**).
    - o Changes its text color to **gray-400** (that is, **`text-gray-40`**).
    - o Moves two point down from top (that is, **`top-2`**).
    - o On *Dark theme*, background color of the label will be **`slate-800`** that is, **`bg-slate-800`**) and text color will be **`gray-100`** (that is, **`text-gray-100`**)

- Following is the **`div`** block and a form element where all the input fields will be present, inclusive of all these comprise a complete contact us form:

```
<form method="POST" id="contact_us_form" onsubmit="return submitForm();">
    <div class="space-y-5 my-5 px-3 md:px-0">
        /// all input fields
    </div>
</form>
```

- The *Contact us form* contains the following elements:
    - o **First name**: Text input
    - o **Last name**: Text input
    - o **Email address**: Email address input

We have added a validation rule for this and error messages will be displayed using peer-invalid state modifiers.

- o **Mobile number**: Number input
- o **Query**: Textarea input
- o **Submit** button

- The following are the snaps of the rendered result of this code block in desktop devices:

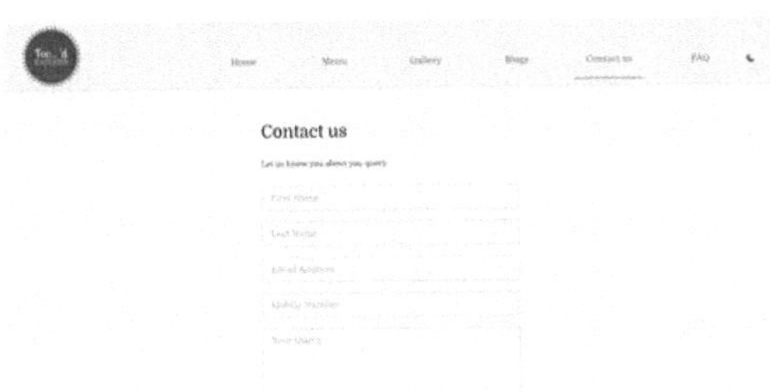

6.3 (a)

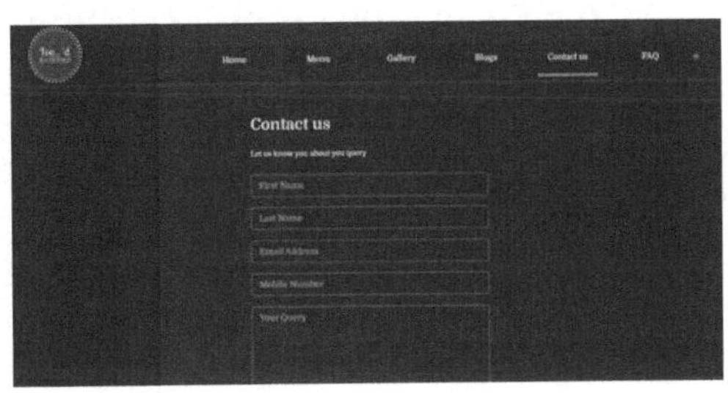

6.3 (b)

Figure 6.3: *Contact us page images in both light (a) and dark (b) themes in desktop devices*

- The following are the snaps of the rendered result of this code block in mobile devices:

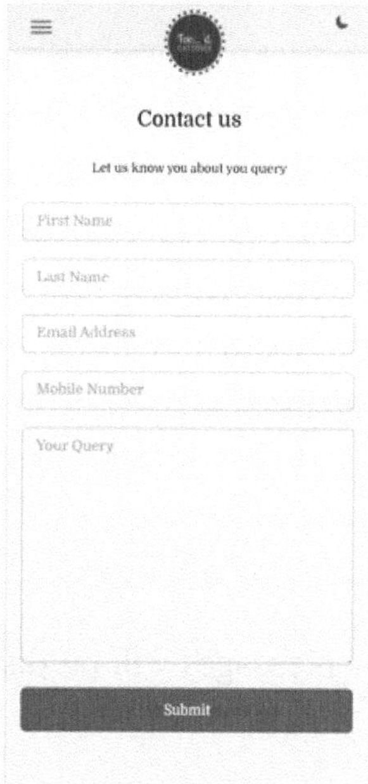

6.4 (a)

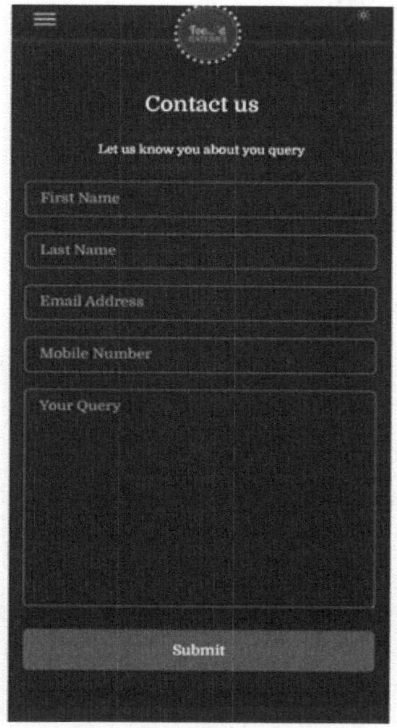

6.4 (b)

***Figure 6.4**: Contact us page images in both light (a) and dark (b) themes in mobile devices*

The complete HTML file can be found at this link:

https://github.com/iamkartikbhat23/tailwindCSSWebsite/blob/main/contact_us.md

FAQ page

This is the page that has a list of questions and answers; these are common aspects that customers ask in general. Instead of querying by filling out the form, customers can clarify doubts or other information by looking into these questions and answers.

Here, we are developing these *Question-and-Answer elements* using **<details>** and **<summary>** tags available in the HTML. By designing these tags using Tailwind CSS utility classes to make them look approaching.

The following piece of HTML shows a single *Question and Answer element* developed using **<details>** and **<summary>** designed using Tailwind CSS:

```
<div class="w-full px-2">
```

```
    <details class=" open:bg-white dark:open:bg-gray-900 ring-1 ring-gray-600
                        dark:ring-gray-100   dark:open:ring-gray-200
            open:shadow-lg
                    p-6 rounded-lg">
        <summary class=" text-sm leading-6 text-slate-900
                        dark:text-white font-semibold select-none">
            Popular recipes of the restaurant?
        </summary>
          <div class="mt-3 text-sm leading-6 text-slate-600 dark:text-slate-400">
            <p>
                   Lorem Ipsum is simply dummy text of the printing
                   and typesetting industry. Lorem Ipsum has been the
                   industry's standard dummy text ever since the 1500s,
            </p>
        </div>
    </details>
</div>
```

Highlights we can observe from the given piece of code:

- We are using a **summary** tag for displaying the question and a **div** tag below it contains an answer for the question, as surrounded by tags with **details** tag. On render, it shows only a **summary** tag and by clicking it, we can observe a **div** tag that contains the answer.
- Added **ring** attribute for the details tag that covers both question and answer in the same block.
- Added **leading-6** class to display the texts of question and answer loosely.
- Added **select-none** class for both question and answer so that user cannot select them using the mouse cursor.
- Repeating the preceding piece of code as many numbers of times as wished with different questions and answers generates a full FAQ page.
- The following figure shows snaps of the FAQ page in the desktop viewport.

- Add **open** attribute to the details tag to keep the open answer on the page load itself (HTML default attribute):

6.5 (a)

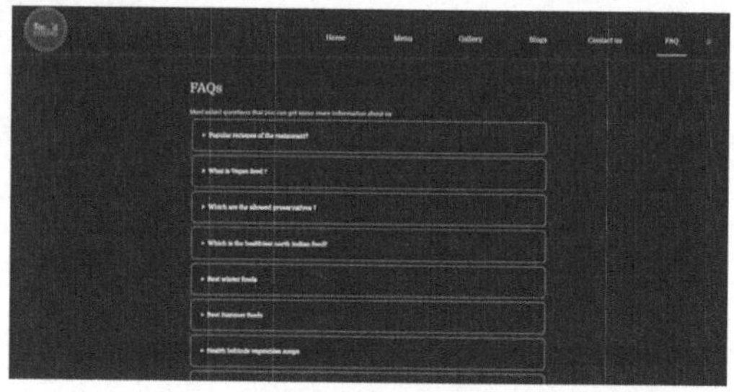

6.5 (b)

***Figure 6.5**: FAQ page images in both light (a) and dark (b) themes in desktop devices*

- *Figure* 6.6 shows snaps of FAQ pages on mobile devices:

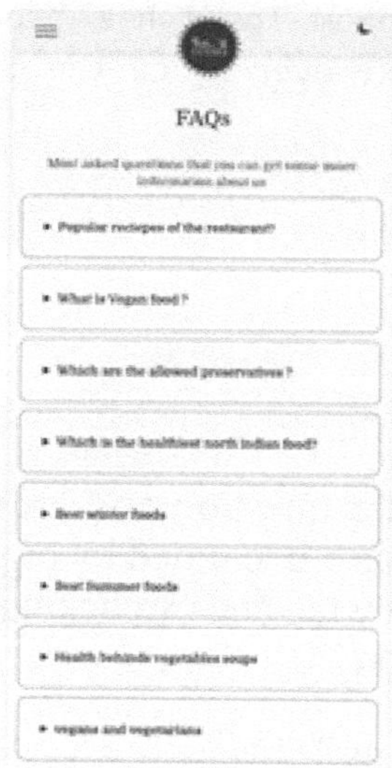

6.6 (a)

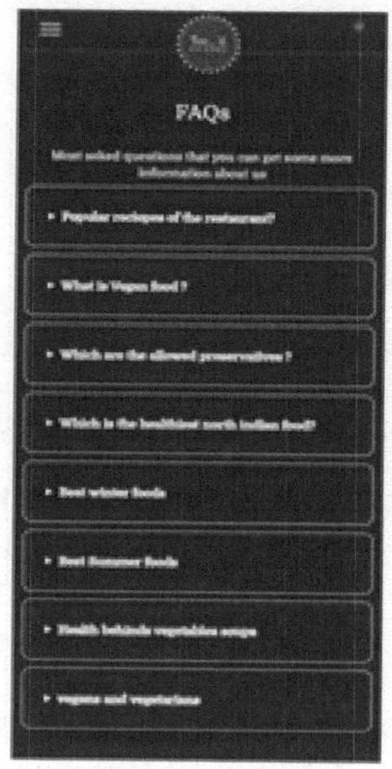

6.6 (b)

***Figure 6.6**: FAQ page images in both light (a) and dark (b) themes in mobile devices*

A complete HTML code can be found at this link:

https://github.com/iamkartikbhat23/tailwindCSSWebsite/blob/main/faq.md

This completes the development of a complete website with six webpages. We tried to cover possibly a good number of utility classes that you learned from the initial chapters. We hope you have gained at least some knowledge of website development. We expect you need to go through carefully on each element of the HTML where we applied various utility classes to achieve the expected user interface. Understand the usage of utility classes, and try it again them your webpage to digest things more deeply. Hope you identified that we haven't used a single line of CSS directly in any of our web pages, Tailwind CSS never made us think about writing our CSS rules. *Isn't it?*

As we completed the development, now it's time to deploy this website on GitHub pages so that anybody can view it on the internet. As a beginning step let's begin with some simple concepts of GIT.

GIT: a brief note

GIT is a popular version control system. In general, it is used to track changes in the set of files. When multiple developers work on the same project or source code, they will use it as a collaboration tool to share the codebase with each other. GIT is a *free* and *open-source tool.*

GIT makes data integrity easy with good speed and a support for distributed systems made it popular among the huge developer community. It was launched in the year 2005 by *Linus Torvalds* (creator of the Linux operating system kernel) and maintained by *Junio Hamano* and others. The currently running version is 2.39 (in *March* 2023).

GIT working flow

The following points explain how GIT works in a local machine:

- Create a repository (`project/folder`) with a GIT hosting tool (for example, GitHub, Bitbucket, and so on):

  By signing in to the GIT hosting tools you can create repositories that hold your source code. These hosting tools store files of your project called as **repository**. You can get various setting-up options while creating the repository from that hosting tool. For example, you can keep your repository as public so that everybody can access the project files or as private so that either only you or a specific set of people/developers mentioned by you can access the files of the repository. This hosting tool may provide its file editor as well to edit files directly online. These hosting tools will communicate with GIT installed in a local machine/ computer.

- Clone or download that repository to the local machine:

  Cloning or downloading the repository in the sense, you are creating an instance to communicate with a GIT hosting tool from your local machine. Changes you made to the code will be integrated with the hosting tool from this instance.

- Add/create files to the repository and commit (save) the changes to the repository:

  After cloning the repository, you can add files to the repository of your wish then you need to *commit* or *save* the changes to the repository so that these changes will be ready for uploading to the hosting tool of the source code. (Assume you have added *two* files – *file* A and *file* B)

- Push the new changes to the hosting tool again:

  After committing or saving you are now ready to upload or to push the change to the hosting tool after this step change you made will be reflected to the hosted repository.

  When you clone or download again the repository at different locations in your local system. It contains all the changes you made/pushed last time to the repository.

This completes a normal flow of source code management. Further, let us see how this GIT works with multiple users/developers on the same project or source code:

- After *Developer* 1 completes the preceding steps, there are two files (*file* A and *file* B) available in the hosted repository.
- *Developer* 2 will clone or download the repository and he will get those *two* files (*file* A and *file* B) added by the developer into his local system then he adds another *one* file (*file* C) to the repository, then commits the changes and push or upload the files to the hosted repository.
- Here as *Developer* 2 hasn't made any changes on those two files (*file* A and *file* B) added by *Developer* 1 and he just added a new file (*file* C) to the repository so GIT will push/upload only the new change he made on the repository instead of uploading other *two* files already present in the repository along with a new one – this makes push communication fast as it only looks for **changes** made on the local machine.
- This completes one cycle of source code management for *Developer* 2, now the local repository of *Developer* 2 is up to date with the hosted repository as he made a push operation on the hosted repository at last.
- Now, *Developer* 1 needs to pull/download the repository to get that new file (*file* C) added by *Developer* 2. Here as well, as the local system of *Developer* 1 already contain those *two* files (*file* A and *file* B) and they are unaltered by *Developer* 2 GIT will not pull them again and it pulls

only a new change (*file* C) to the *Developer* 1's local system- this makes pull communication faster because it only looks for changes made on the repository for pulling instead of pulling complete repository.

- Then, *Developer* 1 can make changes to his wish and repeat the commit and push operation and update the hosted repository. Further *Developer* 2 pulls them to his local system to get those changes and he continues to add his changes to the repository. This process continues as part of source code collaboration.
- GIT makes this process very clear to save time for the developers.

Some of the terms present in GIT

GIT has lots of concepts, which provides lots of flexibility to its user to work with source code management. Explaining all the terms may require deep dive into the GIT concepts that are out of the focus of this book. So, let us look into the basic and majorly used terms of the GIT:

- **Clone**: It is the word used for downloading the repository, as it creates a copy of the hosted repository it is called cloning.
- **Branch**: It is the version of the source code present in the hosted repository or local repository.
- **Remote**: This represents the hosted repository URL; local system repository refers to this URL to push and pull the source code.
- **Add**: This adds/tracks the files added to/edited from/deleted from the repository.
- **Commit**: This term is used to save the changes made on a local repository, further, these files will be pushed to the hosted repository.
- **Push**: This term represents the upload operation of the repository.
- **Pull**: This term represents the download operation of the repository.
- **Master**: This is the default branch of the hosted repository.
- **Origin**: This term represents the hosted instance (URL) of the repository.
- **Status**: This term represents the list of tracked files from the local system repository.

You can download the GIT tool from the following URL, an official download page from GIT:

https://git-scm.com/downloads

GIT operations

GIT supports multiple ways of communicating with a hosted repository; here we can see how the command line approach works.

Following are the commands and their brief explanation of each. **`git`** keyword should be there with all the commands that we want to execute **`git`** operations. These commands should be executed within the **`project`** folder:

- **`git clone <remote-repository-url>`**

  This command is to clone or download the remote repository.

- **`git add -- all`**

  This command tracks all the changes you made on your local repository.

- **`git status`**

  This command is used to list the tracked status of the files in the repository. The *green* list indicates tracked files and the *red* list indicates untracked files in the repository.

- **`git commit -m "<commit_message>"`**

  This command is used to save the changes made on a repository, **`-m`** indicates the next parameter will be a message of the commit, then we need to write a message suitable for a change we made on a repository.

- **`git push origin <branch_name>`**

  This command pushes/uploads all the changes saved by the **`git`** commit to the hosted repository. Origin indicates a remote repository and **`<branch_name>`** indicates a branch of the repository. For example, **`git push origin master`**.

- **`git pull origin <branch_name>`**

  This command pulls all the new changes available on the hosted repository which are not there in the local system. Origin indicates a remote repository and **`<branch_name>`** indicates a branch of the repository. For example, **`git pull origin master`**.

- **`git branch`**

  This command is used to list all the branches available in the local system. Similarly, to get all the branches on a hosted repository we need to pass **`-r`** argument to the command.

That is, **`git branch -r`**.

to list out branches from both local and remote pass **`-a`** argument.

- **`git checkout "<branch_name>"`**

  This command is used to switch between *branches*. Need to provide branch name to be switched from the current branch.

- **`git init`**

  This command initiates a GIT instance on the repository. This creates a **`.git`** folder in the project folder. To perform any GIT operation on a local repository it should contain a **`.git`** folder.

- **`git remote add <repository_name> <hosted_repository_url>`**

  This command is used to link an existing local repository to the existing hosted repository. After this remote repository holds changes made to the source code from the local repository.

  - **`repository_name`**: Indicates local repository name.
  - **`hosted_repository_url`**: Indicates hosted repository URL.

GitHub

Starting from the explanation of the concepts of GIT we are mentioning the word hosted repository. In general, it is a place on the internet where our source code is stored. There are various hosted repository services that exist today to store our source code that communicates with GIT installed on the local system, for example, **GitHub**, **BitBucket**, and so on.

Here we are using GitHub as a platform for our hosted repository. GitHub provides much more features than just *repository hosting*, like *bug tracking*, *feature request*, *task management*, *continuous integration*, and so on.

As we already developed a website or restaurant now we will store it on GitHub using GIT installed in our local system. Then in addition to that, there is a feature called GitHub pages from GitHub that deploys a website as a subdomain. So, that anybody with a URL can access the website on the internet.

GitHub account

You need to create an account in GitHub, to host your source code there. By providing your email address you can create an account with GitHub.

Here we are providing snapshots of the account creation process (as of *March 2023*):

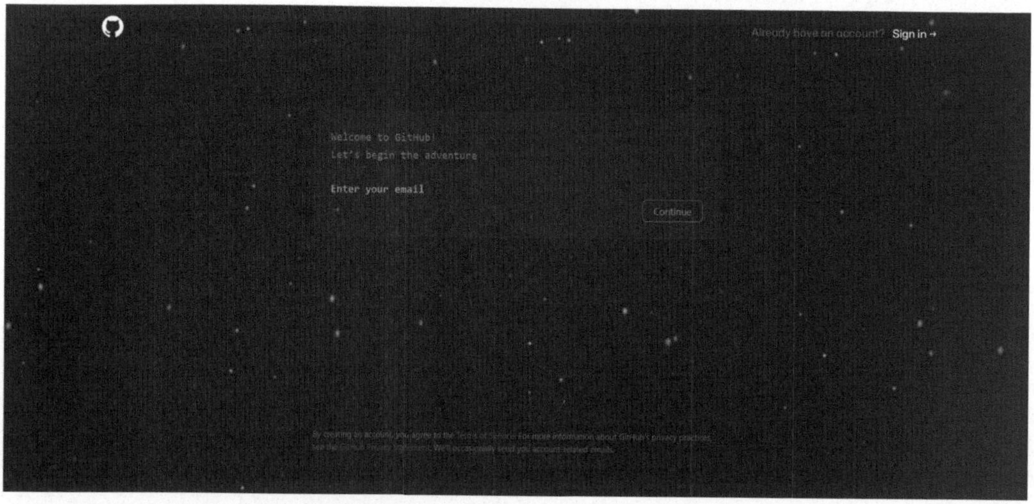

Figure 6.7: *GitHub account creation*

After entering an email, if it is not registered before it will ask for a password for your account and a username of your preference, it validates the availability of the *username* if available it will ask for a **captcha validation**. Then after clicking on the **Create account** button, it will shoot an email to your email address with a CODE to confirm your account.

After verifying the CODE, you can see your profile on your browser. The following image shows the same:

Figure 6.8: *GitHub profile*

Figure 6.9 shows how a new repository can be created here; this is what we call a **hosted repository**.

There is a file called `.gitigore` which comes at the root location of the source code or project. It holds a list of file names with their path within the repository. While doing GIT operations (`commit`, `push`, `pull`, and so on) these files will be ignored from the process.

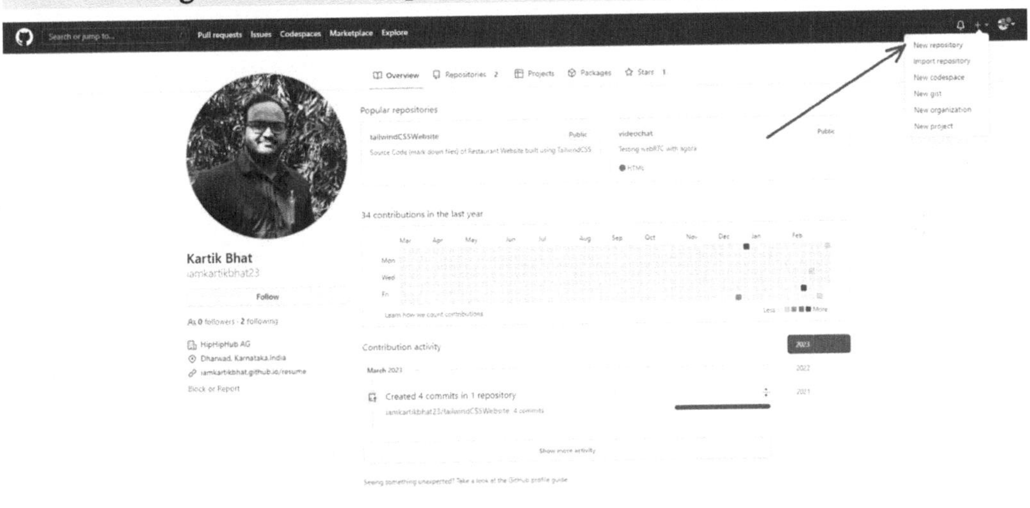

Figure 6.9: *GitHub - way to create a new repository*

After clicking on the new repository, you can see a form where you can enter details of your repository.

Here, we enter the repository name as **`restaurant-website`** and will add a brief *description* for that. Then we choose a repository to be publicly accessible. Then after clicking the **Create repository** button, GitHub creates a repository in your account.

Figure 6.10 shows the create repository form:

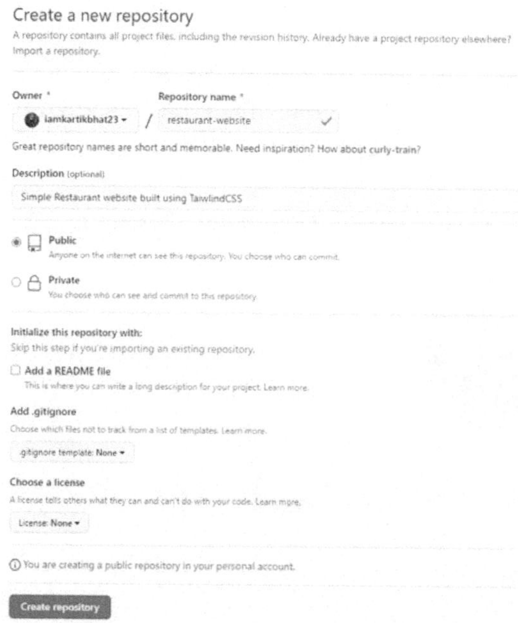

Figure 6.10: *GitHub - create new repository form*

After this step, it creates a repository to host our website; it will be hosted repository for our restaurant website; after the step, GitHub shows a page that contains steps you can follow to push your code to this online repository.

The following image shows the created repository, from the steps mentioned there we need to follow the *second* approach to push our existing project to this created repository (the first step clones created repository as it has no files in it):

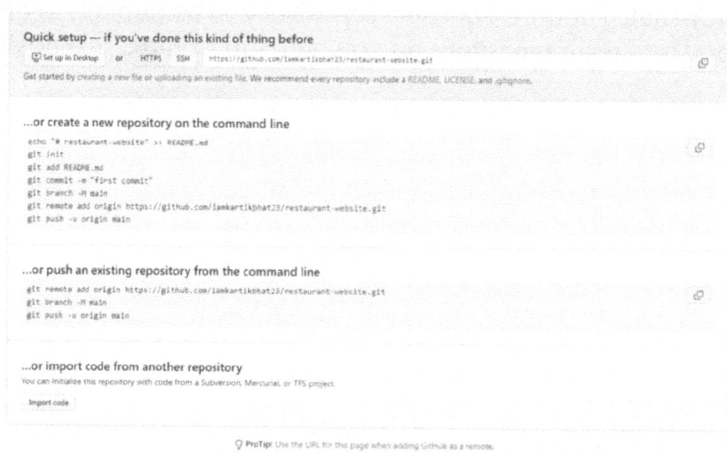

Figure 6.11: *GitHub - created new repository with further steps*

Whenever GitHub repository shows these steps, it indicates that no files are existing within the repository and when it receives files by communicating GIT installed in the local system of the developer it shows all of them along with the date and commit message added to them.

Now we need to execute the following commands to push our restaurant website code to the **`restaurant-website`** GitHub repository.

Before this, make sure you have configured your *email* and *username* in the Command Prompt to get access to your GitHub repository.

Run these commands in the Command Prompt opened in our website source code folder:

```
git init
```

This command initiates a GIT instance in the **`project`** folder by creating a **`.git`** folder making it ready for GIT command executions:

Figure 6.12: *Image of Command Prompt after executing git add command*

Figure 6.13 shows repository items in the local system before and after running the **`git add`** command. Without this folder, the local repository cannot communicate with the GitHub-hosted repository:

Figure 6.13: *Project root folder before and after running git init*

Now you can add remote to this repository:

```
git remote add origin https://github.com/iamkartikbhat23/restaurant-website.git
```

(Do not add the preceding URL itself in your local system for your source code repository, the URL should be grabbed from your GitHub account and a repository created by you).

Let's switch to a branch called **main,** by executing the following command:

```
git branch -M main
```

This command suggests moving to the **main** branch of the repository. (If it does not exist it creates a branch called **main**), then at last there is a **push** command that pushes all the files to the GitHub repository.

Then execute, **git status**.

This command lists all the untracked files of the local repository:

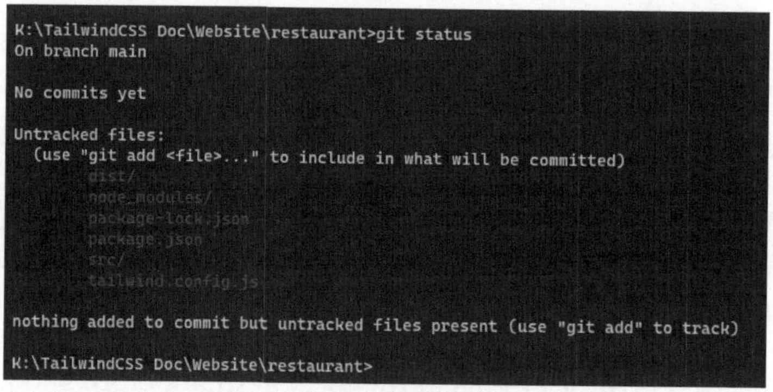

***Figure 6.14**: git status response on the local repository*

Now run, **git add -all**.

This adds/tracks all the files from the local repository; then runs again **git status** to check all tracked files:

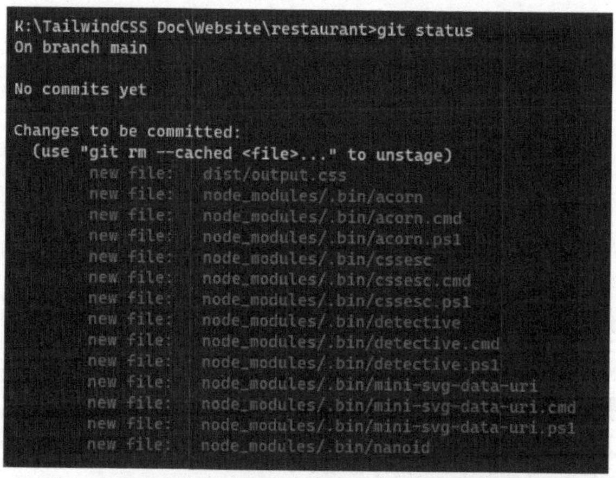

***Figure 6.15**: git status response after git add --all*

Now commit all the tracked files, by executing the following command:

`git commit -m "Source code added"`

This command saves all the tracked files for pushing to the GitHub repository *Source code added* will be a message that we see on the GitHub repository. This responds to files created with the **`chmod`** permission of it:

```
K:\TailwindCSS Doc\Website\restaurant>git commit -m "Source code added"
[main (root-commit) a273c99] Source code added
 1196 files changed, 207924 insertions(+)
 create mode 100644 dist/output.css
 create mode 100644 node_modules/.bin/acorn
 create mode 100644 node_modules/.bin/acorn.cmd
 create mode 100644 node_modules/.bin/acorn.ps1
 create mode 100644 node_modules/.bin/cssesc
 create mode 100644 node_modules/.bin/cssesc.cmd
 create mode 100644 node_modules/.bin/cssesc.ps1
 create mode 100644 node_modules/.bin/detective
 create mode 100644 node_modules/.bin/detective.cmd
 create mode 100644 node_modules/.bin/detective.ps1
 create mode 100644 node_modules/.bin/mini-svg-data-uri
 create mode 100644 node_modules/.bin/mini-svg-data-uri.cmd
 create mode 100644 node_modules/.bin/mini-svg-data-uri.ps1
 create mode 100644 node_modules/.bin/nanoid
 create mode 100644 node_modules/.bin/nanoid.cmd
 create mode 100644 node_modules/.bin/nanoid.ps1
 create mode 100644 node_modules/.bin/resolve
 create mode 100644 node_modules/.bin/resolve.cmd
 create mode 100644 node_modules/.bin/resolve.ps1
```

Figure 6.16: *git commit command with response*

Now, it's time to push the tracked changes of the local repository to the GitHub repository. Run the following command to achieve it:

`git push -u origin main`

Figure 6.17 shows the response to push command execution:

```
K:\TailwindCSS Doc\Website\restaurant>git push -u origin main
Enumerating objects: 1387, done.
Counting objects: 100% (1387/1387), done.
Delta compression using up to 8 threads
Compressing objects: 100% (1284/1284), done.
Writing objects: 100% (1387/1387), 56.76 MiB | 3.89 MiB/s, done.
Total 1387 (delta 177), reused 0 (delta 0), pack-reused 0
remote: Resolving deltas: 100% (177/177), done.
To https://github.com/iamkartikbhat23/restaurant-website.git
 * [new branch]      main -> main
Branch 'main' set up to track remote branch 'main' from 'origin'.
```

Figure 6.17: *git push command response*

After executing this **push** command, you can see all the files of the local repository pushed to the GitHub repository. Open your GitHub repository and check it:

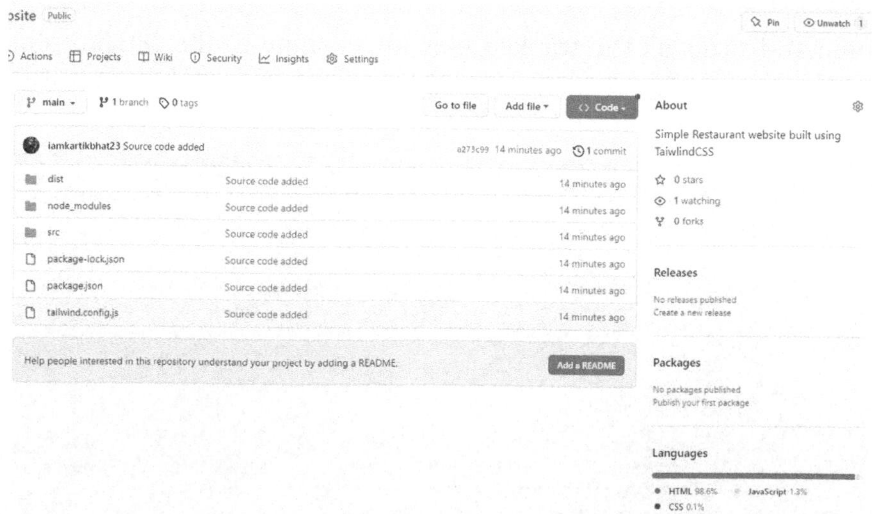

***Figure 6.18**: GitHub repository with all the files pushed*

This completes pushing your local repository to the GitHub repository, if others clone the GitHub repository to their local system they will get all the files available in the repository.

If you made any changes on the local repository, then you need to follow:

- **`git add  --all`**
- **`git commit -m "<suitable_message>"`**
- **`git push origin main`**

To make it available at the GitHub repository so that if another developer pulls the GitHub repository, he will get new changes into his system.

The following image shows a list of commits you made and files you have changed in that commit:

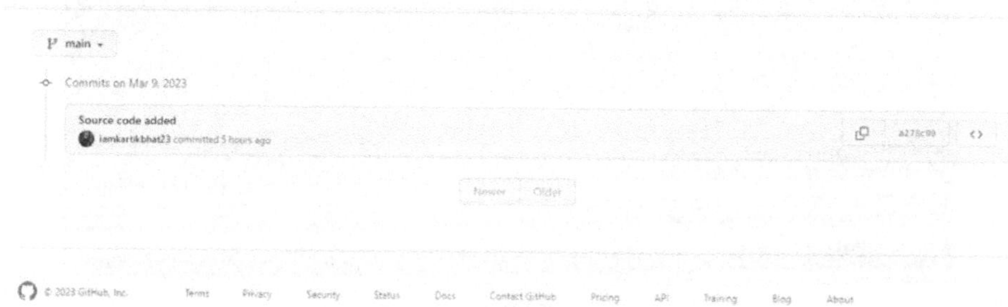

***Figure 6.19**: GitHub commits tree*

As you already read the GIT tool tracks (**add/edit/delete**) changes to make them pushed or pulled instead of pushing and pulling the whole repository each time, that is why GIT saves a lot of time and provides good performance. In a *real-time project*, multiple developers are working on the same GitHub repository by *cloning*, *pushing*, and *pulling* the change multiple times.

git tracks the changes in the sense it captures change from the local repository of multiple developers and merges it with the GitHub repository. Then it will raise a question: *what if two developers made the same change on the same file*? Yes, GitHub still tracks the changes and merges changes with the hosted repository. But, whenever *two developers* made changes on the same file and at the same line, the one who pushes first will not face any problem because GIT never knows the same change may come from other developers as well, it completes the *push operation* successfully and then when other try to push the code, it first asks for *pull*, if there is already new changes available in the GitHub. Then after merging the GitHub repository changes with the local repository, it encounters changes that already exist at the same file and the same line. This is called **merge conflict**.

Conflicts are needed to resolve carefully by rectifying whose source code is correct and needs to be retained. Only after resolving, all the merge conflicts the other developer is eligible for pushing his code. While merging he has *three* options, he can make any of his choices as per code correctness it brings:

- Keep only his changes
- Keep other developer changes
- Keep both the changes

Let's do minor edits to our website source code and will do all required GIT operations again, assuming that the other developer has already pulled your previous changes to his local repository.

Open **`menu.html`** from the local repository and edit the title of the page **`Foo…'d Eateries`** to

`Foo…'d Eateries - for you`

Then, run **`git status`** command on the Command Prompt, you can see **`menu.html`** in **`red`** color. It confirms that you made changes to this file, and it is still untracked.

Now, run **`git add -all`** command to track the changes you made on **`menu.html`**. Then, run again **`git status`** command to check and confirm menu.html is being tracked.

Run **`git commit - m "menu page altered"`** command to save the changes to GIT. Finally, run **`git push origin main`** command to push new changes to the GitHub repository.

You can cross-check the commit from the GitHub commits tree page.

Figure 6.20 shows an updated commit after executing the preceding commands:

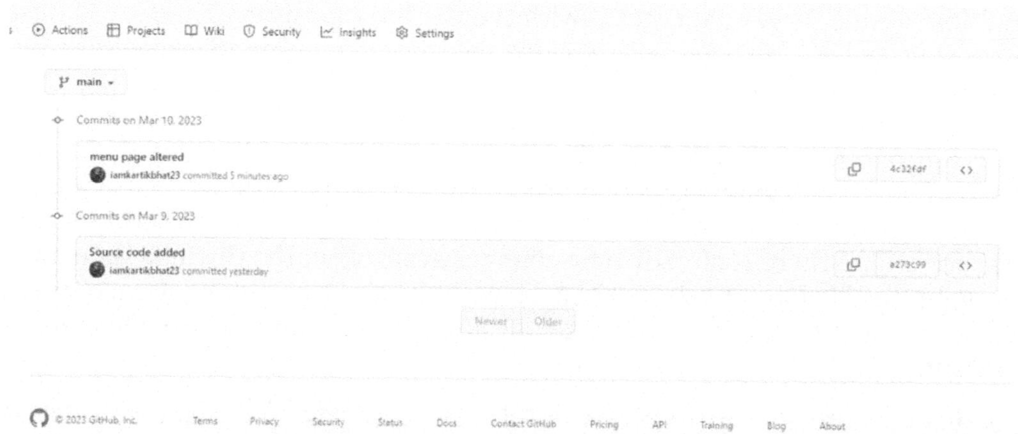

Figure 6.20*: GitHub updated commits*

Deployment

As we mentioned in the beginning of the chapter, we are deploying our restaurant website using the GitHub pages feature provided by GitHub.

It's a free service available in GitHub that publishes a repository for public access by providing a URL for it. URL will be a subdomain of github.io along with the repository name. GitHub creates a subdomain of your username of the GitHub account. Then it points to the repository mentioned for deployment.

Currently, you can host any executable project that has only **HTML**, **CSS**, and **JS** files in it. As we developed our restaurant website within the same context, it is eligible for GitHub page hosting.

Let's deploy the website now (this explanation is as per the GitHub interface in *March* 2023).

After opening the project repository on GitHub on the top navbar, there is a menu called **Settings**, click on it:

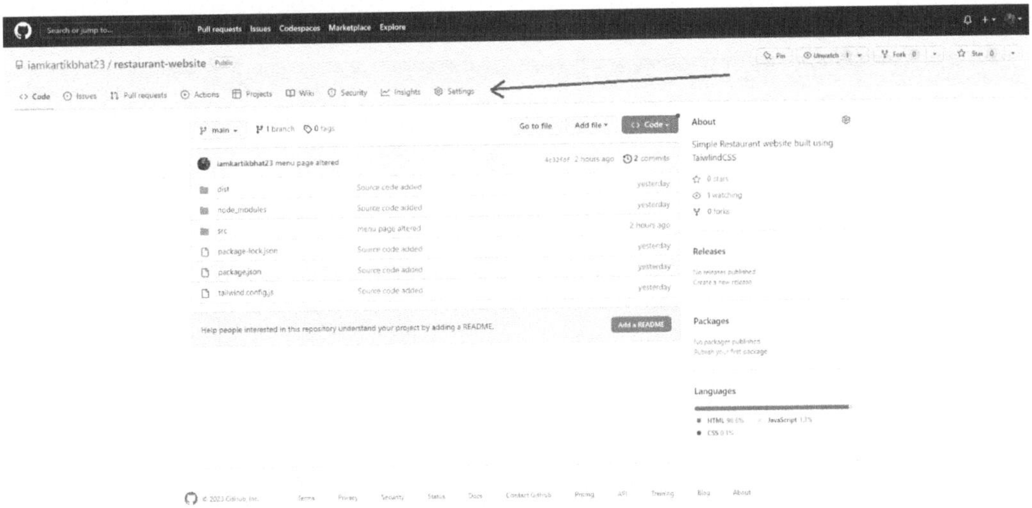

Figure 6.21: GitHub settings tab

When you click on it opens a page, and it shows a sidebar with different options, among those you need to click on **Pages** under **Code and Automation**. It then opens the interface of GitHub pages. There you can see the context of the usage of GitHub pages.

Then there is a section behind it called **Build and deployment**. It is the main section of the deployment process. The first section asks for a source, it is the way GitHub needs to make deployment. By default, it will be **Deploy from a branch**, which means deployment will happen from a branch belonging to the repository. We can keep this as it is. Then in the next step, we need to pick a branch for deployment.

In our GitHub repository, as we have only one branch, we need to pick it.

So, pick the branch **main** from the dropdown. Then you need to pick the **root** folder as deployment source from the dropdown. Then, click on **Save** for deployment setting up.

The following figure shows the interface of the same:

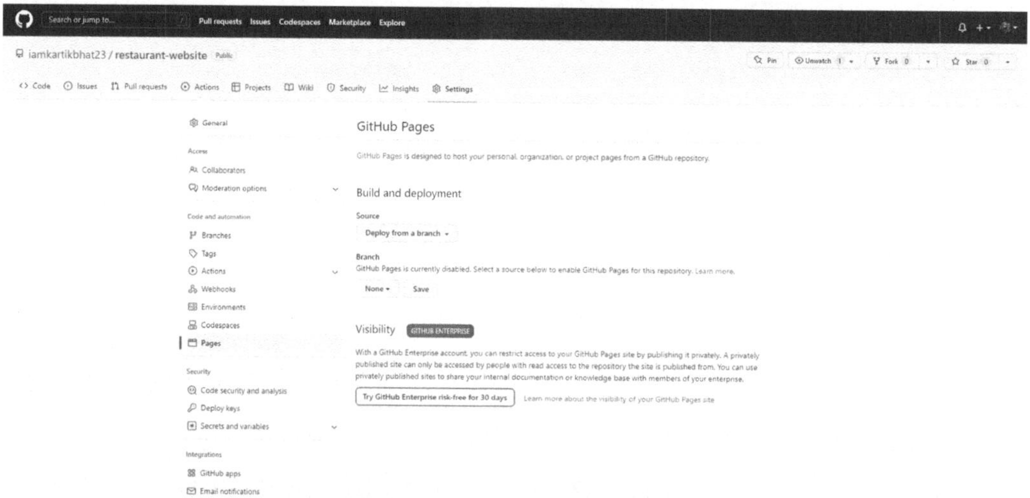

Figure 6.22: *GitHub pages deployment interface*

After a few minutes, if we refresh the page we can see the deployed response of the repository and a URL generated for it:

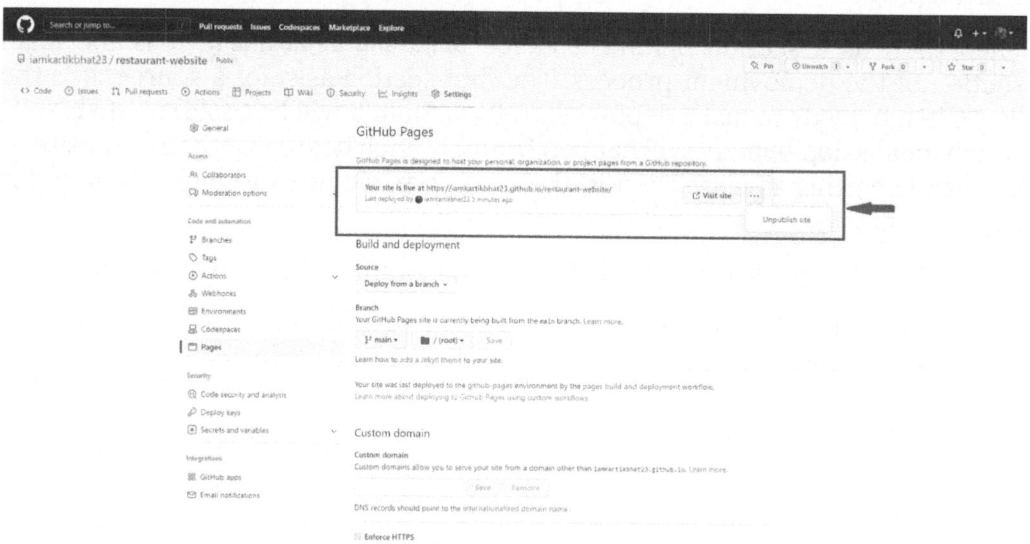

Figure 6.23: *GitHub pages deployment status*

Now, we are ready to visit the following URL in your browser, so that we can see restaurant websites developed by us. It is the deployed URL of the repository.

https://iamkartikbhat23.github.io/restaurant-website/

After visiting this URL on the browser, we are getting the following page:

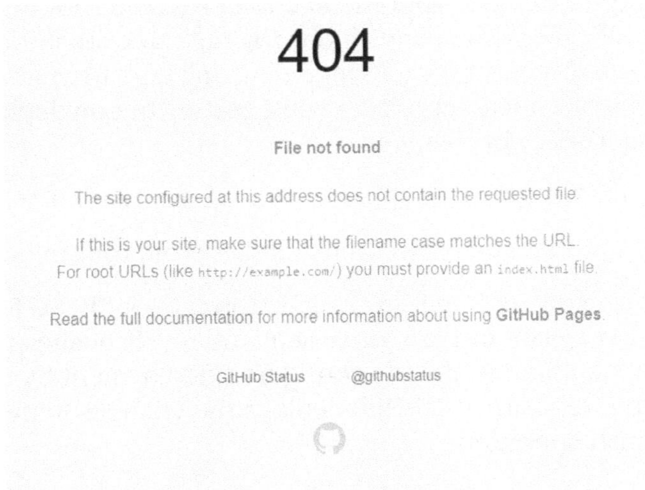

***Figure 6.24**: 404 not found page*

Instead of showing the website why it is showing 404 pages? Do you know why?

While doing a deployment, we specified the **`root`** folder of the repository. Then, GitHub searches for an **`index.html`** file in the **`root`** directory as a beginning page. Now, let's revisit our local repository:

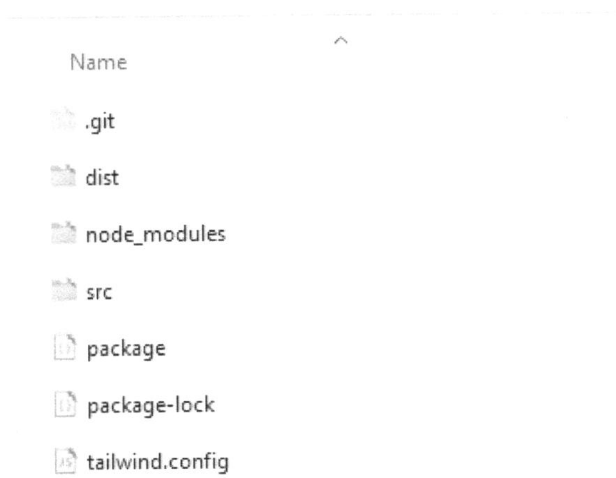

***Figure 6.25**: Root structure of local repository*

It clearly shows that here there is no **`index.html`** file present in the root location, while developing the website we put all our HTML files inside the **`src`** folder.

Now let us modify our local directory structure to keep the files structure clean for proper deployment.

Now move all the HTML files from the **`src`** folder to the root folder, make sure you will replace all **`/src`** with **`src`** in all the **`img`** tag's **`src`** attribute among all the HTML files and **`/dist`** to **`dist`** for CSS including link tag's **`href`** attribute (this will not give any problem in local repository while testing but on deployment it does) and on **`tailwind.config.js`** change:

`content: ["./src/**/*.{html,js}"]` to **`content: ["*.{html,js}"],`**

so that Tailwind CSS class be listed utility classes from root folder files as well.

Now, it's time to execute **`git add -all, git commit -m "HTML files moved out from src"`** and **`git push origin main`** sequentially. It pushes the code to the GitHub repository and as we already configured deployment by referring to the **`main`** branch of the repository, GitHub deploys the changes immediately after it completes the push operation.

GitHub takes some minutes to reflect newly pushed changes into the deployment. The following image shows the deployment status of the repository in a GitHub interface. When that yellow dot turns to a *green check* mark then it confirms deployment is completed:

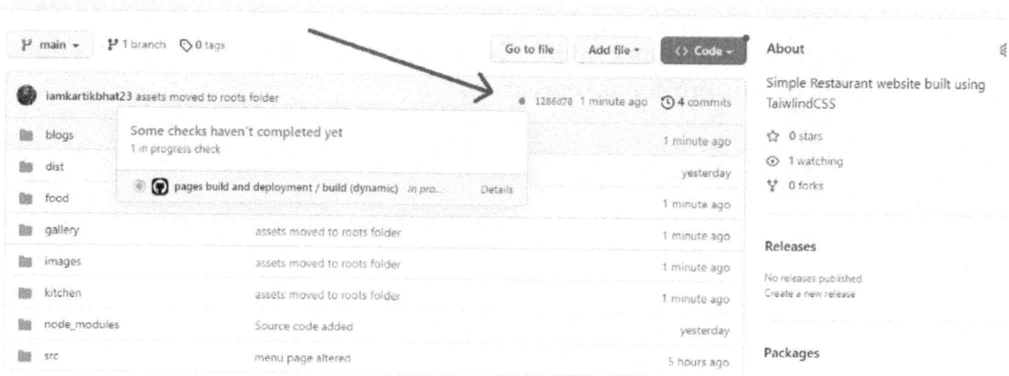

Figure 6.26: *GitHub deployment status*

Remember that whenever you make changes in your local repository and push them to the GitHub repository's main branch it will be deployed automatically, and you can see your changes by visiting the deployed URL of the repository.

Now revisit or refresh the URL **https://iamkartikbhat23.github.io/restaurant-website/**.

To experience the perfect working of the website. This completes the concept of deploying a website on GitHub pages. Feel free to test this website in mobile and desktop devices to confirm its responsiveness and a dark theme toggle as well.

If you observe, none of the HTML pages are having title tag, *which shows on the browser tab as a page name right*? You can make this change and repeat the GIT operation sequentially to deploy a new version of the website.

Conclusion

This chapter provided information on the development of three more web pages as a continuation of the previous chapter with a context of website development. Hope you feel more flexible about the usage of Tailwind CSS at the end of the development of different web pages. Exploring utility classes and source code present in our repository may boost your confidence in the usage of Tailwind CSS for your projects. As we even explained, a free source for deployment (GitHub pages) of your website may be a good choice for showcasing your work online.

Hope we covered enough resources to make you feel fit, to begin with Tailwind CSS or use it in a more intuitive way that makes your user interface development easy. In the next chapter, we are providing finishing concepts to keep in mind for you and some of the Tailwind CSS components designs for you.

Points to remember

- **Website**: Set of webpages.
- **Peer utility classes**: These are used to control other neighbor elements.
- **Git**: A tool used to communicate with hosted repositories from the local system.
- **GitHub**: Repository hosting platform.
- **GitHub Pages**: Repository deployment feature.

Multiple choice questions

1. **On, git commit - <message>, -m indicates**
    a. Commit message comes next
    b. Repository modified.
    c. Repository moved
    d. None of these

2. **GitHub pages deploy source code by referring:**
    a. push
    b. branch
    c. commit
    d. clone
3. Branch is:
    a. Part of the repository that holds the source code.
    b. Part of the local system that holds the folder.
    c. Commits tree of GitHub.
    d. None of these.
4. Domain of GitHub pages hosting:
    a. git.io
    b. github.io
    c. github.com
    d. git.code.io
5. Version of TailwindCSS we used in this book:
    a. 2
    b. 1
    c. 3
    d. 0

Answers

1. **a**
2. **b**
3. **a**
4. **b**
5. **c**

CHAPTER 7

Best Practices for Tailwind CSS

A glance

Throughout the *six* chapters of this book, we hope we have provided enough basic knowledge on Tailwind CSS right from its fundamental concepts to building a simple website by using it. We believe we have ignited a spark about the specialty of using Tailwind CSS to develop user interfaces more systematically and easily.

We expect you need to use Tailwind CSS in your projects to feel more fulfilled about this gem for user interface development. You cannot feed all the utility classes in your head just by reading the documentation, instead, start developing the web application, or a website to gain a clearer idea of when to use which utility class to get the expected output. You will remember utility classes properly when you use them at a proper point of development.

As and how Tailwind CSS frameworks grow in the future some more utility classes may get added and some classes may be removed and some may get renamed. So, understand what you need to do to get an expected user interface design in a theoretical way (deciding on components that require padding or a margin, big font size or more font weight, and so on) then look into the suitable utility class. Doing trial and error with utility class is a good and enjoyable way of learning the framework but once you understand identifying an actual requirement of the user interface component, you should remind the correct/suitable utility class instead of trying with different or nearly matching utility classes for it. Doing this is not a crime but then you need to forget the word rapid development that is linked with Tailwind CSS. *Cool.*

Following is a glance at all the information we provided and their importance.

- Basics of website

  Before learning Tailwind CSS you should know what Tailwind CSS indicates. By looking into the name, we can guess it is something related to CSS if you know what CSS well before. So, to avoid possible loopholes between basic knowledge and the knowledge you will gain, that's why we have covered most of the basics that are required to understand before learning Tailwind CSS.

  This section may act as a foundation for web development for those who are in the initial stage of learning. We tried to elaborate on the point that HTML, CSS, and JavaScript are the pillars of webpage development.

- Fundamentals of Tailwind CSS

  Further, we explained the features available in Tailwind CSS, explained most of the **Utility** classes, and provided pictorial examples wherever possible. This is to let you know about how Tailwind CSS handles everything using classes. If you understand this well then creating user interface components for webpages will be easier.

- Website development

  By digesting the concept of utility classes in Tailwind CSS we have built a simple but fully responsive website that showcases the power of usage of Tailwind CSS for the rapid development process. It's a kind of practical activity covered by the knowledge you gained from previous chapters. As we said in the beginning, *we will develop the website, without writing a single line of direct* CSS *code* we made it possible.

Keep it in mind

The following are some of the things that you need to keep in mind while learning and after learning too:

- Framework changes

  Frameworks are nothing but systematical usage of existing technologies, here for example **Tailwind CSS** is a framework of CSS, **Laravel** is a framework of PHP, **Django** is a framework of Python, and so on. All the fundamentals of the respective programming language remain the same but those will be arranged in such a way that features can be used easily and efficiently.

Frameworks adopt changes as new requirements arise or a new efficient way opens for a particular feature. Whenever a new framework enters the market, in the beginning, they were only ready for providing a feasible solution for a problem, as and when they grow, they will concentrate on improvising the existing logic that improves code efficiency, and they may introduce more approaches that its audience expects, and they may remove redundant features which have no or least usability. In the lifetime of any framework these are the common procedures that usually happen. These are called *minor* or *major versions* of the frameworks.

In our case, as we built a website with *Tailwind* CSS *v*3, here 3 indicates the version of the Tailwind CSS, we are using and the currently active *TailwindCSS is* 3.3.1 (on *April* 2023) it indicates third major version and within that, their minor versions present among those 3, is the first level minor version and 1 is the second level minor version.

As and how versions got released, framework developers do certain changes compared to its previous release that brings efficiency to the user of that framework in various aspects. Previous versions of Tailwind CSS (say *v*1 or *v*2) have a smaller number of utility classes available compared to *v*3 which released a new set of utility classes that its users expected. It continues in future versions as well.

Be always ready for adopting changes that the framework brings on its new versions if you wish to move along with framework updates. Framework becomes stagnant when its developer community dissolves, or it fails to retain its users.

- Framework is not everything

  As we said frameworks are called a systematic way of using a programming language it doesn't mean that it covers all the corners of the programming language. Frameworks always concentrate on providing easy and efficient solutions to common problems that its audience is experiencing. For more common features, the framework has a rich level of solution whereas on the other hand they may not touch those features which are not important in a *real-time* usage of the programming language.

  As the framework becomes popular in the market it keeps on adding new efficient ways that its users request. It is the basic cycle of the framework, until there is a request from its audience framework may not pick up certain features. So, understand that learning framework is nothing, but you are learning a part of programming language/technology, not a complete programming language/technology.

- Do not stop learning CSS

  In this book, we have provided one of the interesting and easier ways to develop a user interface using the framework Tailwind CSS. As you already understood utility classes are the heart of the Tailwind CSS, it provides a class name that can be used to get an appropriate style by adding it as a parameter for the class attribute of the HTML tag. Behind the scene, there are CSS rules provided by Tailwind CSS for those utility classes.

  Even though Tailwind CSS provides a rich set of utility classes to build user interfaces it doesn't cover all the style possibilities that CSS alone can do. As Tailwind CSS grows, CSS grows gradually. The growth of Tailwind CSS is dependent on the growth of CSS itself to some extent. Those new style possibilities will be first introduced in the CSS then based on the need for that style Tailwind CSS brings respective utility classes to the audience.

- Think first always

  As you learned in the development of a user interface using Tailwind CSS in this book, the user interface, more technically a frontend development, is not a few lines of code that decide a logic as we do in backend programming languages (Java, PHP, Python, and so on). As developers need to deal with HTML and style classes, they should think properly about how to arrange and nest the tags to yield an expected user interface design rather than just doing a workaround for everything. The arrangement of HTML tags and styles (utility classes in Tailwind CSS) will impact the efficiency of code readability and page load. Deciding on what to use to get expected solutions rather than just beginning with development, and fixing design issues requires more time and patience for beginners as they need to add/delete utility classes repeatedly until reaching a proper one.

- User interface is not alone

  The user interface is a section where data will be systematically represented to the user on his device (desktop, mobile, and so on). Systematic representation requires the usage of different *colors*, *fonts*, *images*, and so on these will be provided by CSS (utility classes in Tailwind CSS) front-end developer develops or writes code to make it possible by referring to the design provided by the designer. But it is not the ultimate truth that a *front-end developer* just needs to develop the design provided by the designer. He needs to be careful about design logic as well as to decide whether to go in hand with representation of data provided/ fetched from the backend developer. Design just says how data will be displayed that makes a proper impact on users and back-end returns the expected data of the user, but in between these two a frontend developer needs to develop/write the code by keeping proper integrity of the throughout process.

Bonus

Here some of the components are provided which you can use to understand the possibilities of designing better or can use them in your projects.

Component 1

Figure 7.1 shows **Component 1**:

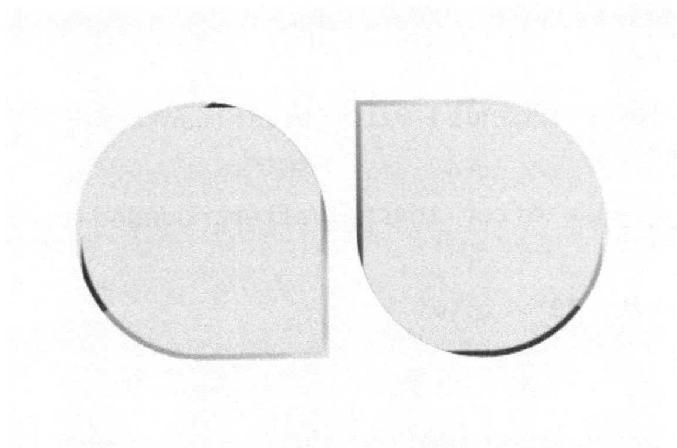

Figure 7.1: *Component 1*

When you execute the preceding component on a browser you can observe an animating border around both the elements of the components. The code is given as follows:

```
<div class=" flex min-w-full min-h-screen items-center justify-center overflow-
            hidden bg-slate-100 gap-5">
  <div class="rounded-t-full rounded-br-full relative h-44 w-44
                overflow-hidden   bg-gray-300   before:content-['']
     before:absolute
           before:w-44 before:bg-[conic-
                gradient(#3A1078_120deg,transparent_240deg,#E96479_
          360deg)]
           before:h-60 before:shadow-lg before:animate-spin-slow
```

```
            before:rounded-full after:content-[''] after:absolute
          after:bg-
            gray-300 after:inset-1 after:rounded-t-full after:shadow-
          lg
            rotate-[270deg]"> div>
   <div class="rounded-t-full rounded-br-full relative h-44 w-44 overflow-
hidden
            bg-gray-300 before:content-[''] before:absolute before:w-44
            before:bg-[conic-
                gradient(#3A1078_120deg,transparent_240deg,#E96479_
          360deg)]
            before:h-60 before:shadow-lg before:animate-spin-slow-
          reverse
            before:rounded-full after:content-[''] after:absolute
          after:bg-
            gray-300 after:inset-1 after:rounded-t-full after:shadow-
          lg
            rotate-90"></div>
    </div>
```

On *config*, we have extended **animation** and its **keyframe** for border animation:

```
animation: {
        'spin-slow': 'slow 4s linear infinite',
        'spin-slow-reverse': 'fast 4s linear infinite',
},
keyframes: {
        slow: {
          '100%': { transform: 'rotate(360deg)' },
        },
        fast: {
          '100%': { transform: 'rotate(-360deg)' },
        }
}
```

From this component, you can understand how before and after states can be achievable with Tailwind CSS.

Component 2

Following is a component that has a vertical flipping effect on hover, it feels like you are flipping a real card.

Figure 7.2 shows **Component 2**:

(a)

(b)

Figure 7.2: *(a and b) component 2*

image source: ***https://media.istockphoto.com/id/696094594/vector/minimal-elephant.jpg?s=2048x2048&w=is&k=20&c=6l_ZQ9WVVCZ7ghirkUzZp5lHRhkHqbEvK3Lp-_0NmyY=)***

You can observe the usage of group utilities with HTML elements, also you can understand how arbitrary values can be passed as utility classes, code is given here:

```
<div class="flex min-h-screen items-center justify-center bg-slate-100">
  <div class="group h-80 w-80 [perspective:500px]">
    <div class="relative h-full w-full rounded-xl shadow-2xl transition-
all
                duration-500 [transform-style:preserve-3d]
                group-hover:[transform:rotateX(540deg)]">
      <div class="absolute inset-1">
        <img class="rounded-xl shadow-xl shadow-blue-600/60
                    group-hover:shadow-none"
          src="https://media.istockphoto.com/id/696094594/vector/
```

```
            minimal-elephant.jpg?s=2048x2048&w=is&k=20&c=6l_ZQ9WVVCZ7gh
            irkUzZp5lHRhkHqbEvK3Lp-_0NmyY=" alt="" />
        </div>
        <div class=" absolute inset-1 rounded-xl bg-blue-300 px-12 text-
center
                 [transform:rotateX(540deg)]                  [backface-
            visibility:hidden]">
          <div class="flex w-full min-h-full flex-col items-center justify-
center
                 text-2xl bg-blue-300 font-semibold text-blue-800 ">
            I'm an Elephant
          </div>
        </div>
      </div>
    </div>
</div>
```

Component 3

The following is the button component that opens other text on hover and closes on moving away from it.

Figure 7.3 shows **Component 3**:

***Figure 7.3**: (a and b) Component 3*

This component provides a hint on the usage of positioning and translating using utilities, code is given as follows:

```
<div class=' min-h-screen flex items-center justify-center max-w-md
           mx-auto space-y-6'>
    <div class='group relative inline-flex items-center justify-center
                 cursor-pointer  h-12  border-2  border-solid  py-0  px-6
```

```
          rounded-md
            overflow-hidden z-10 transition-all duration-300 ease-in-
          out
            outline-0 bg-gradient-to-r from-purple-500 to-pink-500
            text-white border-purple-500 hover:text-purple-500 font-
          medium'>
    <div class='group-hover:hidden'>Hover to uncover</div>
    <div class='hidden group-hover:block'>Opened Text Info</div>
    <span class='absolute bg-white right-0 w-0 left-1/2 h-full
                -translate-x-1/2 transition-all ease-in-out
                 duration-500 group-hover:w-[105%] -z-[1]'>
    </span>
  </div>
</div>
```

Component 4

Following is the *pendulum clock element*, the *pendulum*, and *seconds hand* move simultaneously.

Figure 7.4 shows **Component 4**:

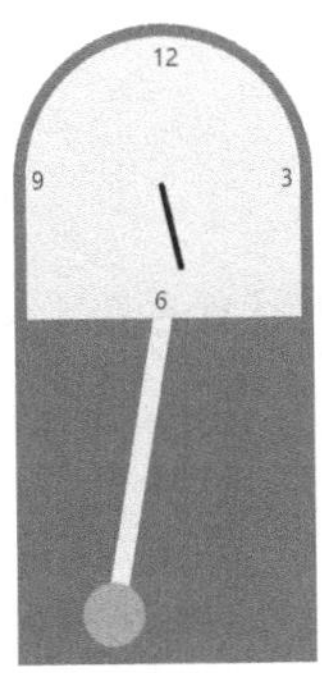

***Figure 7.4**: Component 4*

From this component, you can observe how border radius can be used to design expected corner shapes. The code is given as follows:

```
<div class='min-h-screen flex flex-col items-center justify-center
           max-w-md mx-auto '>
  <div class="p-2 w-fit bg-gray-500 rounded-t-full relative">
```

```
      <div class="w-44 h-44 bg-gray-200 z-20 rounded-t-full relative">
        <div class="absolute top-[20%] left-[49%] origin-bottom w-1 h-14
                    bg-black animate-seconds rounded-md">
        </div>
           <div class="absolute left-[47%] flex flex-col justify-between
h-full">
          <div>12</div>
          <div>6</div>
        </div>
        <div class="absolute top-[43%] flex justify-between w-full px-1">
          <div>9</div>
          <div>3</div>
        </div>
      </div>
      <div class="flex flex-col items-center justify-center origin-top
                 animate-pendulam -mt-1 z-10 rounded-full">
        <div class="w-3 h-44 bg-slate-200 "></div>
        <div class="w-10 h-10 bg-slate-400 rounded-full -mt-1"></div>
      </div>
    </div>
</div>
```

On configuration, we have extended the following utilities:

```
animation : {
     pendulam:'revolve 2s linear infinite',
     seconds:'slowspin 60s linear infinite',
     minutes:'slowspin 3600s linear infinite',
},
keyframes : {
     revolve : {
       '0%, 100%' :  {
          transform: 'rotate(14deg)'
```

```
        },
        '50%': {
           transform: 'rotate(-14deg)'
           },
         },
      slowspin: {
         '100%' :  {
            transform: 'rotate(360deg)'
      },
   }
}
```

Component 5

This component shows the arrangement of similar **div** elements in a systematic way as if they look like arranged cards.

Figure 7.5 shows **Component 5**:

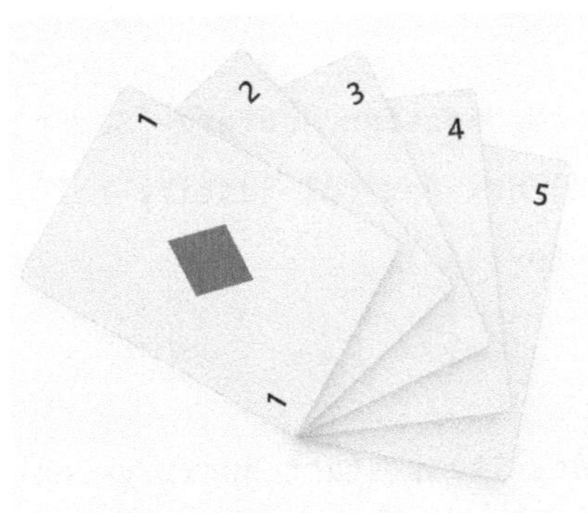

Figure 7.5: *Component 5*

Following is the code for this component:

```
<div class="  flex min-h-screen items-center
            justify-center bg-slate-800 px-5 relative shadow-lg">
  <div class="card-design hover:shadow-gray-300  rotate-[12deg]">
    <div class="card-text">
       5
```

```
      </div>
    </div>
    <div class="absolute card-design -rotate-6">
      <div class="card-text">
          4
      </div>
    </div>
    <div class="absolute card-design -rotate-[24deg]">
      <div class="card-text">
          3
      </div>
    </div>
    <div class="absolute card-design -rotate-[42deg]">
      <div class="card-text">
        2
      </div>
    </div>
    <div class="absolute card-design -rotate-[60deg]">
      <div class="h-[100%] flex flex-col justify-between">
        <div class="card-text">
          1
        </div>
        <div class="p-3 flex items-start justify-center w-full">
          <div class="h-12 w-12 rotate-45 bg-red-500 skew-x-12"></div>
        </div>
        <div class="card-text justify-start">
          1
        </div>
      </div>
    </div>
</div>
```

From this code, you can observe that there is a class called **card-design** and **card-text**, these are not default utility classes of Tailwind CSS, we have created these classes in our input CSS file where we extended base, components, and utilities of Tailwind CSS. We are adding a layer on components where we define utility classes required to form **card-design** and **card-text** components:

```
@layer components {
  .card-design {
   @apply  w-44 h-64 bg-gray-200 rounded-md z-40 shadow-lg hover:shadow-
2xl
origin-bottom-left hover:shadow-gray-500 border border-gray-400/30;
  }
  .card-text {
    @apply p-3 flex items-start justify-end text-2xl font-semibold;
  }
}
```

Component 6

The following component also refers to the above created/extended components, here cards are arranged horizontally:

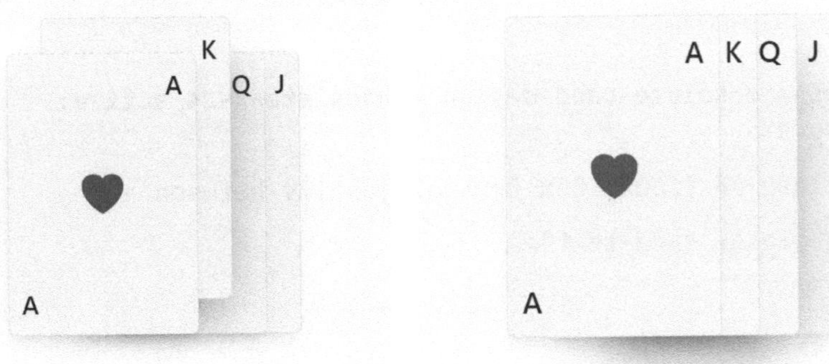

(a) (b)

Figure 7.6 (a & b): *Component 6*

From this component, you can observe how the active state of the HTML element can be handled from utility classes. Here, when you click on any card it moves up and when you release the click it moves down again; see the following code:

```
<div class=" flex min-h-screen items-center justify-center bg-slate-100
px-5
             relative shadow-lg">
  <div class="card-design hover:shadow-gray-300 active:-translate-y-8">
    <div class="card-text">
        J
    </div>
  </div>
  <div class="absolute card-design -translate-x-8 active:-
translate-y-8">
    <div class="card-text">
        Q
    </div>
  </div>
  <div class="absolute card-design -translate-x-16 active:-
translate-y-8">
    <div class="card-text">
        K
    </div>
  </div>
  <div class="absolute card-design -translate-x-24 active:-
translate-y-8">
    <div class="h-[100%] flex flex-col justify-between">
      <div class="card-text">
        A
      </div>
      <div class="p-3 flex items-start justify-center w-full">
        <svg xmlns="http://www.w3.org/2000/svg" fill="red" viewBox="0 0
24 24"
            stroke-width="1.5" stroke="red" class="w-12 h-12">
          <path stroke-linecap="round" stroke-linejoin="round"
                d="M21 8.25c0-2.485-2.099-4.5-4.688-4.5-1.935 0-3.597
            1.126-
```

```
                4.312 2.733-.715-1.607-2.377-2.733-4.313-2.733C5.1
                3.75 3 5.765 3 8.25c0 7.22 9 12 9 12s9-4.78 9-12z"
                />
      </svg>
    </div>
    <div class="card-text justify-start">
      A
    </div>
  </div>
 </div>
</div>
```

In the preceding code, you can observe we have used SVG element for a heart icon. These icons can be found at **heroicons.com** which was developed by Tailwind CSS's creators itself.

Component 7

This element shows how polygons can be drawn using utility classes:

Figure 7.7: Component 7

Image resource: (iStock Images) **https://media.istockphoto.com/id/965307792/photo/chimpanzee-face.jpg?s=2048x2048&w=is&k=20&c=foruAGheQRRfncHPcqavbyebYUnSdf5V2Hg3T0V0Hkw=**

Following is the code for the drawing the polygon:

```
<div class="min-h-screen flex items-center justify-center">
  <img class="w-80 rounded-lg shadow-lg object-cover object-center mb-0
mr-6
            [clip-path:polygon(20%_0%,80%_0%,100%_50%,70%_80%,0%_80%)]"
```

```
src="https://media.istockphoto.com/id/965307792/photo/chimpanzee-
face.jpg?s=2048x2048&w=is&k=20&c=foruAGheQRRfncHPcqavbyebYUnSdf5V2Hg3T-
0V0Hkw="
  />
</div>
```

Component 8

The following element shows the arrangement of elements based on *z-index*, hovering on each element they will get a higher z-index:

Figure 7.8: *Component 8*

```
<div class="flex min-h-screen items-center justify-center bg-slate-300 px-5
            relative shadow-lg">
  <div class="flex -space-x-10 border-2 border-gray-400 p-10">
    <img
            src= https://images.unsplash.com/pho-
            to-1533725920959-5cd2c514d898?ixlib=rb-4.0.3&ixid=M3wxM-
            jA3fDB8MHxwaG90by1wYWdlfHx8fGVufDB8fHx8fA%3D%3D&auto=for-
            mat&fit=crop&w=870&q=80 class="z-50 img-design"/>

    <img
            src= https://images.unsplash.com/photo-1517849845537-
            4d257902454a?ixlib=rb-4.0.3&ixid=M3wxMjA3fDB8MHxwaG90by1wY
            WdlfHx8fGVufDB8fHx8fA%3D%3D&auto=format&fit=crop&w=735&q=80
            class="z-40 img-design"/>
    <img
            src= https://images.unsplash.com/photo-1615807713086-
            bfc4975801d0?ixlib=rb-4.0.3&ixid=M3wxMjA3fDB8MHxwaG90by1wY
            WdlfHx8fGVufDB8fHx8fA%3D%3D&auto=format&fit=crop&w=654&q=80
            class="z-30 img-design"/>
```

```
    <img
            src= https://images.unsplash.com/photo-1527153857715-
            3908f2bae5e8?ixlib=rb-4.0.3&ixid=M3wxMjA3fDB8MHxwaG90by1wY
            WdlfHx8fGVufDB8fHx8fA%3D%3D&auto=format&fit=crop&w=788&q=80
            class="z-20 img-design"/>
    <img
            src= https://images.unsplash.com/pho-
            to-1509987300714-11c90a6d40e7?ixlib=rb-4.0.3&ixid=M3wxM-
            jA3fDB8MHxwaG90by1wYWdlfHx8fGVufDB8fHx8fA%3D%3D&auto=for-
            mat&fit=crop&w=687&q=80 class="z-10 img-design"/>
    <img
            src= https://images.unsplash.com/photo-1614027164847-
            1b28cfe1df60?ixlib=rb-4.0.3&ixid=M3wxMjA3fDB8MHxwaG90by1wY
            WdlfHx8fGVufDB8fHx8fA%3D%3D&auto=format&fit=crop&w=786&q=80
            class="z-0 img-design" />
  </div>
</div>
```

You can observe a utility class called **img-design**, we have defined it as a component under the **input.css** file:

```
@layer components {
  .img-design {
      @apply w-32 h-32 rounded-full object-cover border border-white
      hover:z-[60]
              hover:shadow-xl hover:shadow-gray-700 hover:scale-125;
  }
}
```

Component 9

The following component is color-changing animation on hovering an element:

***Figure 7.9**: Component_9*

On hovering an element each **div** changes its color after a specific delay, then on hover out changes its color back to the original. Following is the code for it:

```
<div class=" flex min-h-screen items-center justify-center bg-slate-300 px-5
            relative shadow-lg">
  <div class="grid grid-cols-5 grid-rows-5 gap-2 group">
      <div class="box2 delay-0"></div>
      <div class="box2 delay-[50ms]"></div>
      <div class="box2 delay-100"></div>
      <div class="box2 delay-[150ms]"></div>
      <div class="box2 delay-200"></div>
      <div class="box1 delay-[425ms]"></div>
      <div class="box2 delay-[375ms]"></div>
      <div class="box2 delay-[325ms]"></div>
      <div class="box2 delay-[275ms]"></div>
      <div class="box2 delay-[225ms]"></div>
      <div class="box1 delay-[450ms]"></div>
      <div class="box1 delay-[475ms]"></div>
      <div class="box2 delay-[500ms]"></div>
      <div class="box2 delay-[525ms]"></div>
      <div class="box2 delay-[550ms]"></div>
```

```
      <div class="box1 delay-[550ms]"></div>
      <div class="box1 delay-[525ms]"></div>
      <div class="box1 delay-[500ms]"></div>
      <div class="box2 delay-[475ms]"></div>
      <div class="box2 delay-[450ms]"></div>
      <div class="box1 delay-[225ms]"></div>
      <div class="box1 delay-[275ms]"></div>
      <div class="box1 delay-[325ms]"></div>
      <div class="box1 delay-[375ms]"></div>
      <div class="box2 delay-[425ms]"></div>
      <div class="box1 delay-200"></div>
      <div class="box1 delay-[150ms]"></div>
      <div class="box1 delay-100"></div>
      <div class="box1 delay-[50ms]"></div>
      <div class="box1 delay-0"></div>
  </div>
</div>
```

box1 and **box2** are the components that we defined under **input.css**:

```
@layer components {
  .box1 {
    @apply w-20 h-20 bg-pink-500 group-hover:bg-green-400 transition-all;
  }
  .box2 {
    @apply w-20 h-20 bg-green-400 group-hover:bg-pink-500 transition-all;
  }
}
```

Component 10

This component is an example of multiple animations in action. You can observe *rotating squares* in opposite directions along with that there is a *red circle* that translates in various directions:

***Figure 7.10**: Component 10*

Its code is given here:

```
<div class="flex min-h-screen items-center justify-center bg-white px-5
            relative shadow-lg">
  <div class=" w-96 h-96 relative z-0">
    <div class="h-full w-full bg-gray-300 rounded-md shadow-2xl
              animate-slowspinreverse duration-1000"></div>
   <div class="absolute inset-0 h-full w-full rounded-md bg-slate-300
             rotate-45 shadow-2xl shadow-slate-500 animate-slowspin
              duration-1000 p-3 border-2 border-dotted border-green-500">
      <div class="w-16 h-16 bg-red-500 rounded-full animate-move">
      </div>
    </div>
  </div>
</div>
```

Its animating **keyframes** for utilities **slowspin**, **slowspinreverse** and **move** are as follows:

```
animation : {
        slowspin : 'slowspin 10s linear infinite',
        slowspinreverse : 'slowspinreverse 10s linear infinite',
        move: 'move 8s ease-in-out infinite'
},
keyframes : {
        slowspin : {
          '0%': {
            transform: 'rotate(0deg)',
            background: '#99f6e4'
          },
          '50%': {
            transform: 'rotate(180deg)',
            background: '#d4d4d4'
          },
          '100%': {
            transform: 'rotate(360deg)',
            background: '#99f6e4'
          },
        },
        slowspinreverse : {
          '0%': {
            transform: 'rotate(360deg)',
            background: '#d4d4d4'
          },
          '50%': {
            transform: 'rotate(180deg)',
            background: '#99f6e4'
          },
```

```
      '100%': {
        transform: 'rotate(0deg)',
        background: '#d4d4d4'
      },
    },
    move : {
      '0%,100%': {
        transform: 'translate(0%,0%)'
      },
      '20%': {
        transform: 'translate(450%,200%)'
      },
      '40%': {
       transform: 'translate(10%,250%)'
      },
      '60%': {
       transform: 'translate(190%,20%)'
      },
      '80%': {
       transform: 'translate(450%,450%)'
      },
    }
}
```

Component 11

This component is an example of how the utilities can be applied to a peer element from an element:

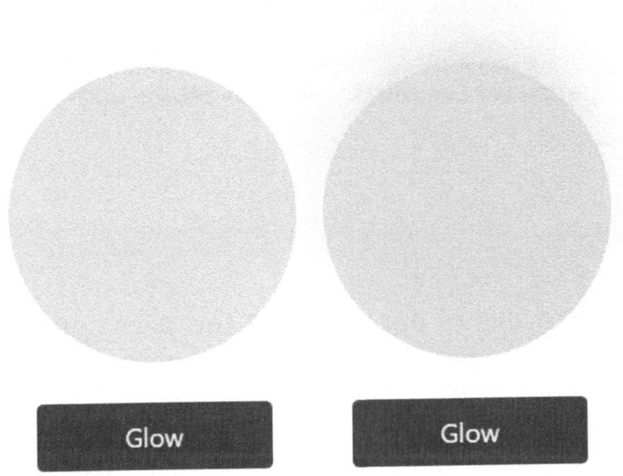

***Figure 7.11**: Component 11*

When you click on **Glow** button *below the circle*, the circle element identifies the click state and changes it utilities. Following is the code for the same:

```
<div class=" flex flex-col min-h-screen items-center justify-center bg-white
            px-5 space-y-3">
  <div class="grid grid-cols-2 gap-4">
    <div class="flex flex-col-reverse items-center justify-center gap-6">
     <div class=" w-36 h-10 bg-blue-800 rounded text-white text-center py-2
                  cursor-pointer peer">
                  Glow
      </div>
      <div class="flex-grow p-8 w-44 h-44 rounded-full bg-blue-200
                 peer-active:bg-blue-600 peer-active:shadow-2xl
                 peer-active:shadow-blue-400 rotate-180">
      </div>
    </div>
    <div class="flex flex-col-reverse items-center justify-center gap-6">
      <div class="w-36 h-10 bg-blue-800 rounded text-white text-center
                 py-2 cursor-pointer peer/bulb">Glow</div>
      <div class="flex-grow p-8 w-44 h-44 rounded-full bg-yellow-100
```

```
                  peer-active/bulb:bg-amber-300 peer-active/bulb:shadow-
            2xl
                  peer-active/bulb:shadow-amber-400 rotate-180"></div>
    </div>
  </div>
</div>
```

Provided two different ways of approaching the *peer* concept of utilities, look into it carefully.

Conclusion

This chapter concludes the book. It will help you learn about Tailwind CSS so that you can try it for your academic/hobby projects. Being the author of this book, I felt that I tried to ignite the knowledge of Tailwind CSS in you, I assume you will try more and more utilities that make you ready for rapid development of user interfaces using this gem Tailwind CSS.

Index

C

D

H

I

J

L

M

N

O

P

R